Manipulated

Manipulated

Inside the Cyberwar to Hijack Elections and Distort the Truth

Theresa Payton

ROWMAN & LITTLEFIELD

Lanham • Boulder • New York • London

ROWMAN & LITTLEFIELD

An imprint of The Rowman & Littlefield Publishing Group, Inc.
4501 Forbes Blvd., Ste. 200
Lanham, MD 20706
www.rowman.com

Distributed by NATIONAL BOOK NETWORK

British Library Cataloguing in Publication Information available

Library of Congress Cataloging-in-Publication Data

Names: Payton, Theresa, 1966– author.
Title: Manipulated : inside the cyberwar to hijack elections and distort the truth / Theresa Payton.
Description: Lanham : Rowman & Littlefield, [2020] | Includes bibliographical references and index. | Summary: "Stories from the Frontlines of the Global Cyberwar Cybersecurity expert Theresa Payton tells battlefront stories from the global war being conducted through clicks, swipes, internet access, technical backdoors and massive espionage schemes. She investigates the cyberwarriors who are planning tomorrow's attacks, weaving a fascinating yet bone-chilling tale of Artificial Intelligent mutations carrying out attacks without human intervention, "deepfake" videos that look real to the naked eye, and chatbots that beget other chatbots. Finally, Payton offers readers telltale signs that their most fundamental beliefs are being meddled with and actions they can take or demand that corporations and elected officials must take before it is too late" — Provided by publisher.
Identifiers: LCCN 2019048507 (print) | LCCN 2019048508 (ebook) | ISBN 9781538133507 (cloth ; alk. paper) | ISBN 9781538133514 (epub)
Subjects: LCSH: Elections—Corrupt practices. | Espionage. | Disinformation—Political aspects. | Internet in political campaigns. | Internet—Security measures. | Cyber intelligence (Computer security)
Classification: LCC JF1083 .P39 2020 (print) | LCC JF1083 (ebook) | DDC 364.1/324 —dc23
LC record available at https://lccn.loc.gov/2019048507
LC ebook record available at https://lccn.loc.gov/2019048508

♾™ The paper used in this publication meets the minimum requirements of American National Standard for Information Sciences—Permanence of Paper for Printed Library Materials, ANSI/NISO Z39.48-1992

Contents

Prologue

I have something to admit to you. I'm what many would consider a conspiracy theorist. Growing up, my sweet gram often would say to me, "I haven't voted since *They* killed the Kennedys." I once asked her respectfully (but in exasperation), "Just who are *They*?" She nodded and said, "You're too young to understand now, kiddo, but you will. Pay attention. Always question. Never believe what They tell you, and you'll be okay. Read lots of different sources. Don't let Them tell you how to think. Ever." RIP Gram. That wisdom shapes how I do my job today. It's not that I don't believe what people tell me; I believe *they* believe it's true. I'm often quoted saying, "It's only paranoia if it's not true." Yes, I am skeptical of everything now, and I study the manipulators of these social and political issues on your behalf. The collective They may not be any one specific group, but know this: They are manipulating you. They are trying to divide us, because They hate democracy—the idea that the power is held by the people versus the concentrated few. I am convinced we all need to put on our conspiracy hats to spot the manipulators conducting their tradecraft and to not fall prey to their schemes due to our confirmation biases. Authoring this book is one of most important pieces of work I have undertaken in my career. I pray and hope I got it right.

Foreword

General James F. Amos, USMC, Retired

I first met Theresa Payton through her cybersecurity work for some of the world's most important global companies. Theresa's passion to protect and defend our nation, allies, businesses, and citizens comes as no surprise for those who know her well. It's in her DNA to serve. Much of Theresa's family has served in the US armed forces, including her dad and maternal grandfather, who served as Marines. Theresa's husband, a Naval Academy graduate, was a surface-warfare officer with the Navy. She worked in the White House for President George W. Bush in cybersecurity. Knowing that Theresa was working on this book, I told her that I wanted to read it first. My wife accused her of never sleeping: we don't think she does; you see, Theresa is a patriot on a mission.

As both the assistant commandant and later the commandant of the Marine Corps, from 2008 to 2014, I saw from the front lines that we were fighting a cyberwar against adversaries old and new. I'd watched manipulation campaigns evolve over time, moving from solely a ground game to a ground and digital game in the late 1990s. By 2000, we in the military had observed cyber campaigns jump the line from nation-states trying new military tactics into a global digital arms race. Today, instead of focusing solely on hacking equipment or stealing data, the latest tactic is to make us doubt what we hold to be true and to distort that truth through misinformation and manipulation campaigns. Now with only technical equipment and small teams, a person can conduct a battle with the click of a mouse or the swipe of a finger.

My successor as commandant wrote in his 2014 *Strategic Plan for the US Marine Corps* that

> Globalization will continue to increase interdependence between nations, placing a premium on access to the world's commons—land, sea, air, space, and cyber. . . . As

difficult as the physical and fiscal aspects of operations will be, the evolving information environment and cultural terrain will be even more challenging. The rapid development of new technologies coupled with easy access to cyber-based capabilities and advanced precision weaponry further empower state and nonstate actors and amplify the risks to US and allies' interests. Therefore, the ability to comprehend and shape these dimensions of the modern operating environment will be integrated into the development of the force.[1]

Although written in 2014, this endures and applies to today's threats. I studied military history throughout my time as a Marine. Today's influence campaigns represent the logical progression of centuries of manipulation between warring rivals, enemies, and friends, within and across countries. The digital age has only sped up the game and raised the stakes. As frightening as the potential hacking of our voting booths is to consider, Theresa is right when she says that the manipulation of our civil and social discourse may well be even more dangerous.

In *Manipulated*, Theresa takes the reader right into the trenches of today's hackers. From her time serving in the executive office of the president of the United States to her years of fighting cybercrime as founder and CEO of Fortalice Solutions, she knows who the operatives are and how they conduct their tradecraft. From "zombie computers" to "sock puppets" to "bots," she describes what the buzzwords mean and how these new tactics are leveraged against ordinary people. Theresa's exclusive interview with an unnamed hacker reveals the real anatomy of a manipulation campaign—firsthand—from the person who actually ran the operation. The story is both a page-turner and an eye-opener.

Finally, after reassessing the 2016 and 2018 US elections, Theresa offers her predictions for where we are headed in 2020. Given her seeming clairvoyance in early 2016 that manipulation and misinformation campaigns would be a thing, and that the "Internet of things would be leveraged to harm the Internet infrastructure," we would do well to heed her words.[2] What will the world look like if this meddling continues unabated? Theresa emphasizes that our country needs to act now—and to do so with our global allies. The fight will require not just government actions but also the commitment of social-media companies, tech giants, and global citizens, all working together. *Manipulated* concludes with a how-to guide to empower the reader to take action.

Theresa has dedicated her life's work to this mission—keeping each of us safe from manipulation campaigns through awareness and by pushing for solutions. *Manipulated* is both entertaining and informative—in some cases, even shocking. A must-read, it serves as a wake-up call for all of us.

General Amos served as thirty-fifth commandant of the US Marine Corps, retiring in December 2014 after forty-two years of active service. During his tenure as member of the Joint Chiefs of Staff, the Department of Defense recognized the magnitude of cyber threats facing the United States and US military services and established the US Cyber Command, officially acknowledging cybersecurity as a war-fighting domain.

General Amos currently serves on corporate boards, both public and private, and is actively involved in several nonprofits that care for US military veterans and their families.

Introduction

The 2016 Oxford Dictionary word of the year was *post-truth*.[1]

There's more to the war for free and secure elections than meets the eye. The United Kingdom and United States may have "outed" Russian meddling in elections around the globe, but the use of misinformation campaigns, fake personas, and political espionage shows no signs of slowing down. In fact, they seem to be escalating. According to a 2017 report on Internet freedom, manipulation and disinformation tactics deployed by several cybercrime groups and nation-states played an important role in elections in at least eighteen countries over the past year, including in the United States.[2] I call the techniques and tactics "the manipulator's playbook." Perfected by the Kremlin and directed toward disrupting election integrity and the democratic process, the playbook is being used against citizens around the world and in all aspects of our lives. It's not solely about elections. What I have uncovered through years of research is that these manipulation campaigns can be driven by multiple motives, from the ideological to the financial.

This election-meddling playbook has worked so well for the Russians that the United States has dedicated over two years investigating it, and as I write this book the significance of the meddling is still hotly debated. Countless hours have been spent grilling Silicon Valley teams over how the meddling was allowed to happen and what could have been done to prevent it. Hours of testimony on C-SPAN from Capitol Hill and BBC coverage of parliament in the United Kingdom have aired. Special Counsel Robert Mueller indicted dozens of Russian citizens, companies, and intelligence officers. But even with this scramble after-the-fact to figure out what has really been going on, can we truly believe what we are being told about it?

What if the election-espionage operation is still alive and well, while our government has publicly claimed victory in naming a couple dozen operatives? What if the dozen names listed within Mr. Mueller's indictment are the ones Russia *wanted* us to find, while they continue to covertly push their agenda—the destabilization of capitalist economies and democratic societies? What if other countries such as Iran, North Korea, and China become Russia's protégés and improve upon the manipulator's playbook with new plays of their own? What if the playbook is also being used by anyone who wants to push an extremist ideology or a specific political or social agenda? What if all this time the endgame was not just about influencing the 2016 US elections, Brexit, and Spanish separatists but about making free citizens everywhere doubt the very foundation that makes them free? What if the goal is an all-out war to hack into our minds, manipulating the way we see an issue at hand, a company's brand, or the underpinnings of free markets?

So how can we detect when we are being manipulated? While speaking to one local high school's honors English class, I asked the students where they get their information. They told me they consumed news from many sources—television, radio, printed news publications, and online at news websites—but mostly from the social-media newsfeeds of family and friends. This is alarming, as all it takes is one person inside a trusted circle to fall prey to a manipulation or misinformation campaign for the rest to be tempted to follow. Of the many bright students assembled before me that day, only one said they primarily trusted TV news, citing Lester Holt of *NBC Nightly News*. (Great parenting; Lester Holt is a favorite of mine.)

I then taught these students how to spot a misinformation or manipulation campaign and then put them to the test, presenting known fake personas, fake accounts, and fake organizations that promoted misinformation and manipulation campaigns around vaccination, Blue Lives Matter, Black Lives Matter, and political campaigns. After some training and awareness, the teens were able to successfully spot the amateur fake, forged, or false information—with one caveat: Internet memes proved harder to spot. This generation sees memes as a basic form of communication and assumes most are harmless opinions, not orchestrated malicious attempts to influence. To the students, the more unpolished the meme, the more authentic (benign) it reads. When it came to interpreting memes pertaining to social issues and to political themes, the majority of these smart digital natives still fell for misinformation, mistaking Russian-produced memes as truly American, because they didn't look "overproduced." My test shows that while many of us can be trained to spot less-sophisticated manipulation campaigns, the targeted and nuanced ones can often slip by us.

So how do we safeguard ourselves against the next iteration of the manipulator's playbook?

We need to wake up. We have hit the snooze button too many times, and now it may be too late for us to protect ourselves in time for the next election cycle. You may assume that 2016 was the first time the US voting process was subject to computer hacking by a hostile nation, but there is a long precedent for such attacks. For example, during the 2008 presidential-election cycle, both the Obama and McCain campaigns were reportedly hacked by China. I have spent the last several years as a cybersecurity expert asking what I could do to stop this worrisome trend of election interference. My work on the front lines has taught me a great deal, and, although I never discuss nor name our clients publicly, I can share what I and my team have learned from years of experience.

Right now, one of the biggest threats we face is the security of the looming 2020 elections, both in the United States and around the globe. So far, no digitally collected vote in the US federal elections of 2016 or 2018 has been reported as being hacked or changed. And yet Silicon Valley knows that voter-registration hacks, ballot tampering, and potential voter disenfranchisement are real threats. Thankfully in the United States, voting systems are decentralized within states, which makes it harder to manipulate at scale. Election officials know that in order for your vote to count, it has to be accurately recorded and protected. Yet much of our election infrastructure—from voting machines to voter-registration databases—is driven by the private sector.

Everyone involved in the election lifecycle that I have met and worked with knows they are racing against the clock: it's only a matter of time before our elections are compromised. The threat comes from many fronts—hacked election campaigns, the theft of political-party e-mails and other communications, hacked voting machines, tampering with registration rolls, and, yes, manipulating voters' minds before they enter the booth. The level of dedication and concern applied by election workers is fierce and intense, yet the effort to secure the elections process is often a thankless job for the many state employees, board of elections officials, Silicon Valley engineers, and law-enforcement agencies.

To boost democracy and improve voter turnout, many have even called for wider and easier ways to vote, such as creating automatic registration or allowing citizens to vote by one's phone or computer. It is easy to see the appeal. Why shouldn't we strive for 100 percent participation in the democratic process? However, before we rush to further digitize the voting process, let's examine the risks. In America currently, only a limited group can vote online—those serving overseas in the military or some US expats registered to specific states. This population is small enough that manual spot checks can be performed and processes put in place to ensure accuracy. However, I believe it's too risky to roll out widespread online voting, given the technology is not fully secure and that elections are prime targets for domestic and international meddlers.

Promising advances like highly encrypted blockchain technology may one day mean moving the election process online would be a safe proposition. But for now, countless potential forms of attack can tamper or cast doubt on the legitimacy of an election. First, known Russian-led hacking attempts have already been made to penetrate state voter-registration databases, which could potentially alter or remove people from the rolls.[3] Second, since all technology is hackable, the electronic voting machines we now use that connect to the Internet could be manipulated to actually change votes. Instances of this sort of tampering have never yet been reported by officials, and this sort of fraud is more difficult to perpetuate on a widespread basis since there are more than ten thousand election jurisdictions in the United States, all with their own decentralized voting machines; but smaller races could certainly be swung by this kind of malicious interference. Finally, any voting machine that permits remote tech support or software updates is potentially insecure.[4]

We've already had a few close calls: In September 2018, the State of Washington disclosed that the web page allowing its voters to register, update personal information, and view voter guides online had inadvertently been made accessible to anyone through the website's development code. As far as the state knows, there was no data-security breach, but it just goes to show that state election systems are potentially quite vulnerable. Similarly, in July 2017 it came to light that a campaign contractor out of Virginia had stored voter data in the cloud and misconfigured access, exposing the personal information of almost two hundred million US voters.[5]

This is why some responsible for voting security are going "back to the future," promoting the idea that we should all vote using the old-school method: paper ballots, which, they argue, can be audited and checked. And yet, paradoxically, the only claim of votes being potentially tampered with in the US 2018 election cycle came from an investigation into paper-based absentee ballots in North Carolina, which had been gathered inappropriately and were possibly discarded.

So where do we go from here?

WHY WE NEED TO ACT NOW

Warren Buffet says cyber warfare is the greatest threat to mankind . . . even more so than nuclear weapons.[6] In an increasingly interconnected world, where nearly all adults have access to robust computers in their pockets through smartphones and tablets, the next frontier of security isn't physical—it's digital. As threatening as the hacking of our voting booths or election processes is to consider, the manipulation of our minds may be worse.

Misinformation campaigns spreading slightly altered or completely fictional news reports are cost effective and pay off: Research shows that a false story about any topic, not just politics, reaches 1,500 people six times faster than does legitimate news. As Jonathan Swift noted in 1710, "Falsehood flies, and truth comes limping after it." A lie or a twist on the truth regarding politicians or political issues is the most likely to engage social-media communities and go viral.[7]

Disturbingly, you don't even need someone to slip a lie into your circle of trust for you to fall victim to misinformation—we do it ourselves. Researchers have found that social-media users will continue to repeat a story they know is fake and not speak up to correct the inaccuracies they're spreading, so long as it supports their version of the story. Researchers reviewed Twitter-based rumors following several high-profile news events, such as the December 2014 Sydney hostage situation and the 2015 Charlie Hebdo shooting in Paris. What they found was astonishing: Social-media users were more likely to share unsubstantiated news, also known as *rumors*, they had picked up than they were to pass along news from trusted and vetted news organizations. They were also less likely to share that something they had posted, commented on, or reposted previously had been since been found to be misinformation or purely a farce.[8] Why let the facts get in the way of broadcasting your own point of view? Even after social-media users were educated on fake stories and misinformation, roughly 30 percent still posted or reposted stories they knew to be untrue.[9]

How widespread was the use of the manipulator's playbook during the 2016 US elections? Facebook revealed in 2017 that an estimated 126 million of their users were exposed to content promoted by Russian operatives—a twelvefold increase from initial estimates that only 10 million users had been affected.[10] We later found out the spread of misinformation on their subsidiary, Instagram, had been even worse, approaching 187 million engagements, according to a 2018 report by research firm New Knowledge.[11] Over one thousand videos on YouTube, over a million Tweets, and posts on Pinterest, Reddit, Tumblr, and beyond disseminated Russian-originated disinformation.[12] It's not a case of who saw it; it's a question of who *didn't*.

Increasingly, government experts and social-media companies warn that Russia is not the only player in global election interference; other countries have adopted the manipulator's playbook, too. Facebook announced in August 2018 that it had shut down 652 pages, groups, and accounts tied to Iran for "coordinated inauthentic behavior," while Twitter announced that it had shut down 284 Iranian-linked accounts.

We're running out of time.

Iran, North Korea, China, Russia, and other election meddlers and social-media disinformation peddlers are undermining confidence in the globe's democratic institutions and—ultimately—our way of life. The enemy has entered the gates. They pretend to be our neighbors and fellow citizens; they are inside our digital infrastructure and are shaping what we believe, the way we get our news and make our purchases, and, as we will see, even our most personal decisions, such as whether or not to vaccinate our kids. As you will learn later in this book, it's not just foreign military operations targeting your mind; the manipulator's playbook has gone local and is deployed by governments against citizens; and, yes, my research has revealed that US citizens are using the manipulator's playbook against their fellow citizens.

When it comes to securing our minds and elections and resisting this manipulation, our political leaders and heads of technology companies can no longer afford to delay. We need a comprehensive strategy across countries and the private sector to protect democracy from foreign adversaries and put an end to election interference. We also need to ensure that countries can share, in real time, threats that could have an impact on other election processes. Citizens need to act now to secure the freedom and integrity of elections, our civic discourse, and the democratic process.

Unlike other books on the market covering the manipulation of the 2016 US election, this book shows what you can do to make a difference and how you can protect your mind. Your reaction to issues in your daily life, and your vote from malicious influence. The following pages will reveal techniques used by cybercriminals and cyber operatives that play just inside the gray area of the law. You will discover how they do their work, from launching social-media bots to selling password credentials on the dark web. You will learn how to spot a fake news video or ad like a pro, preventing your falling prey to election-related schemes, fraud, and identity theft. You will be given a personal toolbox of strategies to safeguard yourself and your loved ones from the mind games that come straight out of the manipulator's playbook.

1

How Did We Get Here?

Covert political interference is nothing new: Today's influence campaigns are the logical progression of centuries of manipulation between countries. The writings of Sun-Tzu, military strategist and philosopher of ancient China, contain subversive techniques, military-intelligence gathering, and deception strategies. Rabbinic texts and the Bible tell the story of Rahab, a woman who used her position as a sex worker to spy for the Israelites.[1] In Japan, as early as the eighth century BCE intelligence gathering was undertaken by ninjas. Reviewing influence campaigns from the past, from the ancient Greeks even to the modern-day Cold War era, we find the groundwork on which our current predicament of political interference—how the digital age's advent of artificial intelligence, machine learning, ubiquitous Internet, and social-media networks lend a devastating new twist to an age-old problem.

COUNTRIES HAVE ALWAYS MANIPULATED ONE ANOTHER'S CITIZENS—AND THEIR OWN

Although the terms *influence campaign, misinformation campaign,* and *manipulation campaign* might seem to describe modern concepts, covert political activity truly dates back to ancient times. Throughout the ages, humans have been manipulating other humans to convince them to agree with their point of view, to produce more loyal subjects to govern, and to incite them to act in one way or another. According to the American Historical Association's "Story of Propaganda," by professor of journalism Ralph Casey, one of the earliest examples of a well-run influence campaign can be found in Ancient Greece. As the citizens of Athens developed their civic life, differences of opinion began to divide the populous on societal issues such as religion, politics, marital practices, and more.[2] Alas, the Greeks predated modern social media, so we can only imagine Socrates engaging in a Twitter flame war.

Socrates Tweeted
The only true wisdom is in knowing you know nothing. #Wisdom #UKnowNothing

We have learned that governments, political parties, families of influence and wealth, and any others creating propaganda have always put in place labor-intensive ground games and alternate communication channels to reach their audiences. In fact, ancient Greeks wielded influence through entertainments such as games, poems, plays, and social gatherings. Homer's *Iliad*, for example, serves as propaganda to uplift the Greeks, who are depicted as an organized civilization, with all other societies portrayed as barbaric and backward.[3]

Leveraging influence campaigns was integral to Greek governing. Reading Aristotle, we see that persuasion is a part of what we now call manipulation, influence, or propaganda. In *Rhetoric*, his treatise on the art of persuasion, written in 350 BC, Aristotle defines the three types of persuasion a speaker can employ: using one's authority is *ethos*, using an emotionally based approach is *pathos*, and using logic to promote a campaign is *logos*.[4] The Greeks laid the cornerstone for some of the most effective propaganda campaigns later to come.

Interestingly, while the term *propaganda* may have taken on a negative connotation in the modern age, it has ostensibly noble origins. In 1622, in an effort to spread Catholicism across the world, Pope Gregory XV established in Rome the Sacred Congregation for the Propagation of the Faith. This propagation of the faith—or *propaganda*—was entrusted to a handpicked group of cardinals. In subsequent years, the congregation further developed under Pope Urban VIII, who in 1627 founded the Collegium Urbanum to train missionaries to convert as many people as possible.[5]

ESPIONAGE, PROPAGANDA, AND DISINFORMATION

With the eve of the modern era, new methods and technologies were increasingly enlisted to influence the minds of the populace—from postcards and posters to radio broadcasts and, eventually, television. During World War I, the United Kingdom determined that the first government to disseminate their version of the news about the war might actually win the war—or, at least, the propaganda war. And so UK operators cut Germany's undersea communication cables, effectively silencing the German press and allowing the United Kingdom's message to reach the American press without real-time competition from Germany. Further, the United Kingdom established their own government-run press agency, Wellington House, to produce stories and other news copy sympathetic to their national interests and to quash dissenting points of view from German media and elsewhere.[6]

On the advent of World War II, the United Kingdom knew it would be a tough sell to ask its own citizens to go to war again so soon, and they knew they could not successfully oppose the Nazis without help. Thus they needed to enlist the United States. But as late as 1940, polls showed 80 percent of Americans were isolationists and opposed to entering the war. And so the British Security Co-ordination was established, a spy agency of nearly three thousand agents, which created a mock news agency and radio station to feed pro-British and anti-Nazi news into the United States in an attempt to sway the Americans to their side. Also, in the war's earliest days, the United Kingdom reconstituted a successful news-creation and -dissemination operation they had used during World War I to push propaganda in their favor. This time, the Ministry of Information, as it was called, pushed anti-Nazi themes. For example, one cartoon postcard created by the MOI depicted Nazis running off with chests of gold after German forces had looted Hungary's government. Another depicted various countries with unhappy citizens and Nazi soldiers glowering like evil overlords.[7] In addition to leveraging traditional forms of propaganda in posters and newspapers, the MOI also branched their operations out to include newer technologies, in radio broadcasts and even films: Comic-book characters were fighting Nazis and Japanese warriors, Walt Disney's Donald Duck had a nightmare that he had become Hitler, and Hollywood heartthrobs showed cinemagoers across the heartland that patriotism was heroic.[8]

Once the United States finally entered the war, it also used disinformation tactics to get the edge. Turning to the labor force it had on hand—women—the US military, mainly the Army and Navy, called approximately ten thousand American women into service to try to decipher codes and foil the enemy's plans.[9] The intellectual and problem-solving teams of women, mainly working out of Washington, D.C., and northern Virginia, were able to decipher Nazi messages pertaining to ship movements, providing vital data points that allowed the US Navy to target and sink many enemy supply transports. And these code-breakers were essential to shifting momentum to the Allies' favor: The Germans, who had long waged propaganda and disinformation campaigns themselves to devastating effect, were thoroughly deceived when before D-Day the United States created fake radio traffic about the Allied landing site, allowing forces to storm the beaches of Normandy while the greater part of German forces were diverted elsewhere.[10] This ruse shifted momentum of the war, and not fifteen months later, the war was won, the Nazis defeated.

THE STASI OF POST-WAR EAST GERMANY

Of course, even with the conclusion of the World Wars, ample opportunities for state manipulations remained: After all, a government can choose to maneuver its own citizens as well as attempt to sway those of another country. The Stasi—considered to this day to be one of the most efficient and effective spy agencies of the Cold War era—was the secret-police agency of the German Democratic Republic. Headquartered in

East Berlin, the Stasi worked closely with the KGB of Russia to conduct surveillance and promote manipulation campaigns; it is estimated that as many as one in six East Germans served as a spy or informant for the state.

Initially, the Stasi employed overt tactics of oppression and persuasion, such as arrests and torture. But they eventually began to utilize more insidious forms of manipulation, ranging from psychological attacks to smear campaigns, designed with the goal of plausible deniability.[11] A psychological attack could involve breaking into a home and making subtle changes to furniture or belongings, to gaslight the residents. Victims shared with historians that smear campaigns involved falsified documents—for example, delivering an anonymous letter to a spouse, showing their partner in a convincingly doctored, compromising photograph. The Stasi was so sinister and effective, history shows, that many who were targeted by the state's manipulation campaigns never resisted, having no idea that the Stasi were behind their torments. Many victims suffered from depression and mental breakdowns as a result, and many chose suicide rather than endure further suffering.[12] East Germany was so brutally effective in large part because, as a satellite state of the USSR, they had learned at the feet of the masters of manipulation.

RUSSIA: FROM THE COLD WAR TO MODERN DAY

> Twenty years ago the Russians had to recruit journalists to find people to disseminate something. Nowadays they just have to start a meme.
>
> —John Schindler, former NSA analyst[13]

Russia has long aimed to perfect tactics of influence and exploitation, and today they command the respect—however grudgingly—of cybercriminal syndicates, hacktivists, and government-directed cyber operatives around the globe. In fact, they invented disinformation. Under the leadership of Joseph Stalin, the USSR created a specific agency that took propaganda campaigns to a more organized and professional level. The approach, or *dezinformatsiya*, comes with a playbook to sharply and cunningly plant manipulation campaigns of truths and lies to purposely mislead citizens within a given country—be it another or one's own.

During the Cold War era, Russia, the seat of Soviet power, developed a strategy of global influence to direct public discourse surrounding topics of interest to the USSR. They called their campaign *aktivnyye meropriyatiya*—or "active measures."[14] The government strategy transcended military action to include disinformation campaigns as well as a ground game to distribute forged documents, recruit talent, and plant misinformation.[15] According to research conducted by the Center for Strategic and International Studies, Russia's attempts to sway US elections predates 2016: When they hoped for the defeat of US presidential candidate Richard Nixon in 1968, they secretly offered financial aid to his Democratic opponent, Hubert Humphrey. Humphrey, notably, turned it down. And it should come as no surprise that Russia actively opposed President Reagan's reelection.[16]

During the administrations of US presidents Ronald Reagan, George H. W. Bush, and Bill Clinton, Richard A. Clarke served as key advisor on intelligence and counterterrorism. Today he puts his national-security expertise to use as chair of Good Harbor Cyber Security Risk Management and author of countless books on cybersecurity. Over the decades his career has spanned, Clarke has seen a shift in Russian tactics. "When I started out early in my career," he told me,

> I was annoyed to hear a new role was created to battle misinformation campaigns launched by the Russians but did not realize at the time how necessary this role was. The Russia playbook of *dezinformatsiya*—disinformation; *kompromat*—compromising material; and *agitprop*—propaganda, have all been modified with the use of the Internet and social media.
>
> What's changed from decades past, though, is that now with just a click—or a like or a share—disinformation can spread at an astonishing pace. The Internet and social-media platforms are being used in a new way, and in effect we have a national-security crisis on our hands. The United States and other countries need to take heed. Our election process and [ability to prevent] social discord as a nation is not secure unless we have an effective defense against these informational weapons.[17]

Historically, the Soviet Union needed to groom people who would write, promote, and deliver the falsehoods within propaganda posters and news media. The boots-on-the-ground approach would then feed the stories into the news cycle of their own country and any targeted countries that they wanted to disrupt. This was expensive and time-consuming yet often successful. For example, in the 1980s the Russians used dezinformatsiya an attempt to convince the world that the United States had invented AIDS.[18]

In Operation Infektion, as they called their campaign, Russian operatives first devised their story, which they then sent to a Soviet-backed Indian newspaper in the form of an anonymous letter to the editor, which outlined the theory that the United States had developed the AIDS virus for nefarious purposes. The Indian newspaper ran the opinion piece in July 1983, and it was reprinted in a Russian magazine and then picked up by Russia's government-controlled news service TASS. In September 1986, a Russian-affiliated biophysicist released a report corroborating the AIDS theory with vague medical conjecture. By 1987, the story was making the global rounds, and eventually anchor Dan Rather reported its circulation on *The CBS Evening News*.[19]

Richard Clarke had an inside view to the devastation the disinformation was inflicting, as at that time he was serving as deputy assistant secretary of state for intelligence. He told me, "The Soviets, conducting dezinformatsiya, bought off and bribed reporters and newspapers in Africa and ran these stories. By the time we realized that the Russians had Africa convinced that America had created HIV deep inside the Wistar Institute in Philadelphia, it was too late. It took us decades to undo the damage."[20]

Seeing the success of their disinformation campaigns, the Russians pressed on, adapting their offensives with new emerging technologies. With the increased usage of the Internet in the late 1990s through early 2000s, they began leveraging chat rooms and e-mail chains. Social networking further eased the ability to study and interact with global citizens. With the launch of social-networking sites like Myspace (2003), Facebook (2004), YouTube (2005), Twitter (2006), VK (2006),[21] WhatsApp (2009), Instagram (2010), Snapchat (2011), and other social-networking platforms, Russia's ground game—using spies that moved into your neighborhood, obtained jobs in the workplace, and attended social events—was enhanced and in some cases replaced. Why not spare the expense of a foreign operative who can be spotted on camera and arrested in a sting operation when you can instead transform into a virtual operation, headquartered in a building anywhere in the world?

Today's new and improved dezinformatsiya playbook is streamlined, modern, and incredibly effective in swaying public opinion on social issues and politics. The tactics follow a discernible pattern: (1) Russian cyber operatives study and place disinformation in key user groups, using fake personas. (2) They then publish this propaganda using their state-sponsored news outlets, such as the network RT. (3) They then push their fabricated stories to citizen reporters and alternative media sources. (4) And finally they advance the stories through their boots-on-the-ground operations, mixed with the use of fake online personas.

The Russian playbook is so masterful that countries dedicate media time just to debunking it: Latvia has a popular Sunday-night television show with a feature that recaps the week in "Russian lies."[22]

The advent of artificial intelligence and machine learning enables Russian cyber operatives to fake, edit, and forge documents, videos, and audio clips. RT, formerly known as Russia Today, uses its funding from the Russian government to broadcast worldwide, including to the United States, and has a fast-growing global viewership. In fact, between 2015 and 2017, RT's YouTube channel grew faster than CNN's and Fox News's outreach, with impeccable timing, to impact the US presidential elections and establish a foothold for influencing US votes in 2020.[23]

Russia's pattern of attempting to covertly influence the United States is well-established. But the historical record also reveals US operations to undermine and influence.

THE US MANIPULATION PLAYBOOK

We've been doing this kind of thing since the CIA was created in 1947. . . . We've used posters, pamphlets, mailers, banners—you name it. We've planted false information in foreign newspapers. We've used what the British call "King George's cavalry": suitcases of cash.

—Loch K. Johnson, former special assistant to the chair of
the Aspin-Brown Commission of 1995–1996, inquiring into the
activities of America's covert-intelligence agencies, and Regents Professor
Emeritus of Public and International Affairs at the University of Georgia[24]

Before we indict Russia for its misdeeds, let's admit we in the United States are no angels. Throughout history, America has done its share of meddling in politics of foreign nations and their elections. As Scott Shane reports in the *New York Times*, Carnegie Mellon scholar Dov H. Levin has researched overt and covert election-influence operations conducted between 1946 and 2000 by both the USSR generally, and Russia specifically, and the United States. Levin concluded that the United States was supreme in influence campaigns, clocking in with eighty-one incidents, Russia trailing with approximately thirty-six known operations.[25]

Certain US attempts to manipulate global elections between the 1940s to the 1990s stand out: Consider, for example, campaigns waged in Italy, Iran, Guatemala, and Nicaragua. In the two decades after World War II, when Italy seemed to be in danger of sinking into communism, the United States found ways to support non-Communist political candidates through influence campaigns and financial backing. During the 1950s, the mysterious and clandestine Central Intelligence Agency was instrumental in regime changes in both Iran and Guatemala. And in the lead-up to 1990 elections in Nicaragua, the CIA devised and disseminated news stories of corruption in the ruling leftist Sandinista government; the opposition won.[26] Whether or not this was due to the CIA campaign would be hard to prove or disprove. That's the point.

But these US campaigns to promote democracy abroad are not always conducted on the sly, historians note. During the 2000 elections in Serbia, the United States quite openly helped defeat nationalist leader Slobodan Milošević. In addition to providing top-notch political operatives and consultants to assist Milošević's opponent, Vojislav Koštunica, the United States provided millions of stickers stamped with the symbol of the Koštunica campaign: a clenched fist and the words "He's finished" in Serbian.[27]

And although it is widely debated by Russian media, there exists good evidence that the United States intervened in 1996, in Russia's presidential reelection of Boris Yeltsin. In the uncertain period immediately following the collapse of the Soviet Union, Russia was suffering economic troubles, and the United States worried that the country could easily slip back into communism. Various opinion polls were showing Yeltsin trailing the pack in fifth place among the candidates, while Communist Party candidate Gennady Zyuganov topped the list and was favored to win.[28] The United States felt if Yeltsin could show he could secure international funding, his standing with the Russian electorate would stabilize. And so the United States lobbied on behalf of Russia to receive an International Monetary Fund loan of $10 billion. The United States also provided Yeltsin with political consultants to assist in focusing propaganda and messaging in the race. With cash infusions, the Yeltsin campaign leveraged Russian media to promote positive stories, and Yeltsin ultimately won.[29]

And US attempts to influence elections isn't a thing of the past. As recently as January 2018, Tehran accused newly seated US President Donald Trump, Vice President Mike Pence, and the US State Department of encouraging the Iranian people to march in the streets in protest of the sitting government. It also alleged that the State Department was communicating with anti-Iran regime protesters using Farsi on Facebook pages and Twitter accounts.

Through financial backing, expert advice, traditional-media bombardment, and now social-media influence campaigns, the United States and other countries have an arsenal at their disposal to promote regime changes worldwide.

DIGITAL DISSEMINATION OF DISINFORMATION

> The use of propaganda is ancient, but never before has there been the technology to so effectively disseminate it.
>
> —Natalie Nougayrède, journalist[30]

From ancient times, state campaigns to propagandize have meant establishing ground games where the message is developed and promoted using human resources and social venues, like plays and posters. In the modern era, as technology developed, television and radio were increasingly exploited. But the onset of the digital age changed everything: The manipulators handbook has become scalable, more affordable, and easier to deploy than ever.

1990s: MISINFORMATION

With the increased availability and usage of the Internet at businesses and homes across the globe, the 1990s saw an explosion in alternative news sources, satire or comedy news, and newly created online media organizations. These new media also meant a new way to test out misinformation campaigns while hiding in plain sight.

The most popular campaigns of the day involved targeted e-mail letters. Everyone remembers the lonely Nigerian prince whose loyal legal director was casting far and wide for help, offering to send money to any recipient so kind as to assist them with their banking dilemma.[31] Lucky you!

Another particular scam letter that regularly made the rounds was headed, "From Mother Theresa." She wrote this e-mail just for you! Weird that she misspelled her own name, though.[32] This e-mail claimed with authority that anyone receiving it needed to recite the prayer attached and forward it along. If they did not comply immediately, they would lose a loved one. Having followed the great works of Mother Teresa, who since her canonization has been known as Saint Teresa of Calcutta, I knew this was a scam. The manipulation campaign was so convincing that my contacts felt better to have that heavenly insurance and would pass it on to me. When I would call them on the phone to admonish them that these could be used to gather e-mail account information or infect all of us with computer viruses, they said they knew it had to be a scam but, despite their better judgment, thought it would do no harm to send it. This is a mostly harmless example of how human nature is gullible to manipulation campaigns.

Social and political satire—once mostly relegated to plays, nonprimetime television, and printed sources—also changed in the digital age. Satire and traditional media were once easy to discern from one another. Chances are nobody has ever confused *Mad Magazine* with *Newsweek*. But just as the technological evolution of the 1990s brought e-mail scams, it also saw the advent of incredibly popular satire creations that blurred the lines between legitimate news and entertainment. *The Daily Show* began airing episodes in the mid-1990s and was followed a few years later by the digital launch of the satirical newspaper *The Onion*. Initially *Onion* stories were often mistaken as true news stories, because in those days both satire and news stories shared online and filling up our e-mail accounts were new phenomena. Instead of the clearer divisions between legitimate news and satire, the two sat together on our computer screens. One popular *Onion* headline declared "KIM JONG-UN NAMED *THE ONION'S* SEXIEST MAN ALIVE FOR 2012." Two Asian newspapers, the *People's Daily* of China and the *Korean Times*, both thought the story legitimate and republished it.[33]

The lines between real news and satire so blurred, an opening was created for misinformation campaigns to insert altered news stories into the Internet's unceasing wave of news. Responding to this trend, the 1990s also saw the creation of Snopes. com (1994), which started the challenging work of proving or debunking e-mail chain letters or crazy claims on websites to help confused Internet users sort out fact from fiction. Snopes remains one of my go-to sources today to point out manipulation campaigns to my family, friends, and colleagues.

SPREADING FALSIFIED NEWS

With the frenzy of a new Internet-fueled twenty-four-hour news cycle, it became easier than ever for manipulated information to slip past journalistic guardrails. In 2013, a fake press release was accidentally promoted by trusted news outlets, damaging one company's reputation and its bottom line. The false release indicated that ANZ bank was withdrawing $1.2 billion of funds from the company Whitehaven Coal, and a wire journalist rushed to put it out before getting confirmation from the source.[34]

It turned out that the person responsible for the forged press release was anticoal activist Jonathan Moylan, who had an agenda to damage Whitehaven Coal. Moylan had sent the fake release with a real ANZ bank executive's name but changed the phone number to his own, so he could handle any media inquiries into the news.[35] Spooked investors dumped stock in Whitehaven Coal, the value of the stock plummeted, and US$300 million was erased from Whitehaven Coal's company value before anyone was the wiser.[36] With so many independent news groups and journalists racing to break news round the clock, let's hope the stock markets and the media have learned a valuable lesson.

2000s: SOCIAL MEDIA ARRIVES

Remember the ALS Ice Bucket Challenge? This innovative fundraising campaign created by the ALS Association ran during the summer of 2014 and has become one of the best examples of a social-media campaign going viral organically. To participate in the challenge, a person would record themselves pouring a bucket full of ice water over their head—or having someone else dump it with great flair over their head; drenched and chattering, the challenge taker would talk about raising money to research amyotrophic lateral sclerosis, a debilitating neurodegenerative disease. People naturally put twists on their own video submissions, which they would upload and share on social media, tagging their friends and nominating them to take the challenge. I was tagged numerous times, and, yes, I did take the ALS Ice Bucket Challenge. ALS is a terrible disease that has hit my circle of friends at work.

Not only did the ALS Ice Bucket Challenge increase awareness of the disease, it also raised the charity's social-media profile and fundraising to a new level. According to some reports, over seventeen million people took the challenge, including household names like Rafael Nadal, Cristiano Ronaldo, George W. Bush, Oprah Winfrey, and Tom Cruise. The ALS Ice Bucket Challenge received 2.2 million retweets on Twitter and 1.2 million videos posted to Facebook. The year prior, ALS had raised $1.7 million United States; with the help of their viral campaign, ALS raised $11.4 million.[37] It's probably safe to assume the campaign's success was beyond the ALS organization's and the video-campaign creator's wildest dreams.

So what is viral marketing? According to finance-education website *Investopedia*, "Viral marketing seeks to spread information about a product or service from person to person by word of mouth or sharing via the Internet or e-mail. The goal of viral marketing is to inspire individuals to share a marketing message to friends, family, and other individuals to create exponential growth in the number of its recipients."[38]

Viral messages spread quickly on the Internet, often shared via social-media platforms. Some photos and videos go viral in an organic and accidental way, while others are made to deliberately go viral by social-media influencers, marketing firms, and corporate communications teams. Before the emergence of online social media, viral-marketing campaigns took time to develop and disseminate via expensive television ads, radio ads, and newspaper and magazine placements. While these "old-school" methodologies are still used, social-media platforms such as YouTube, Instagram, Twitter, Snapchat, and Facebook provide a less-expensive, more-immediate launch option.

Whether created by individuals, professional marketing teams, hacktivists for a cause, or state-sponsored cyber operatives, viral-marketing campaigns are somewhat formulaic. Winning campaigns typically comprise three parts: (1) a central message that evokes an emotion, (2) an attention-capturing messenger, and (3) a receptive audience.

THE TWO SIDES OF VIRAL SOCIAL-MEDIA MARKETING

In the future, everyone will be world-famous for fifteen minutes.

—Andy Warhol[39]

One of the tools manipulators hide behind is the viral-marketing campaign. To see how impactful viral-marketing campaigns can be, let's look at a recent movie release. In the world of movie promotions, opening-week ticket sales are crucial, and in April 2019, *Avengers: Endgame* debuted to record sales and crowds. The movie's promotional campaign is one of the best examples of modern-day viral marketing. In the week of its debut, the film received more than 9.6 million social-media mentions, totaling 40.5 million engagements across original posts, shares, likes, and retweets. The fourth-most-popular Twitter hashtag in the weeks just following the movie release was #DontSpoilTheEndgame, tallying more than 330,000 mentions.[40] One YouTube video of the Avengers cast singing "We Didn't Start the Fire" on *The Tonight Show Starring Jimmy Fallon* received over twenty million views.[41]

But there can be a dark side to viral campaigns. In 2018, a campaign urging viewers to bite into a Tide laundry-detergent pod and post videos on social media went viral. The campaign was not created by Tide PR but by a group of people wanting to become "Internet famous"—a peculiar sort of celebrity, often sudden and transitory, conferred by Internet notoriety. When the news media began running stories that children were becoming sick or dying eating Tide Pods, Tide found itself dealing with a public-relations nightmare. The company diffused this situation by creating its own viral-marketing response campaign. One video featured Rob Gronkowski, the well-known and easily recognizable tight end for the New England Patriots. In a humorous video that garnered almost eighty-five thousand retweets, "Gronk" discouraged fans from biting into and eating Tide Pods.[42]

CASE STUDY: THE OBAMA CAMPAIGN

We have seen the power of how a viral message can spread to make us want to see a movie, support a charitable cause, or do something dumb like eat laundry detergent. . . . Now, what if that messaging were applied to politics? In 2007, then-senator of Illinois Barack Obama forever changed how political strategists would approach election campaigns. The Obama campaign not only leveraged social media to promote the candidate's platform but truly understood the power of viral marketing. Obama's campaign took grassroots fundraising to social media, often raising as little as $5 per donation, from millions of Americans.[43]

President Obama's 2012 reelection campaign again revolutionized how to reach the electorate, regardless of socioeconomic status, leveraging the power of viral marketing. During the course of the campaign, the Obama team's social-media and viral-marketing tactics changed several times, leaving other candidates flat-footed.

According to campaign manager Jim Messina, the approach was not scattered but, rather, carefully measured the effectiveness of every viral-marketing campaign and social-media platform. "This campaign has to be metric driven," he explained in a 2011 YouTube video. "If something's working, we're going to go do a bunch of it. If it's not working, we're going to go throw it out. . . . If we just run that same [2008] campaign, we stand a good chance of losing. We've got to run a new campaign."[44]

Time magazine reported that the Obama reelection campaign had an analytics department five times the size of its previous election team.[45] The campaign would run champion-challenger campaigns, testing which message resonated most with different groups. For example, they would run a message delivered by First Lady Michelle Obama or Vice President Joe Biden and then determine to which each demographic responded best. The campaign also used Internet- and social-media-behavior information at a new level to understand which messages best motivated people to take action, such as telling a friend, donating money, or voting. One of the biggest and boldest moves made by Obama's campaign team was moving from a viral-marketing campaign to a very detailed, customized, pinpointed grassroots-marketing campaign. Did it work? President Obama served a second term, and his reelection campaign raised $1 billion.[46]

Rival campaigns are not the only ones that have taken notice of this successful approach. Today companies, political organizations, nonprofits, and even world leaders all strive to replicate this strategy to microtarget individuals and interest groups to promote their product, service, or agenda.

POLITICAL "ASTROTURFING"

> The 2020 presidential race is just around the corner, and we would all be wise to be skeptical of every message and every candidate. The more scrutiny we place on supporters and candidates alike, the more confidence voters gain in the choice they're making.
>
> —Josh Rivera, reader-engagement and Opinion NOW editor at *USA Today*[47]

Political astroturfing is the practice of masking a deep-pocketed campaign as having grassroots supporters. The first known reference to *astroturfing* is attributed to US Senator Lloyd Bentsen of Texas in 1985, describing the creation of the illusion that the actions of a company, individual, or movement are organic and grassroots when in reality they are the result of a small operation of savvy manipulators. "A fellow from Texas can tell the difference between grass roots and AstroTurf . . . this is generated mail," Bentsen reportedly said, describing letters his office received that had clearly been generated by insurance-industry lobbyists posing as concerned individuals. In the United States, astroturfing tactics have been used to fight the development of wind turbines off Cape Cod and to halt antitobacco legislation.[48]

Astroturfing an opponent has never been cheaper, more effective, and harder to tie back to a campaign or person than it is now. When on April 14, 2019, *USA Today* asked its readers, "Which 2020 [presidential] candidate is standing out to you, and why?" they noticed signs of an astroturf campaign on behalf of Andrew Yang, one of the twenty-two Democratic candidates running for the party's nomination. Yang had barely registered in April 2019 general polling, but in this new *USA Today* poll, roughly 80 percent of the responses focused on three names: Andrew Yang (38 percent), Marianne Williamson (27 percent), and Bernie Sanders (16 percent). *USA Today* also noted that it received many responses and e-mails supporting Yang, despite his low polling elsewhere, and that a significant portion of it seemed canned.[49] It's important to note that nobody is accusing Yang or his campaign of intentionally skewing polls; this could very well be the work of an overenthusiastic supporter.

And it's not just a domestic phenomenon. According to *Foreign Policy* magazine, political astroturfing can also be seen globally in tactics deployed by such parties as the Bharatiya Janata Party in India and across the Bay of Bengal to the Great Indonesia Movement Party. The BJP and other political machines have the option to outsource proxy armies of real humans to curate social-media feeds, legitimate news sites, and even WhatsApp groups to devise campaigns, produce legitimate and self-promoting content, and disseminate biased and partisan content. A Reuters investigation found that Indonesian citizens had been subjected to astroturfing messages from both of the political parties facing off in that nation's 2019 presidential elections. Astroturf writers for hire, called "buzzer teams," claiming to be working for either party were paid to spread misinformation and promote religious divides leading up to elections in the world's third-largest democracy.[50] Mafindo, a Jakarta-based organization working to counter fake news, reported that between December 2018 and April 2019, incidents of astroturfing had increased by 61 percent.[51]

Brazil has similar issues. In 2017, an independent investigation found that disinformation campaigns were used to support then–presidential candidate Jair Bolsonaro.[52] The majority of pro-Bolsonaro messages pushed via WhatsApp were sent to citizens in a way that made it seem like the messages were coming from friends of friends.

The lack of action by global entities such as the United Nations and NATO and by governments around the globe means that world leaders have deferred fixing the problem of manipulation campaigns to big-tech and social-media companies—the same tech executives that time and again seem unable to stop viral misinformation and manipulation campaigns until it's too late. This allows users of the manipulator's playbook to operate almost freely, including practicing political astroturfing. Citizens are not equipped to deal with the dynamic and creative manipulation and misinformation campaigns targeting them daily. Entrusting social-media firms to spot these campaigns and arbitrate between the fake and the authentic is foolish at best and dangerous to democratic ideals at worst.

"Things are going to get worse before they get better, but humans have the basic tools to solve this problem, so chances are good that we will," noted Sandro Hawke, technical staff at the World Wide Web Consortium. "The biggest risk" to the solution, Hawke notes, "as with many things, is that narrow self-interest stops people from effectively collaborating."[53]

WHAT'S THE ENDGAME?

In power struggles the world over, manipulators seek every advantage. The development of new media means people looking to exploit other people have a whole slew of new tactics to use, from viral marketing to microtargeting. While the players vary, their aims remain universal: to control you for their own ends.

Manipulators strive to hijack your mind—bombarding you with disinformation and propaganda, making you distrust everything you see, and dividing you and your loved ones. Why? Perhaps they want to drive you to embrace their ideologies—or at least alienate you from opposing ideologies. More likely still, they want to "gum up the works" of the opposition. And when the player is a foreign state actor and the aim is to influence regimes, the stakes are raised and the manipulations grow even more insidious.

These actors seek to divide you from your loved ones on social and political issues. They want to muddy the waters—distort the truth. Confusion breeds suspicion and mistrust. And if you mistrust your institutions, those institutions destabilize. And once they topple, guess who's left standing?

As we will see in the coming chapters, bad-faith actors hope to manipulate you into distrusting the sanctity of democracy and the security of election processes. The endgame is to make you doubt everything you believe—which leaves you open to believing anything.

The head of the Syrian Electronic Army waits in a darkened room in a rural area of Syria, smoking a cigarette and nervously checking his mobile phone. The SEA has just assigned their latest task to a team composed of their best hackers, and something is about to happen: A test. A small test that may or may not work, but an interesting test, nonetheless.

A world away, on Wall Street, it's a brisk, busy day at the New York Stock Exchange in lower Manhattan. Elite traders shout over one another and crowd each other out with frantic hand signals, initiating million-dollar transactions. Every so often, they'll leave the paper-littered trading floor for a quick smoke break or to make dinner reservations at a high-end restaurant.

Back in their hideout, the Syrian team—four men and one woman—shuffles in, sipping from cups of steaming, fragrant *zouhorat shameea*. They know their goal and the plan and are anxious to get to work, but the timing has to be just right.

The head of the SEA nods to the team leader, and the command is given. The team gets to work hacking into the Twitter feed for @AP—the handle for the Associated Press. The attack is initiated. The tweet has been sent. The hackers murmur quietly among themselves. Could they really influence American perception of the stock market and the economy through social media? Could their actions have an impact on the day's trades? They're about to find out.

The hacked tweets suggest that a bomb has detonated at the White House and that the president might be hurt or even dead. This news is picked up by automated, live-trade models that conduct buy and sell orders with little to no human intervention. Those carefully chosen words under the official @AP Twitter handle spark a sharp momentary sell-off, with the Dow plummeting 143 points, from 14,697 to 14,554, erasing $136 billion in the span of three minutes.

The hoax is eventually revealed, and the market rights itself before the closing bell, but the mission is deemed a success. The head of the operation stamps out his cigarette and smiles. Promising, indeed. The strike was small this time . . . but what about the next?

Dramatization of actual events.

2

Motives and Targets

Manipulation in a Post-Truth, Post-Trust Era

You think we are living in 2016. No, we are living in 1948. And do you know why? Because in 1949, the Soviet Union had its first atomic bomb test. And if until that moment, the Soviet Union was trying to reach agreement with [President Harry] Truman to ban nuclear weapons, and the Americans were not taking us seriously, in 1949 everything changed, and they started talking to us on an equal footing. . . . I'm warning you: we are at the verge of having "something" in the information arena [that] will allow us to talk to the Americans as equals.

—Senior Kremlin advisor and special representative
of the president for international cooperation in
the field of information security, Andrey Krutskikh[1]

Why would a remote nation try to tamper with our stock market or hack our news media? For that matter, why would a nation care to influence our presidential elections?

We are all by now too familiar with the evolving media storyline confirmed by the Mueller report conclusions that Russian GRU military units 26165 and 74455 meddled in the 2016 US election, releasing e-mails stolen from the Clinton campaign and the Democratic Congressional Campaign Committee to discredit Hillary Clinton, and injecting fake news stories into American social-media feeds to further damage the Democratic candidate's reputation and stoke partisan division.[2] "We assess that only Russia's senior-most officials could have authorized the recent election-focused data thefts and disclosures, based on the scope and sensitivity of the targets," reads a joint statement put out by members of the Senate Armed Services Committee.[3]

But to what end?

Was it Putin seeking revenge on Clinton after she'd impugned the fairness of Russia's elections?[4] To tip the election and create a "useful idiot" in a President Donald Trump? And if either of these theories is correct, what to make of the perplexing news that some of these Russian troll sites also promoted *anti-Trump* rhetoric? And why continue meddling after the election was over? According to a Senate report released on December 17, 2018, Russian-led social-media sites posting activity actually *spiked* six months after the election was over.[5]

Why are these bad actors meddling in American affairs? Is it possible the true motive for those hacking our election and manipulating our minds is far more important—and disturbing—than previously imagined? The true target, I have come to believe, is democracy itself. And Russia is not the only aggressor nation. Not by far.

What I call the manipulator's playbook has likely already been adopted by nations hostile to democracy like China, North Korea, and Iran. "Until there's real action, Vladimir Putin will . . . continue to use a playbook which becomes the same playbook used by other countries—notably Iran," warned Democratic Senator Richard Blumenthal in August 2018. "I believe there will be news about Iranian aggression in the cyber domain."[6] The stated objectives and tactics employed across these countries may be different, but they all revolve around the fundamental ideal that democracy is inimical to their aims and that they therefore need to weaken democracy.

Why do autocrats around the world want to make democracy look as unappealing as possible? Because they lower the risk that their people will rise up and revolt against authoritarian controls if government by the people is discredited—made to look like it's an innately unfair system that basically creates social havoc. Consider the case of Hong Kong.

Back in 1997, the United Kingdom handed over control of the colony of Hong Kong to administration by China. Despite having agreed to protect certain freedoms the people had enjoyed under British administration, China's president Xi Jinping began taking measures to control the Hong Kongese and slowly erode their autonomy. In the summer of 2019, the government of Hong Kong introduced a bill that would have left its citizens vulnerable to imprisonment in China. But the people began pushing back against the encroachment of socialist Beijing, whose rigid control stood in stark contrast to the democratic society Hong Kong had known under the British. Realizing their democratic freedoms were at stake, protestors rioted in the streets, even stopping traffic at the airport with a sit-in.[7] Now imagine if democracy were thoroughly unappealing to the people of Hong Kong. Problem solved, right?

It's not just politicians in Beijing who find democracy threatening. During an interview with Vladimir Putin, Chris Wallace of Fox News pressed the Russian president to explain why he was bent on destroying democracy and silencing those who oppose him. From the interview transcript, we have Putin's own explanation for why bad things happen to people who get in the way of his Russian government.

WALLACE: You say nothing happened to you, but I need to ask you, domestically—not internationally, domestically, inside Russia—why is it that so many of the people that oppose Vladimir Putin end up dead or close to it? Former Russian spy and double-agent Sergei Skripal, the victim of a nerve agent attack in England. Boris Nemtsov, a political opponent, gunned down near the Kremlin. Investigative reporter Anna Politkovskaya, murdered in an apartment building. Why is it that so many people who were political enemies of Vladimir Putin are attacked?

PUTIN: Well, first of all, all of us have plenty of political rivals. I'm pretty sure President Trump has plenty of political rivals.

WALLACE: But they don't end up dead.

PUTIN: Well, not always— Well, haven't presidents been killed in the United States? Have you forgotten about— Well, has Kennedy been killed in Russia or in the United States? Or Mr. King?[8]

Putin does not end his attacks on democracy with the close of that interview. He continued to take democracy to task at the G20 Summit in 2019 and said in interview about democratic movements across the globe that democracy—which he calls *liberal democracy*—does not work. "Liberalism is obsolete," he told the gathered world leaders.[9]

Furthermore, we now know that candidates not aligned with Putin and his party were struck from the ballot by authorities citing technicalities with their registration. In other words, if you're not running as part of the Putin party and platform, you're not going to get a chance to be elected.[10]

The more chaotic, unstable, and arbitrary democracy looks, the easier it is for autocrats to maintain their tight hold, their power, and their vision.

The ways to mortally wound democracy are many: shut down civic discourse and suppress voter engagement, create strife and discord among our citizenry, generate mistrust in independent news sources, cripple our financial institutions and economy, and sow doubt in our most core beliefs.

In other words, these state aggressors don't promote misinformation just for the thrill of showing you something fake or to convince you to ascribe to their point of view. Instead, they promote misinformation—or what Russia calls *dezinformatsiya*—to encourage populations to doubt what they believe. They push dezinformatsiya so convincingly and at scale so that people begin to believe that nothing they see, read, or hear is true. And what could destabilize a democracy more thoroughly than eroding the support of its citizens?

According to the *New York Times*, "The fundamental purpose of *dezinformatsiya* is to undermine the official version of events—even the very idea that there is a true version of events—and foster a kind of policy paralysis. What the Russians are doing is building narratives; they are not building facts. The underlying narrative is, 'Don't trust anyone.'"[11]

You may already sense this growing uncertainty in areas of your own life. Have you grown uncertain whether your trusted news source is telling you everything? Have you read that there are more bots posting on the Internet than real people? Have you abandoned your Facebook page, disturbed by the company's mishandling of users' privacy and algorithms permitting bias to run rampant in your newsfeed? Or are you dubious that anyone has the power to control what you believe—despite the $200 billion spent annually on advertising that would argue the contrary? If any of this resembles how you are thinking, you are not alone. I have talked to countless experts, friends, family, and work colleagues during my years of researching for this book, and very rarely did they feel that information was free of manipulation. Interestingly, younger generations seem less likely to believe "news" posted on social media but remain susceptible to manipulation tactics delivered via memes. The manipulators know this and tailor their approach to meet their targeted demographic.

The state of affairs is so alarming that research group Freedom House devoted its 2017 *Freedom on the Net* report to the notion that so-called disinformation campaigns are now rampant. "Governments around the world have dramatically increased their efforts to manipulate information on social media over the past year," the report concludes. "The Chinese and Russian regimes pioneered the use of surreptitious methods to distort online discussions and suppress dissent more than a decade ago, but the practice has since gone global." Their survey of sixty-five countries concludes that thirty of them—including Venezuela, the Philippines, and Turkey—used "armies of 'opinion shapers' to spread government views, drive particular agendas, and counter government critics on social media."[12]

"The number of countries where formally organised social-media manipulation occurs has greatly increased, from twenty-eight to forty-eight countries globally," says Samantha Bradshaw, coauthor of a 2018 Oxford Internet Institute working paper exploring the manipulation of public opinion online. "The majority of growth comes from political parties who spread disinformation and junk news around election periods," says Bradshaw. "There are more political parties learning from the strategies deployed during Brexit and the US 2016 presidential election: More campaigns are using bots, junk news, and disinformation to polarise and manipulate voters."[13]

What legal, political, or military recourse do we have to this tampering? Very little. Some believe that political espionage, conducted via cyberattack, should be a punishable offense, either via military action or through an alliance such as NATO or the United Nations. However, US law has lagged far behind the advance of cyber weapons and capabilities. The United States can publicly accuse cybercriminals of digital crimes and impose sanctions, but US law around engaging military action to respond to such an incident are unclear. Declaring that a remote nation has tampered with election doesn't seem to do much other than prompt a flurry of media headlines and arguments on Capitol Hill.

International law struggles to keep up as well. NATO regularly publishes a guide on how to handle international cyberattacks, the *Cooperative Cyber Defence Centre of Excellence's Tallinn Manual*.[14] However, even with the guidance laid out in this manual, it is not clear that the attack on the Clinton campaign's infrastructure, and subsequent posting of e-mails and communications via WikiLeaks and other venues, would be considered illegal in the United States or international courts.[15] As someone who has personally vowed to protect and defend our nation, businesses, and citizens from digital break-ins, I find this lack of legal recourse highly objectionable. But the manipulators play in the gray spaces of the law and international-extradition treaties, knowing that often they will not be named or singled out. The Russian operatives named in the Mueller report and countless other unknown parties clearly broke laws: They stole information and dumped it on the Internet. But is it a crime punishable with jail time, or more akin to a "terrorist" attack? Or simply a case of "cyber vandalism"?

"Social-media manipulation is big business," conclude Sarah Bradshaw and coauthor Philip N. Howard in their 2018 Oxford working paper. "Since 2010, political parties and governments have spent more than half a billion dollars on the research, development, and implementation of psychological operations and public-opinion manipulation over social media. In a few countries this includes efforts to counter extremism, but in most countries, this involves the spread of junk news and misinformation during elections, military crises, and complex humanitarian disasters."[16]

Let's step back and consider the various targets the manipulators pursue, starting with the greatest one of all—the democratic process.

HIJACKING ELECTIONS

As of this writing, in 2020 there will be more than twenty democratic elections around the globe, including in countries in the European Union, Canada, the United States, and the Asia-Pacific regions. Leaders are bracing for foreign interference through cybercrime and social-media manipulation. This tactic has proven to be low-cost, scalable, hard to detect, and hard to trace back to individuals.

It also works.

"Manipulation and disinformation tactics played an important role in elections in at least seventeen other countries over the past year, damaging citizens' ability to choose their leaders based on factual news and authentic debate," noted the authors of the 2017 Freedom House report.[17]

In 2018 a report released by the UK Digital, Culture, Media, and Sport Committee highlighted that misinformation and manipulation campaigns—also known as fake news—are a danger to society and to elections with the "relentless targeting of hyper-partisan views, which play to the fears and prejudices of people, in order to influence their voting plans."[18] The committee invited countries such as Argentina, Belgium, Brazil, Canada, France, Ireland, Latvia, Singapore, and the United States to participate in the research they conducted for the report. The report indicates that their research shows an attempt to influence citizens of the United Kingdom as far back as 2010. And as we will see in detail in chapter 8, recent global attempts to hijack elections have also targeted France, Spain, Sweden, and many more countries.

CASE STUDY: CAMBRIDGE ANALYTICA

Coming out of the winter doldrums of 2018, the world was shocked to learn that voter-profiling firm Cambridge Analytica had logged the data of Facebook users in a database used by political campaigns. In this grave breach of public trust, the information of fifty million Facebook users had been collected, unbeknownst to them directly, and used by this company. Users' social-media patterns of likes, friends, friends of friends, and more were leveraged as part of the firm's microsegmentation targeting.

Cambridge Analytica, which closed its doors in 2018 in response to outrage over the scandal, aimed to provide its clients insights into consumer or voter patterns and behaviors by using tools that track audiences or customers by segments and break them down into the smallest groups possible. Per their website, "Combining the precision of data analytics with the insights of behavioral psychology and the best of individually addressable advertising technology, you can run a truly end-to-end campaign."[19] Political clients of Cambridge Analytica reportedly included global campaigns and parties, including the Congress Party in India, the Labour Party in Malta, and the John Bolton Super PAC in the United States.[20]

During undercover reporting on this issue, the United Kingdom's Channel 4 found that Cambridge Analytica's executive team was proud of the fact that their data could be used to target audiences with misinformation and manipulation campaigns.[21] Although the data set and its application to political campaigns were purported to be used in over two hundred global political campaigns, there was a connection to the 2016 US presidential campaign at the center of the controversy. The controversial advisor to candidate and later president Donald Trump, Steve Bannon, had previously been vice president at Cambridge Analytica and had stepped down to run candidate Trump's election campaign.

The aggregation of Cambridge Analytica's treasure trove of data, used in ways that surprised even Facebook, remains to this day one of the biggest global data breaches that was not labeled a data breach. You may define someone's taking your data and using it to manipulate you as a data breach. But the parties involved—Cambridge Analytica and Facebook—insist that this was not a data breach because no data was *stolen*. Cambridge Analytica claims they paid for the data. Facebook claims the data's use after it had been appropriately gathered was merely a violation of the user agreement. This is yet another example of manipulators operating in the gray spaces of laws and regulations. Your trust was violated, but nobody has been indicted or been sent to a courtroom over this misuse of your digital information.

Chances are, if you love to take Facebook quizzes, you too may have been caught up in the scandal. Researcher Aleksandr Kogan borrowed heavily from the personality-quiz app made by the laboratory at the Psychometrics Centre at the Cambridge University, where he was employed, to create a personality-quiz app on Facebook.[22] Roughly 270,000 people installed the app and accessed it via their Facebook account. At that time, a little-known design flaw allowed developers to take the data of anyone who opted in to their app *as well as their friends' data*, without disclosure or, more importantly and covertly, an ability to opt out. Aleksandr Kogan's app grabbed the data and stored it in a private database.

The database quickly grew at an alarming rate, ultimately grabbing the data of fifty million Facebook users. This is significant, as Facebook's database of its customers could be the largest of its kind in the world; the World Economic Forum reports that approximately one-third of the globe has an account.[23] The information Kogan's app gathered was critical to informing Cambridge Analytica's psychographic voter profiles. This is a reminder to be mindful what companies you and your friends connect to online and trust with your private information.

Cambridge Analytica used the data they collected and built roughly thirty million "psychographic" profiles of US voters. They had data on citizens of various countries and capitalized on the diversity of the data. Although touted as a voter-profile company, Cambridge Analytica reportedly also used their profile database to inform their clients' purchases of targeted online ad buys for the Brexit Vote Leave campaign.

The data analysis and iterative nature of reviewing the information collected in user profiles fed Cambridge Analytica's model of US voters. The company leveraged the Facebook likes of those answering the survey and of any friends connected to them, and then worked backward, reverse-engineering the individual and categorizing them. Sifting through the data elements, the tool would take a best guess at an individual's political affiliations, hot-button issues, and personality types. A refined set of 2.1 million profiled records across eleven states was used to design, test, and adjust ads and messages for political campaigns. The treasure trove taken from Facebook allowed campaigns to target political messages at an astonishing level of granularity: For example, the data could be used to advise an advertiser to write a specifically worded ad to every person it identified as loving the New England Patriots and another ad targeting those who hated the team, and to craft a different message specifically relevant to those users who preferred futbol or soccer.

Similarly, political-platform messages containing phrases like "Lock her up," "immigrant crimes," "more jobs," "tax cuts," "health care," or "border security" could be custom-tailored to each special-interest group. This microtargeting allowed a campaign to connect on an emotional and personal level but also at a customized, individualized scale not previously achievable. It was almost tantamount to a fill-in-the-blank game, where a political message with blanks left open is filled in with the words that will best capture an individual voter's interests.

This customized targeting through appealing to an individual's sense of values worked. We now know about this targeted scheme to influence us with our own digital tracks and information, but it is hard to make the leap from data mining and data modeling to convincing someone how to vote for or against something. Or is it? In 2012, Facebook filed a patent titled "Determining User Personality Characteristics from Social Networking System Communications and Characteristics" for a communication network to mine linguistic data, where "stored personality characteristics may be used as targeting criteria for advertisers . . . to increase the likelihood that the user . . . positively interacts with a selected advertisement."[24]

Were Americans in our presidential elections, the British in the Brexit vote, and perhaps other global citizens coerced by our slanted social-media newsfeeds to act in a way we wouldn't have otherwise? Or did the Russians and other operatives guide our minds in a direction many of us went along with all too willingly?

CONTROLLING ECONOMIES AND FINANCIAL SYSTEMS

As we saw at the beginning of this chapter, one key way to attack the democratic process is by disrupting a nation's economy and its financial institutions. For those countries failing to keep up with the global economy—or that have been backed into a corner by tariffs, trade issues, and sanctions—little recourse remains. One way for some to claw their way toward financial empowerment is to cheat, using digital efforts—like intellectual-property theft, theft of identities to monetize their victims' information, "ghosting" servers across the globe to mine cryptocurrency, and conducting elaborate wire-transfer fraud and ransomware schemes. In fact, Reuters reported that North Korea launched cyberattacks that as of mid-2019 have netted an estimated $2 billion by stealing from financial institutions and cryptocurrency exchanges.[25]

To some degree these types of tactics have helped ease the financial strains faced by certain nations acting in bad faith, but in most cases it's not enough to achieve fiscal stability. By leveraging fake personas online and using them to stoke social unrest, these bad actors can manipulate our minds and disrupt the global economy: It's a philosophy that says, *If we can't rise, at least we can pull you down with us.*

In fact, capitalism is a frequent target. Using social media, disinformation campaigns link causes that young people care about—like Occupy Wall Street in the United States or the yellow-vest movement in France—to the evils of capitalism.[26] And if the government is of the people and the people no longer trust the institutions, the institutions topple, and the government is weakened. And where democracies are weakened, opponents of democracies gain leverage.

Cryptocurrency—for example, Bitcoin—has its own market and its own market value. Though no cryptocurrency is currently tied to any specific global currency, unscrupulous countries and traders can design schemes to create fake demand and fake trading volumes to make cryptocurrency look credible and on the rise. It's also possible to use these same tactics to diminish its value. Many of the legal safeguards in place to protect people who buy a currency or invest in securities are not in place for cryptocurrency. The overarching governance is "Buyer, beware."

One of the tactics that could be used by state-sponsored groups to manipulate markets is to make *wash trades*—whereby you pump up the price of a stock, or in this case, a cryptocurrency, by just trading between your fake personas, essentially trading with yourself. Another tactic used is *spoofing*: talk up a particular cryptocurrency on social media, and then place large orders using fake personas. The crooks then cancel the orders at the last minute when the price jumps. Of course, the entire cryptocurrency market isn't fake, but it's vulnerable to the same tactics used in election meddling. Several *flash crashes* occurred in 2017 and 2018, and although many theories are out there as to who or what was behind the precipitous drops in cryptocurrency values, no single party has been accused—let alone convicted—of driving the secretive market. However, we do know that the world's initial coin offerings for cryptocurrency were mainly launched in Russia, the United States, and the United Kingdom.[27] The Mueller indictment mentions that cryptocurrency was used to fund and hide the tracks of Internet operatives manipulating the world's elections.

What a boon the present state of global trading is to bad-faith actors seeking to hide their tracks. Working under the cloak of anonymity and in the Internet's darkest corners is crucial to parties manipulating markets, minds, and governments, and so it will come as no surprise that diminishing transparency and the impact of journalism becomes one of their primary aims.

DISCREDITING TRADITIONAL MEDIA

If you're doing bad things, you probably don't want people publicizing the fact. As we have seen in chapter 1, manipulating the media is one effective way to control populations. And discrediting it entirely can leave all sorts of bad behavior unnoticed. Trump's mocking a disabled journalist, labeling CNN "fake news," and calling the press "the enemy of the people" is mere child's play compared to how other foreign journalists have been targeted.[28]

Finnish investigative journalist Jessica Aro began looking into Russian troll farms and bots back in 2014 for Finnish broadcast company Yle. As a result, she was targeted for retribution by pro-Russian websites, which began publishing false stories accusing her of drug use, while other online aggressors suggested she was actually a spy. She began receiving death threats, and she was repeatedly doxed, with locations of her upcoming speeches and even her home address distributed online for anyone with a mind to heckle her or worse.

"They wouldn't have attacked me so heavily if this was some sort of small issue, so in a way, with all this brutality and all this campaigning they have only exposed that this whole troll phenomenon is real and it's really serious," she told the BBC in 2017.[29] Luckily for Aro, the Finnish authorities took the harassment seriously, and her original aggressor was ultimately brought to justice in a Finnish court, sentenced to jail, and ordered to pay her compensatory damages.

In other countries the crackdown on the media is enforced by the government, whether by filtering all news through state-run media or even turning off Internet access for its own citizens. The Iranian regime uses a mix of these heavy-handed tactics along with subtler, more-covert manipulation campaigns on social media to spread disinformation and fake news at a velocity and scale that would have been unheard of before the digital age.

Iran's goal is to drive positive news about the regime of Iran, often manipulating its own people to ensure undying support for the mullahs' ideological and international political interests. Iran is using the latest technology to generate and distribute false headlines complete with contrived pictures and falsified videos known as *deepfakes*. Iran also promoted fake news relating to the Iran nuclear deal (officially known as the Joint Comprehensive Plan of Action), trying to persuade the world that their nuclear program existed solely for peaceful use and that its military involvements in countries such as Yemen, Iraq, and Syria were humanitarian.

The theocracy of Iran also attempts to interfere with the public and political sentiments within other countries, using their manipulation machine to stoke anti-Semitic, anti-Saudi, anti-American, and anti-Western emotions. The Iranian state employs native or fluent speakers in English, Arabic, Spanish, and Persian to ensure readers find their propaganda believable. One of these fake sites, *Nile Net Online*, posed as an independent Egyptian news operation based in Cairo's Tahrir Square. The site expressed opinions in opposition to the typical Egyptian media narrative that often celebrates President Trump's positive relations with Cairo. After Trump called out Iran in a speech at the United Nations, *Nile Net Online* posted commentary that President Trump was a "low-level theatre actor" who "turned America into a laughing stock."[30]

In August 2018, Reuters exposed *Nile Net Online* and more than seventy other such Iranian websites run out of Tehran, which were written in over sixteen languages and hiding behind fake personas like news outlets or grassroots organizations. These sites were visited by more than half a million people per month, and the social-media accounts driving traffic to the site had more than a million followers.[31] Bad-faith actors don't only seek to blunt the media's ability to investigate their false dealings. They also wish to co-opt the media narrative into shoring up their reputations at home and abroad to support their interests.

PUMPING UP GLOBAL PR

They are trying to . . . control the discourse and the dialogue about China.

—China expert Bill Bishop, publisher of the *Sinocisim* newsletter[32]

Sometimes influence manipulation happens within a country to impress the outside global community. In order to keep Chinese citizens confident that their government is pursuing the best possible strategy and that the country is headed down the right path, China has made investments in internal manipulation campaigns. The Chinese government goes to great lengths to control its citizens' views of their country's economy so they don't lose confidence and rein in spending, which could cause an economic slowdown nearly impossible to reverse. President Xi Jinping urged members of his party at their nineteenth congress of October 2017 to "tell the China story well and build China's soft power."[33]

China hones its story at home before launching it abroad, believing that by influencing its vast population it can influence how other countries see them and possibly soften tariffs, sanctions, and trade negotiations. Social-media manipulators and Internet influencers are considered a vital part of that strategy. China designed a program called The Good Netizen and asked their youth to get involved through the Communist Youth League of China's Volunteer Campaign to Civilize the Internet.

What conventional wisdom may characterize as social-media manipulation, misinformation, and fake news, China instead calls "public-opinion guidance management."[34] A leak of e-mails in late 2014 from the Internet Information Office of Zhanggong District in the city of Ganzhou revealed the existence of half a million government-paid and -directed citizens promoting pro-China government posts on social media. These progovernment manipulators on social media are referred to as the *wumao*, or fifty-centers. The fifty-centers are known to personally attack Chinese liberals who speak out against China. They were nicknamed the fifty-centers in the early days of the Chinese "One Nation" national Internet strategy because they were allegedly paid 0.50 RMB for every pro-Chinese government message they posted.[35]

In 2017, a watershed report of China's ability to distract its citizens by posting progovernment, pro-China propaganda was released by professors at Harvard University, Stanford University, and the University of California–San Diego. Published in *American Political Science Review*, the article estimated that covert pro-Chinese-government operatives posted more than 488 million fake-news stories and propagandizing.[36] The pro-China online-manipulation army has evolved to include patriots who post in their own free time to support the regime. Referred to as The Little Pinks, members of this group of trolls creates social-media backlash against anyone perceived to commit even small offenses against China's interests.[37] For example, in 2016, when Lady Gaga posted photos of her meeting with the Dalai Lama, who is considered a foe of China, she was attacked on her Instagram and mocked by Internet trolls on the Chinese Twitter equivalent, Weibo. "It's all over for Lady Gaga, a nation trumps an idol," wrote one.[38]

TAKING OVER COUNTRIES WITHOUT ARMIES?

Perhaps harassing a pop star sounds like small potatoes. But taken to an extreme, these manipulation attacks can mean the takeover or unseating of a nation's ruling party. Russia has aimed some of its misinformation and manipulation strategies toward formerly communist countries that now hold up Western ideals and, in cases of Estonia and Ukraine, seek to repatriate countries that have split off from Russia. When key election and policy changes considered inimical to Russian interests are made in Ukraine, Hungary, Slovakia, the Czech Republic, or Poland, for example, Russian trolls come out in force. They launch social-media manipulation campaigns while simultaneously committing cyberattacks against the governments and private-sector infrastructure to foster distrust in their media and elected officials and create an air of unrest among the citizenry.

Leading up to local elections in 2018, Taiwan saw a three-fold rise in high-impact cyberattacks, primarily from mainland China, although some may also have originated from Russia and North Korea. It is suspected that these nations are perfecting their techniques before using them against the United States, United Kingdom, EU countries, and others. China's likely motive was to unseat or undermine Taiwan's sitting president, Tsai Ing-wen, and her Democratic Progressive Party, in retaliation for resisting Beijing's efforts to control or repatriate Taiwan. The Taiwanese government has reported it receives millions of low-level cyberattacks each month, probing for vulnerabilities.[39] In a surprise upset in the November 2018 elections, the Democratic Progressive Party lost major ground, forcing Tsai to resign as party leader and putting into doubt her reelection for a new term starting in 2020.[40] Security-research firm FireEye believes Beijing targeted the Taiwan election cycle with cyber misinformation operations aimed at demoting the president's party while promoting the pro-China opposition party.[41]

The implications are troubling, to say the least. Will we soon see a complete overthrow of a democratic regime through actors using the manipulator's playbook?

Whoosh. The curtains are pulled back briskly inside the one-story bungalow, sending the geckos darting along the outside of the window frame scattering. It's early morning, and the hot Florida sun is bright.

"What a gorgeous day," Sally says aloud to nobody in particular. The local radio station, 1290 WJNO AM, plays in the background, reporting the West Palm Beach traffic and weather.

Sally hums to herself, leaning up against the ceramic-tiled countertop in her kitchen, Tweeting stories about the presidential election she's found on the *Drudge Report*, when the phone rings. It's August 5, 2016. Sally hopes it's a hot new lead for her booming real estate business.

"Yes?" Sally answers.

"Hello?" says a man's voice, and then a second man's voice says, "Hello, is this Sally?"

The men both sound like the men at her local Greek diner, speaking with deep, melodious voices that betray slight foreign accents. "Yes, this is she."

The men introduce themselves as Mike and Joe and tell her they admired her recent posts on Twitter and how clever she was with her comments. "Sally, would you like to help us with a project? We're UCLA students and working with Hollywood on a project."

Sally thinks Joe sounds a lot like Yanni, the Greek composer and musician.

Joe goes on. "We are coordinating our project with the March for Trump group. We want to pay you to be an actress!"

Sally likes what she's hearing so far; she's a big MAGA fan. "Really?" she asks.

Mike responds this time, "Yes. We already have someone to play Bill Clinton, and we'd like you to play Hillary. We have a wonderful MAGA supporter named Hank. He's going to create a prop of a jail and lock you up in it. He's going to take pictures and video of you and the Bill Clinton actor. We're going to make you famous and help get Trump elected. If you want to see our project, just go to our website, *Being Patriotic for Trump*, and take a look.

Sally takes a quick glance at the website and likes what she sees.

"We'll pay you for your time," Mike says. "We'll send you a script. You'll be fabulous! Are you available? Show up on August 20, 1 p.m., outside the Cheesecake Factory in West Palm Beach."

"I'll be there!" Sally says, hanging up the phone and heading to the nearest costume shop in search of a Hillary mask.

Dramatization of actual events.[42]

3

How Do You Know What You Think You Know?

The IRA was fluent in American trolling culture.

—New Knowledge, report on Russia's Internet Research Agency[1]

Consider the Facebook page Heart of Texas, which at its peak managed to attract nearly 250,000 users on Facebook, playing to Texan pride and championing the longtime crusade of some for the state to secede from the Union.[2] Some of its more contentious posts were riddled with typos and grammatical errors, like "The Election is RIGGED, the US are BROKEN," but none of its followers seemed overly concerned.[3]

Leading up to the 2016 US elections, the page's authors also began pumping out anti-immigrant and anti-Muslim rhetoric. In May 2016, Heart of Texas encouraged its fan base to show up at a rally at the Islamic Da'wah Center, a mosque in downtown Houston, for an event they called Stop Islamization of Texas.[4] Some followers avidly agreed with the sentiment, with one commenting, "Need to blow this place up. We don't need this sh*t in Texas."[5] Posts encouraged gun owners to bring their legal weapons, upping the chance of violence.[6]

That day, about a dozen flag-waving followers showed for the rally, bearing "White Lives Matter" T-shirts and AR-15s, chanting "Fascist and proud," and facing down police and fifty counterprotesters organized by a competing Facebook group known as United Muslims of America.[7]

Luckily, despite hot tempers and semiautomatic weapons, no actual violence broke out. But oddly no one affiliated with the Heart of Texas Facebook page seemed to have shown up either. It would take over a year before the reason why would be revealed: Both rallies had been organized by fake personas and websites maintained by a single group of Russian cyber operatives known as the Internet Research Agency.[8] As Senate Intelligence Committee chairman Richard Burr remarked after this event was exposed, "It's hard to attend an event in Houston, Texas, when you're trolling from a site in Saint Petersburg, Russia."[9]

CREATING STRIFE OVER SOCIAL ISSUES

What does this story tell us about what we believe to be true? You may like to think your opinions are carefully cultivated from among your friends' and family's beliefs, what you read online, or what you learned in school. It's unsettling to find that some attempting to influence your opinion on today's most controversial topics—guns, race relations, immigration, health care, energy policy, and climate change—don't wish to inform but instead have a vastly different agenda: to create strife, discord, unrest, and even violence among us.

Did the Heart of Texas Facebook page's 250,000-odd followers ever realize they had been duped?[10] That for the cost of around $200 in online ads, American blood nearly spilled into the streets? Did those who showed up to march for peace realize to their chagrin that they'd been played? Sadly, it's likely those who were manipulated may not even care.

We now know that Russians targeted politically activated citizens on social media, contacted them, and convinced them to participate in manufactured political events. In one mock rally that took place in front of the Cheesecake Factory in Palm Beach, Russians paid local Floridians to be actors in a skit, sent them scripts, and reimbursed them for materials. But when these Americans found out months later from the FBI that they'd been roped into a Russian operation, one of the participants, Anne Marie Thomas—the woman who had impersonated Hillary Clinton—shrugged it off. "I wasn't used as a puppet," she told one *Radiolab* reporter, noting that she had loved the idea so much that she did it on her own again without Russian encouragement, involvement, or payment. "I don't feel like the Russians used me," she later reiterated to the *Palm Beach Post*.[11]

The Russian organization of this US political rally is not an isolated occurrence. It seems Russians were often more successful at rallying US citizens for political causes than were our own politicians. We now know that Russian operatives used Facebook pages such as Being Patriotic and Twitter accounts like @March_for_Trump to promote Trump rallies in seventeen US cities—among them Twin Falls, Idaho, and Fort Meyers, Florida—and in some cases, people showed up in droves. On Instagram, the Russians controlled an account called american.made, which they used to promote issues important to the Tea Party and NRA supporters. In fact, the Mueller report points out several Russian Internet Research Agency–controlled accounts that faked local citizens: The Twitter account @TEN_GOP seems like it would be the Republican Party's account for Tennessee. It wasn't. This account was run by the Russian IRA.[12]

Why? This wasn't merely trolling to "own the libs." The IRA's main goal was to use American disagreement over social causes to create disruption in US social and political discourse. From gun control to firearm supporter, right-leaning evangelicalism to left-leaning ideologies, Bernie Sanders to Texas Separatists, the Russian manipulation machine had you in its sights. They didn't care which side you were on—they played on your passions to get you fighting with your neighbor, your family, your fellow citizens.

"The Russians, and other nation-states want the American people to give up on our system," security expert Richard A. Clarke told me. "They want Americans to perceive ongoing gridlock, [that] their opinion does not matter in Washington, and they want us arguing with each other on every issue. . . . You wonder how a Russian, pretending to be an American saying something on social media, could change a vote: It wouldn't. If the post were microtargeted for a specific time of day, with the right topic hashtags, and focused to hit the perfect demographic, yes, their post could motivate people to take action or change how they vote. It's possible."[13]

How effective were these Russian manipulations? A 2018 New Knowledge study found a staggering 187 million IRA engagements with Instagram users: "Instagram was a significant front in the IRA's influence operation. . . . Our assessment is that Instagram is likely to be a key battleground on an ongoing basis."[14] And although the media and Capitol Hill focused mainly on Russian operatives' use of social-media platforms, their influence fanned out well beyond Facebook, Twitter, and Instagram to Internet gaming platforms and even music-sharing apps. They also followed citizens online through browser extensions as plug-ins to track potential targets and by interacting with players on the popular game Pokémon Go using political phrases as player names.[15] The Russians even jumped into the retail game, selling merchandise with politically divisive messages through do-it-yourself online T-shirt shop Represent.

I caught up with Clint Watts, author of *Messing with the Enemy: Surviving in a Social Media World of Hackers, Terrorists, Russians, and Fake News* and cocreator of Hamilton 68, a dashboard tracking Russian propaganda on Twitter. He recalls realizing how convincing manipulation campaigns can be. "Someone I went to high school with sent me what I had been tracking as Russian propaganda, and he saw it as accurate. He had no idea that he was sending me Kremlin-sponsored content."[16]

Let's look at some of the more hot-button cultural issues we now know were subject to Russian manipulation.

RACE RELATIONS

> While the motivations behind these shootings may not yet be fully known, there are indications that the El Paso shooting follows a dangerous trend: troubled individuals who embrace racist ideologies and see themselves obligated to act violently to preserve white supremacy. Like the followers of ISIS and other foreign terrorist organizations, these individuals may act alone, but they've been radicalized by white nationalist websites that proliferate on the Internet. That means that both law-enforcement agencies and Internet platforms need to come up with better strategies to reduce the influence of these hate groups.
>
> —Former US president Barack Obama's private Twitter account[17]

Dividing the races is a handy way to disrupt any society. Besides stirring anti-Muslim resentment in Texas, Russian operatives also played upon US racial tensions relating to the Black Lives Matter movement. For example, another Russian-masked Facebook page, Being Patriotic, climbed to roughly 4.4 million interactions, with its peak of user engagement hitting in mid-2016 but remaining high through the beginning of 2017. This page knowingly stoked America's racial tensions, promoting violence against minorities in negative and insulting posts including "Arrest and shoot every sh*thead taking part in burning our flag!" and "#BLM vs #USA." (#BLM is the hashtag for the Black Lives Matter protest movement.) The account also advertised a toll-free "Being Patriotic Hotline" to report instances of voter fraud on Election Day. Another account tweeted about an October 2016 clash between 150 black youths and police in North Philadelphia.[18] "Watch 150 black teens attacking white students & police at Temple University in Philly. But deafening silence from the MSM." And Back The Badge, at one point was the most-viewed page on Facebook, purportedly rallied support for law enforcement, even though the owners were the same Russian operatives.

It is important to note that Russians were responsible for fake pages, ads, and events set up to egg on *both* sides of the racial debate. These Russian trolls also posed as left-leaning citizens using monikers such as "Black Matters" or "Born Liberal." According to the New Knowledge report, the Russians' IRA created websites such blackmattersus.com, blacktivist.info, blacktolive.org, and blacksoul.us and an Instagram account @Blacktagram with over three hundred thousand followers.[19] The Russian operatives also bought Google ads to promote its BlackMatters.us website with messages such as, "Cops kill black kids. Are you sure that your son won't be the next?"[20] In a new study, Clemson University researchers found that in 2018 Russian-powered Twitter accounts fostered racial outrage by boosting videos of ostensibly racist incidents by white women in an attempt to send them viral.[21]

However, Russian operatives seemed to have tailored messages for specific groups. These pages steered African American voters away from voting for Clinton, encouraging them to instead stay home and opt out of voting altogether or at least support more left-leaning candidates, like Green Party's Jill Stein, which would likely split the Democratic vote.[22] "These campaigns pushed a message that the best way to advance the cause of the African American community was to boycott the election and focus on other issues instead," researchers of one white paper out of Oxford concluded.[23]

VACCINATIONS

Do you believe in vaccinating your children? While ideally your opinion is shaped by well-established medical advice from your pediatrician, the American Medical Association, and the Centers for Disease Control, heated debate over vaccinations can still be found raging on social media. Although one prominent study that claimed to find a link between the rise of autism and the MMR childhood vaccine was widely debunked in 2010, on any given day in your social-media feed you can find an array of alternative theories supporting vehement opposition to vaccinations, for example, claiming they're unsafe or promoted by a greedy pharmaceutical industry.

This one on Twitter read, "Did you know there was a secret government database of #vaccine-damaged children? #VaccinateUS?"

But yet again, things are not what they seem. Researchers from George Washington University, the University of Maryland, and Johns Hopkins University examined tweets posted from 2014 through late 2017 and reported in the *American Journal of Public Health* that fake persona accounts manned by Russian operatives were behind many of these comments about vaccinations—both for and against. The hashtag #VaccinateUS was particularly favored by these trolls.[24]

Why would Russian hackers care if our kids are vaccinated? They don't. In fact, Russia has almost a 100 percent vaccination rate for its own children. The US Department of Health and Human Services does in fact have an established database for reporting adverse effects from vaccines; it is hardly a secret.[25] The ultimate goal in the Russian trolling wasn't really to reduce vaccination rates in the United States; it was to create a public misinformation campaign, rile up Americans' hostility, and foster unease about the issue, making us distrust those in authority who are trying to tell us what is best for us. "These trolls seem to be using vaccination as a wedge issue, promoting discord in American society," says Mark Dredze, team member and professor of computer science at Johns Hopkins. "However, by playing both sides, they erode public trust in vaccination, exposing us all to the risk of infectious diseases."[26]

ENERGY POLICY

It's contentious times in the fight over energy policy. In the United States, we are divided over climate change, granting land access to oil pipelines such as the Keystone Pipeline, and the safety of fracking—or sourcing natural gas from a rocky ground—to those living in surrounding communities. Again, Russian IRA operatives used these issues to create a wedge in the American electorate. A March 2018 report from the US House of Representatives during its review of four thousand social-media accounts revealed that over nine thousand posts on Facebook, Twitter, and Instagram focused on negative news and fake news regarding pipelines and fracking.[27]

For example, one post read, "Uh oh! Progressive fans of Justin Trudeau might be in for MAJOR buzzkill (Hint: Keystone, Trump, OMG!)"[28]

Why promote fears of fracking? One possible motive would be controlling gas prices. Putin needs to improve Russia's economy and in a world where fuel prices are low he has not been able to count on high prices for his pipeline sales to the European Union to fund his ambitions. One devious way for Russia to control or at least influence pricing on fuel is to create public panic or distrust in alternative-energy sources, such as fracking, or in other countries, such as Canada, as suppliers.

Capitol Hill investigations published by the US House of Representatives' Committee on Science, Space, and Technology found evidence of Russian operatives promoting social-media activism against pipelines between the United States and Canada.[29] These included the Keystone XL, which exports Alberta oil to the United States, and Enbridge Inc.'s Line 5, part of the Lakehead pipeline system that moves Western Canadian oil to Eastern Canada. Information provided by social-media companies such as Twitter and Facebook[30] found again that Russian IRA operatives' posts incited fears around oil spills and pollution. Ironically, the misinformation campaign also promoted alternative-energy use and abandoning using fossil fuels. The operatives did not stop at using social media; they also funded pro-environmental groups, such as the Tides Foundation. Russia's motivation is undoubtedly financial: They want to stop the United States and Canada from being major oil producers and exporters so Russian can control prices and energy flow, leading to their greater global influence.

If you have made conclusions on energy policy based on skimming a few online posts, you should be disturbed to know that your opinion may have been tampered with by forces from beyond our borders.

PRO-PALESTINE

Like Russia, Iran has been using social-media influence operations to discredit democracy for years. In recent US elections, Iranian hackers, also posing as everyday Americans, created websites and pages promoting anti-Trump content. These Iranian Internet trolls posted as if they were Never Trumpers in some scenarios, members of the women's movement in others, concerned Democrats in some instances, and so on and so forth. Their posts used hashtags like #Resist and #NotMyPresident. Some accounts were traced back to Iran as early as 2011, but most of the fake personas pushing anti-Trump propaganda were created after Trump took office. In August 2018, Facebook and Twitter reported that over one thousand accounts with fake personas were being used to promote the Iranian regime across the globe—in the United Kingdom, the United States, Latin America, and the Middle East—and removed the accounts responsible.[31]

One of Iran's attempts at covert manipulation was to establish an organization and website for Liberty Front Press, which described its own membership as anyone who wants to shape the direction of the world toward a better future. They lifted news stories from traditional news organization such as CNN and Politico and began promoting pro-Palestinian articles to attract liberal readers—all while covertly trying to push pro-Iranian messaging.

Facebook was eventually tipped off by California-based security firm FireEye, which noticed that the e-mail addresses to register the site could be traced to Iranian-based Web designers, and ended up suspending Liberty Front Press's account—but not before it had already garnered 155,000 followers across platforms such as Pinterest and YouTube. In hindsight, their messaging was sloppy; they used off-topic, random hashtags like #TheBachelor and #HappyBirthdayJustinBieber to pump up views, which should have been a giveaway to any savvy Internet user.[32]

"Come on, come on! We don't have all day!" Huzaifa shouts in his native Farsi. "Did you push out the newsfeed on WhatsApp?"

Huzaifa was born and raised in the picturesque 1,500-year-old Iranian village of Abyaneh, where he graduated at the top of his class in high school. His gaze briefly falls upon a picture of his lovely wife, smiling in a white floral headscarf, traditional garb in their village. She is framed by a garden of flowering trees, vines, and plentiful mint and chamomile. He smiles back at her, distracted for a moment by her beauty, until he hears the reply.

"Calm down," Buraid shouts back in Farsi, although his family also speaks Kurdish. "Yes! It is perfection." Buraid hails from the village of Palangan in the Kurdistan Province of Iran. Buraid and Huzaifa met in a freshman computer-engineering class at the University of Tehran and soon became inseparable.

"The debate is about to start. You sure this is going to work?" whispers Huzaifa, as if they might be overheard. The two men look around the family apartment anxiously. Both are sweating profusely even though it's not at all warm in the small room they occupy.

"Yes," croaks Buraid. "It will work. Turn on the TV."

To viewers at home, the debate had not started. But inside the university theater where the debate is being held, it is a hive of activity. Buzz! Reporters' cell phones begin to light up with a blast of incoming alerts. Their faces glow a greenish blue as they peer intently over their screens. Many are squinting at the WhatsApp message in disbelief. Some shake their heads. Others look around with wonderment on their faces, subtly glancing left and right, to see if anyone else has received what they've just received.

One reporter scribbles a note and rushes past security toward the moderator up on stage. The moderator nods to the guard to let the reporter proceed and grabs the note with a quick flick of one hand, pushing his reading glasses down with the other. He scrutinizes the reporter's outstretched phone and looks disgusted. He runs his hands through his silky black hair, flashing silver cufflinks that play off his distinguished gray suit and even grayer eyes. He takes his glasses off and grabs the hankie tucked into his front pocket and begins to slowly clean them.

The moderator is the country's best political reporter and has been highly critical of the leading political candidate, Mr. Jaideep. Even without audio, Huzaifa and Buraid can tell through the TV screen that the moderator is contemplating what to do: It's too late to debunk the info, but at any moment the announcer's voice will signal that the debate is about to begin. The moderator is stuck. The producer in his earpiece announces that it's time to begin. The TV camera lights switch to red. The cameraman counts down silently, by holding up three fingers. The producer mouths "Three, two, one—" and then points to the moderator.

They are live! The moderator's left cheek is twitching. He's tapping his pen and his right foot. He's visibly agitated. His familiar voice begins with hardly a waver.

"Thank you, people of India, for tuning in—and to those of you here tonight who came to watch the debate in person. I am disgusted to report that I have just watched video of myself soliciting sex from a prostitute. I wouldn't have believed it, had I not watched the video with my very own eyes. I'm disgusted. But I promise you, I never did that. I never would do that."

The crowd murmurs and the channel goes quickly to commercial break.

The biggest critic of the leading candidate has now been discredited. His wife and mother are in the audience and begin to sob loudly as security rushes them behind stage.

A reporter's reputation is in ruins, an upcoming election is upended, while Iran laughs from nearby.

This is fiction, for now.

4

The Manipulators
and Their Methods

Cyber threat actors, especially nation-state actors, are increasingly interested in cyber-social exploits as opposed to cyber-physical exploits. While cyber-physical exploits can have real-world repercussions, such as floods or blackouts, cyber-social exploits are useful to nation-states as a way to undermine their opponents in an asymmetric way. . . . For a small investment, an actor can cause a disproportionate response from an opponent.

—Optiv Security, "2018 Cyber Threat Intelligence Estimate"[1]

WHO'S SETTING THE RULES OF THE GAME?

During the Cold War, it was obvious how the game was played: The world's superpowers set the rules, and most of the time other countries obeyed. In the period of time after World War II, we knew who was aligned with the Soviet Union and who was in alliance with the United States. The rules of engagement were clear. During the Cold War, decades of global conflicts resulted in a variety of international treaties, rules, and agreements. One of the most studied and well-known were the Geneva Conventions. We knew what constituted a hostile action, how to treat civilians, and what the boundaries were.

But with the advent of the digital age, the treaties, rules, and agreements at best are quaint and at worst arcane. A missile attack on American soil would be declared an act of war, but what about a cyberattack on an American company? It's debatable.

In the new world order, it's not just world superpowers calling the shots: The rule breakers are now setting the rules. The rules are set by tiers of operatives. On the global-political stage, we still have the leaders of nations; the opportunity for adhering to the ideals of their nation are up to them. We have democracies and dictators alike taking advantage of traditional media and nontraditional media to promote their approach to governing; that same framework can also be used for political gain, political payback, and political demise. But no longer is the game only nation to nation. It can be nations to individuals or private companies and vice versa.

PROFILES OF THOSE PULLING THE STRINGS

Although the US media have exhaustively covered the antics of Russia, many of which are revealed in Robert Mueller's report, there are other countries in Russia's line of sight. Putin and his regime have designed a propaganda campaign to discredit Western ideals, press, and more. They meddle everywhere, including in Latin America and the Caribbean. You might think Russia would spend time promoting itself or its national ideals, but its focus is to diminish the standing of democracy and international relationships. The National Endowment for Democracy found that Russia will pursue propaganda campaigns establishing foreign policy goals through a "4D" offensive:

- Dismiss an opponent's claims or allegations,
- Distort events to serve political purposes,
- Distract from one's own activities, and
- Dismay those who might otherwise oppose one's goals.[2]

Russian operatives continue to target US policies around the globe. Clemson University, in partnership with *FiveThirtyEight*, found that Russia used manipulation campaigns to post messages to social media for and against US involvement in Syria. In fact, out of three million tweets gathered that were attributed to Russian cyber operatives we know they covered a wide range of topics.

While Russia still recruits and grooms double agents, it also deploys digital tactics and fake personas to gather and plant fake intel. Russian operatives used more than ten thousand tweets to try to trick US Department of Defense employees into clicking on links hiding malware. This campaign was not a massive spam campaign; it was clever, well-researched, and very targeted. The Russian agents tailored these messages to individual hot buttons and interests so well that click rates hit almost 70 percent. Cybersecurity firm ZeroFOX, called this particular manipulation campaign from Russia "the most well-organized, coordinated attack at the nation-state level we've ever seen. . . . It's [a] harbinger of things to come."[3]

CASE STUDY: THE RISE OF PUTIN

Did Putin single-handedly create the manipulation platform that drives us to the point of fighting in the streets? No. However, the rise of Putin and his approach to amplify the US nation's dialogue, discourse, and disagreements are targeted, unique, scalable, and effective. Russia, with Putin at the helm, created a massive amount of political instability and manipulated beyond anything a political PR firm could ever imagine pulling off. In the process, he took one of the things that makes America wonderful—the ability to be able to disagree—and leveraged it, packaged it, and weaponized it. He profited from it. He turned American democracy against itself.

Before we take a behind-the-curtain look on how Putin and Russian cyber operatives achieved such a feat, we must take a short journey through history to understand how Putin, as a global brand, was able to promote an image of strength and popularity. When Putin came to power in 1999, the use of the Internet was very much in its infancy. Only about 248 million, or less than 5 percent, of global citizens were connected to the Internet then, compared to almost 60 percent of the planet today.[4] Upon assuming the Russian presidency in 2000, Putin and his government used traditional media outlets and their ground game of propaganda to promote a strong image. He succeeded Boris Yeltsin, a middle-aged figure who did not exude vibrancy or strength.

Many of the videos and photographs of Putin released to the public over the last two decades show him enjoying traditionally masculine and outdoorsman activities, such as judo, shooting a gun, riding a motorcycle, hunting, fishing, and, famously, riding horseback, shirtless. Yet Putin has also been portrayed with a softer side, such as in his official 2018 calendar, which features a photograph of the president holding a kitten.[5]

Is anyone buying it? Is he popular? Evidently, his strategy is working. In a 2017 poll, the Pew Research Center found that Putin was seen more favorably than other global leaders, including President Trump. The Gallup World Poll found that Russia's leadership has increased its favorability ratings every year since 2014. In fact, across the world, Putin is held up by some other politicians and political operatives in election campaigns as someone to emulate. In March 2018, Indonesia's congressional deputy speaker Fadli Zon posted this on Twitter: "If Indonesia wants to rise to victory, we need a leader like Vladimir Putin: brave, visionary, intelligent, authoritative."[6]

IRAN

In October 2018, long after the initial Brexit vote and well into the next US presidential-election cycle, Facebook announced that it had shut down over eighty fake personas and groups that had targeted the United Kingdom and US citizens with misinformation and manipulation campaigns since 2016. The nation-state responsible this time was Iran.

Are you beginning to see why this problem will never be solved by the social-media networks? Facebook's revelation came a full *two years* after the revelations that Russia had been using social-media to meddle in global affairs. While Russian accounts had been shut down, these Iranian accounts continued to thrive and successfully target. Iran's new team of digital spies leverage memes and posts about social issues and political agendas and other cultural topics of interest to masquerade as patriotic, passionate, opinionated citizens of other countries. They were found to have commented on issues for and against candidates in US midterm elections and even commented in support of and in opposition to the confirmation of Supreme Court Justice Brett Kavanaugh.

Did these Iranian digital spies really connect with anyone in the United States and United Kingdom? You bet they did: They had over a million followers across the accounts. That'd be the envy of any grassroots campaign, political candidate, or corporate brand. Iran's manipulation campaign, according to Facebook's cybersecurity policy head Nathaniel Gleicher, "was targeting broad division. It was sowing discord and targeting socially divisive issues." The Russian playbook is now the de facto global playbook for other nation-states to emulate, the new gold standard in how to sow the seeds of discord. "This looks like an Iranian operation [that] learned from earlier Russian ones," said Ben Nimmo, a senior fellow at the DFRLab.[7]

NORTH KOREA

If you want a demonstration of how the rules of cyberattacks are fuzzy, consider North Korea's attack on Sony Pictures. In 2014, when Kim Jong-un and his government learned that a movie called *The Interview* was going to be made that was blatantly disrespectful to North Korean leadership, they warned Sony Pictures Entertainment, the production company, not to promote or release the movie. The satirical comedy starring Seth Rogen and James Franco featured an absurdly plotted assassination attempt on Kim Jong-un. Sony Pictures Entertainment chose not to comply with demands to bar the movie. They were then barraged with a complete and total assault against their operations. The attack is considered in cybersecurity professional circles to be a real-life enactment of how a nation-state conducts business and can put the full force of their trained cyber operatives to take out a company. The attackers took Sony Pictures Entertainment offline for months, they dumped confidential internal correspondence on the Internet, they stole movies not yet released and put the material on the net for distribution, and in effect they left Sony Pictures Entertainment inoperable. On December 16, 2014, the group that claimed responsibility, the Guardians of Peace, threatened attacks at any movie theater showing the movie and made references to "9/11." The US Department of Homeland security issued a statement that the threats did not seem credible; however, theaters became concerned and began canceling movie screenings.[8]

Would a missile launch by North Korea on Sony Pictures' Los Angeles studios or New York headquarters constitute war? Based on layman interpretation, yes. If any nation's military were to launch a missile onto US soil, we would respond. But does this "digital missile" attack—or cyberattack—on Sony Pictures' infrastructure also constitute war? Hard to say. There is little legal precedent, other than previous UN and NATO condemnation of digital attacks on private-sector infrastructure.[9]

"Foreign governments don't fly military planes in US airspace without the fear of being interdicted, but they fly military cyber weapons into our networks, e-mail accounts, and electronic communications every day with limited repercussions," says Shawn Henry, former FBI executive assistant director and now chief security officer of CrowdStrike, a cybersecurity firm. "If a tank came across the Canadian border, we know what the government response would be. Yet every day malicious 1s and 0s land in our Internet traffic. Companies are often too reactive, and many don't have the budget or the staff to proactively defend themselves from these sophisticated attacks in a meaningful way."[10] In other words, the sophisticated attacks on businesses, waged using sophisticated cyber campaigns, creates a no-win solution for companies: It's very expensive to put protective measures against the threats into place, and even a great staff and great tools are not going to be 100 percent unhackable.

CHINA

While many Western countries are still debating how to combat cyberattacks, those using manipulation campaigns to knock down other countries are holding training classes on this new kind of warfare. According to *Freedom on the Net 2017*, Freedom House's country-by-country ranking of online freedom, Chinese officials held training seminars on how to manipulate the media, take advantage of new media, and leverage social media for their purposes. Representatives from thirty-six out of the sixty-five countries studied by the report attended these classes![11]

Once "smash and grab," China's cyber-intrusion techniques have become stealthier, combining a ground game of recruits with advanced technology. Based upon US Trade Representative assessments, President Trump has accused China of conducting cyber theft of American intellectual property to the tune of $200 to $300 billion a year. North Korea, known for the 2017 WannaCry ransomeware attack targeting Microsoft Windows operating systems and its cyber aggression against Sony, is also further ramping up its cyber capabilities.[12] And then there's Iran, which staked its claim in the digital realm when it broke into HBO, seizing unaired *Game of Thrones* episodes and demanding $6 million in ransom to be paid in cryptocurrency. Bullets aren't flying here, but we're under siege, deep in the middle of a new type of war.

ALL THE REST

When you think of any country that would attack the United States and our allies through cyberattacks or social media, what names come to mind? When I conducted interviews for this book, the people I talked with would consistently mention the countries detailed above—Russia almost always first, followed by China, North Korea, and Iran.

But surprisingly, new players are also getting in on the action. According to Optiv Security's annual *Cyber Threat Intelligence Report,* Lebanon has been spying on people across twenty countries. How did they do it? They designed a targeted Android malware campaign that allowed them to spy on thousands of people. According to the report, "One of the more notable groups in 2017 was the Lebanese General Directorate of General Security, or Bld3F6. They were identified as being behind the Dark Caracal attacks in which the group used various techniques to harvest data."[13]

In democratic Hungary, there are signs of manipulation campaigns well underway under Prime Minister Viktor Orbán. According to international reporters and the Pulitzer Center on Crisis Reporting project, the Orbán regime controls Hungarian news media either directly or through its connections. The transition began over a decade ago, and it has paid off—not for the people of Hungary, but for Hungary's communist Fidesz party. After winning a majority of seats in 2010, Fidesz held back government ad spending, blocked media mergers, and added new taxes onto media. This incented media outlets to sell, and many of them sold to Fidesz allies or to the government directly. In less than seven years, 90 percent of the media had come under the direct control of the government or by private ownership friendly to Fidesz. It has more recently come to light that, Orbán's Fidesz party creates fake opposition to run against Fidesz candidates to make the party's grip on Hungary's power structures appear fairly and democratically achieved.[14]

In 2015, Hungary recorded 177,000 asylum-seeking immigrants. Orbán played on the fears of anti-immigrant Hungarians and constructed a fence to create a visual declaring his seriousness about halting immigration and to deter migrants flowing over Hungarian borders.[15] He won political support for his actions, and the number of asylum-seeking immigrants fell below thirty thousand the following year. These numbers create a rallying cry for his voting base, and although it's not an issue according the numbers, he uses advertisements, including billboards, to promote a tough immigration stance. His regime-friendly media in Hungary covers any news of immigrants committing crimes throughout Europe, which reinforces the cycle: fear, crackdown, justifying propaganda, fear.

THE METHODS THEY USE TO CONTROL

Limiting What Citizens Can See

In some cases, manipulating a population can mean blocking websites, social-media networks, Internet-based encrypted-messaging platforms, or the Internet altogether. As the Internet becomes more ubiquitously available, authoritarian regimes are scrambling to ensure they have more influence over their citizens. The Open Observatory of Network Interference tracks global access to the Internet and reports that the following countries have all participated in Internet site blocking: Russia, China, Iran, Saudi Arabia, Turkey, India, Indonesia, Greece, Sudan, Belgium, Cyprus, and Korea. In fact, 2018 reached a depressing new milestone, the year that global Internet freedoms declined for eight years in a row. Nonprofit organization Freedom House's 2018 report found that Internet freedom declined in twenty-six out of sixty-five countries compared to the previous year.[16]

Blocking Websites

Blocking websites can be an appropriate action when attempting to shield children from adult content, or restrict access to sites trafficking illicit drugs and goods. However, certain countries and political regimes block websites in order to control their own citizens. Technically, it's not too difficult a task to implement this sort of censorship. A government can staff a team of Internet experts and assign them, for example, to block domain names and websites based upon keywords, filter out websites with specific content, or block a range of Internet protocol addresses. In some cases, security experts have confided in me that they have seen governments use the same software platforms often adopted by schools, places of work, and libraries to protect users from objectionable and inappropriate content while surfing the net and tweak the software to block anything they deem "unfriendly" to their government.

Sometimes countries block web pages temporarily in protest and to shield their citizens from negative information about their country. According to news reports, in 2017 Turkey banned *Wikipedia* when two articles were posted there about the Syrian civil war that implicated Turkey as a supporter of terrorist groups killing Syrians.[17]

In some cases, during periods of crisis countries block the Internet in the name of public safety. It is hard to know whether to support or condemn such actions. One the one hand, such censorship could prevent anyone with nefarious intentions from coordinating widespread attacks during a vulnerable time. On the other hand, censorship limits the ability of citizens to connect, report, and check in on each other. In April 2019, over three hundred people in Sri Lanka were killed in a devastating bombing attack on religious worshippers attending Easter Sunday services. The government responded by blocking access to social-networking platforms, including Facebook, Instagram, Snapchat, and WhatsApp.[18]

Prohibiting the Use of Encrypted-Messaging Apps

Many global consumers want to protect their privacy, so it's no surprise that encrypted apps such as WhatsApp and Facebook Messenger are quite popular. Some people never really use encrypted apps or don't realize they're using one, while others will not conduct anything personal or professional without using an encrypted app. Privacy advocates think more needs to be done to encrypt data, devices, and communications from spies, snoops, and people trying to take a peek into our lives for nefarious purposes. Law enforcement, intelligence groups, and the military counter, saying that encrypted apps prevent the collection of intelligence needed to curb crimes and terrorism. Governments that want to control, or manipulate, how communications are transmitted also aren't fans of encrypted apps. Some countries ban apps altogether, and others ban them on a case-by-case basis.

For example, the government of Bangladesh has been known to shut down Facebook, WhatsApp, and Viber to protect its interests. Russia's president Vladimir Putin wants to build his own separate Internet[19] and, in the meantime, has approved a law that bans technology that will work around any sites that Russia has decided to block. Some encrypted apps, for example, WhatsApp and Facebook Messenger, are limited in function in Saudi Arabia and Dubai, ostensibly to ensure they do not compete with the telephone companies that want to charge for phone calls, video calls, and texts.

According to reports by the Associated Press, during the protests in Hong Kong that began over the summer of 2019, Telegram, an encrypted-messaging app, was hit by Chinese attackers, slowing connectivity as thousands of protesters assembled around government headquarters.[20] China has blocked most popular encrypted apps, such as WhatsApp, Facebook Messenger, Telegram, and Signal. Anyone can try to access encrypted apps while in China using a Chinese-government-approved virtual private network, but chances are the government will know a VPN is being used to access the apps.[21]

These are not the only ways countries flex their muscles and let citizens, dissidents, reporters, and the rest of the world know that they will shut down news they deem inappropriate. In what can only be seen as an intimidation campaign, Egypt instituted a new law for social-media users: Now anyone with more than five thousand followers must to get a license from the Egyptian government.[22]

Restricting Other Types of Apps

In April 2018, the *Wall Street Journal* reported that China was shutting down mobile apps whose content the government deemed offensive in nature or culturally inappropriate. The two agencies in China charged with ensuring that government-friendly comments are supported, as well as with blocking offensive and inappropriate content, are the Cyberspace Administration of China and the State Administration of Radio and Television.[23] In several cases, apps just stopped working on digital devices in China, and some disappeared from smartphone app stores altogether. And in another case, livestreaming on an app from ByteDance, the company behind video-sharing app TikTok, was prevented. The rationale for banning the live-stream capability? Chinese authorities said that underage mothers were streaming videos of themselves, which promoted and encouraged teen pregnancy.

In May 2017 in Indonesia, a presidential decree established the National Cyber and Encryption Agency, which has the responsibility and authority to monitor and block online content.[24] One of the restrictions they placed was on gay and lesbian dating apps.

Censoring Mobile Connectivity

Governments have the ability to constrain cellular services by throttling them, monitoring the traffic, or shutting down the signals—sometimes for valid reasons in time of natural disasters or the need to redirect traffic, but also when they wish to control and manipulate information. In recent years, we have seen governments around the world restrict mobile networks during citizen protests. You can see examples of this in Tehran, Cairo, Moldova, and Belarus.[25] Governments try to justify the shutdowns as a way of preventing protestors from organizing angry and potentially violent flash mobs. In 2012, the government of the United Arab Emirates required that all of its citizens register their SIM cards and link them to their identity. A SIM card—or *subscriber-identity module*, or alternatively *subscriber-identification module*—secures the key and identity of the owner. UAE authorities indicated that the services of anyone found to be out of compliance would have their services cut.[26]

Disconnecting Citizens from the Internet

The West African coastal republic of Benin shares its eastern border with Nigeria, has Burkina Faso and Niger as northern neighbors, and has Togo on its western border. Although considered a democracy, Benin was cut off from the Internet in the weeks leading into its April 2019 parliamentary elections. According to various news media and watchdog groups, the government initially cut off social-media networks Facebook, Instagram, Twitter, and WhatsApp. Additionally, authorities blocked access to other platforms such as professional-networking app LinkedIn and even social dating app Tinder. The social-media censorship eventually extended into a national Internet blackout, with Benin's main Internet service provider, Spacetel, also shut down. Once the elections were over, as of April 29, 2019, it was reported that Internet access to these social platforms had been restored.[27]

DANGEROUS TREND: SUPPRESSING THE NEWS PROFESSION

Designating *Fake News* the 2017 Term of the Year by the Collins English Dictionary

Around the globe, political regimes suppress news and information they do not want their citizens to see. In many cases, when traditional media content is blocked, the government's rationale can range from protecting against criticism of their national religion, muting attacks upon their regime leaders' reputations, preventing the promotion of lifestyles their regime does not agree with, and more. Countries such as Turkey, the Philippines, and Venezuela drown out and suppress the news and opposition through a variety of methods. They have disconnected their country from the Internet, shut down apps, and employed cyber armies of influencers. The influencers spread government propaganda, take on social-media accounts that oppose the regime, and promote their own versions of the news.

When Freedom House began tracking governments and Internet freedoms in 2009, they found that government regimes are better than ever at suppressing the news. How? Due to relatively inexpensive yet advanced technology, they can power social media with bots, create propaganda that looks citizen-generated, and promote their false news outlets.[28] For example, researchers have found that the country of Malta staffs political influencers and media silencers—government employees to both promote the government in power and to specifically target and discredit journalists and activists critical of Malta's policies. This new form of suppressing the news by burying it with false information and armies of bots making more noise than the truth is more difficult to detect and call out as blatant censorship.

Arresting Dissenters

Citizens speaking in opposition to government policy have been detained, arrested, tortured, or killed as long as there have been governments. At an alarming rate, countries are now calling any reports unflattering or critical to their leadership "fake news" and using it as an excuse to imprison dissenters. Human-rights activists, journalists, and others deemed unfriendly to a regime could be incarcerated. Consider some of the more recent imprisonments:

- A Rwandan citizen who wrote online about that nation's 1994 genocide was sentenced to ten years in prison.[29]
- According to both the Associated Press and London-based human-rights organization Al-Qst, as of December 1, 2018, at least sixteen journalists were known to be incarcerated in Saudi Arabia.[30]
- In April 2017, Ugandan journalist Gertrude Uwitware was abducted and interrogated for eight hours before being released. Her abductors' identities remain unknown, but their motive was clear: They disliked her social-media support for a feminist academic who had been jailed for calling Ugandan president Yoweri Museveni "a pair of buttocks.[31]
- South Korean president Park Geun-hye was found to have had compiled a blacklist of dissenters that spanned nearly ten thousand names, including news media, artists, and others critical of her regime. And in an attempt to bury detractors, her administration deployed commenters through the country's National Intelligence Service who were "charged with spreading progovernment opinions and suppressing antigovernment views."[32]

CASE STUDY: A REPORTER'S REPUTATION

One of the most heartbreaking recent cases of a technical attack on a reporter is the case of a female investigative journalist named Rana Ayyub. After an eight-year-old Kashmiri girl was brutally raped, India's nationalist Bharatiya Janata Party had decided to support the man accused. Rana Ayyub publicly condemned the government for defending a pedophile. The manipulation and misinformation campaign that followed has silenced her and will likely cause her lasting emotional harm, not to mention opening her up to possible physical harm.[33]

Internet trolls forged tweets from Ayyub's account that were promoted on social media, attributing to her incendiary statements like "I hate India," "I hate Indians," and "I love Pakistan." Another forged tweet stated, "I love child rapists and if they are doing it in the name of Islam I support them." This was horrible enough on its own, but then her likeness was edited into a deepfake pornographic video that was released online. According to Ayyub, this doctored video was shared over forty thousand times. In order to seek legal redress and have the pornographic videos removed, Ayyub visited a police station, but law enforcement was reluctant to file a police report, which, she feels, is because the personal and vicious attacks against her were somehow tied to the Indian government. The United Nations has had to step in to ask India to protect her.[34]

TECHNICAL ATTACKS AGAINST JOURNALISTS

In another terrible example of the harassment of government critics, watchdog group Americans for Democracy & Human Rights in Bahrain report that Ahmed Mansoor, human-rights activist and vocal critic of the government of the United Arab Emirates, has been targeted with cyberattacks on at least three occasions. Twice it is suspected that Mansoor's mobile device was targeted using tools created by German-British tech-surveillance company Gamma Group and the Milan-based HackingTeam. The initial cyberattack against him, Mansoor believes, was conducted in March 2011. Security analysts evaluated a document he was sent that was laced with spyware known as FinFisher.[35]

The month following the FinFisher cyberattack, Mansoor was arrested, and a UAE court convicted him of insulting Emirati leadership. In 2012, Mansoor was the victim of another cyberattack, this time targeting his e-mail account and laptop. The virus mined communications from his laptop and transmitted them to UAE intelligence. His Twitter account has also been hacked. Mansoor was arrested in March 2017 for posts made on social media and is serving a ten-year prison sentence. Amnesty International is calling for his release.[36]

Unfortunately so many cases exist of reporters and activists being actively targeted, hacked, silenced, and imprisoned by their governments that to detail them all would fill every page of this book.

Social-engineering attacks on reporters are considered the new normal. For those of you readers who are journalists, employ journalists, or care for someone who is a journalist, this section could not be more unsettling. From the research I have conducted regarding attacks on reporters, the cyber operatives seem to have a three-step process to targeting media staff and stealing their information or masquerading publicly as them.

1. Reach out via e-mail, text message, or direct message on a social-media platform.
2. Depending upon the medium of outreach, infect the reporter's phone or computer.
3. Once ownership to accounts and or a device have been established, hide and move on to your next planned tactic.

In many cases, the tools needed to take over a reporter's accounts or device are low-cost or free.

For an example, let's look at a real-life operative who refers to themselves as "Mona A. Rahman." Mona is a complete fraud, and there's a Mona on every digital corner of social media. On November 5, 2018, Mona contacted journalist Ali Al-Ahmed—expert on the Gulf States and the evolving nature of terrorism and critic of the government of Saudi Arabia. As many reporters do, Al-Ahmed's account was open to receive direct messages, and he received one on Twitter from @Mona_ARahman.[37] Mona had used Arabic on the DM to chat politely with Al-Ahmed. She then shared an article from the Belfer Center at Harvard's Kennedy School of Government. The article, just like Mona, was a complete forgery: In the article a quote was planted, also fake, from former director of Mossad Tamir Pardo, accusing former Israeli defense minister Avigdor Lieberman of being a Russian agent. Mona had created a legitimate-looking fake reusing the Belfer Center logo, preferred fonts, and format.

Al-Ahmed had recently been the target of a phishing campaign by hackers impersonating real journalists and was suspicious of the link. He inspected the document closely. A closer look showed the article to be posted on belfercenter.net; the center's actual web address is at belfercenter.*org*. Aha! Gotcha, Mona! Sadly, although the forgery was spotted quickly, this story has no happy ending. This one phishing expedition is representative of a much larger dragnet designed to entrap, discredit, hack, and destroy the truth and reputation of reporters worldwide.

Cyber operatives are conspiring against reporters, and their efforts are working. In the case of Al-Ahmed's attempted entrapment, Iranian cyber operatives were stoking tensions and escalating old contentions between Saudi Arabia, Israel, and the United States. The group has targeted numerous journalists and has been aptly named Endless Mayfly.[38] The FBI and others say cyber operatives in Iran are behind the campaign. The operatives have created fake personas that post and repost accurate news stories mixed in with websites that look like legitimate media outlets but are actually fakes. The fake personas engage with other fake personas in order to look more legitimate. They also reach out and direct message or openly tag journalists, media personalities, and activists. The fascinating thing about Endless Mayfly is that once they propagate a misinformation campaign and get good traction, they delete the fake documents and forged news and send the link to the legitimate site. The Citizen Lab found that the planting of forgeries and fakes by Endless Mayfly has resulted in the media's reporting the misinformation generated through Endless Mayfly as if it were real.[39] The group has changed its tactics but is still effective today. In August 2018, Facebook realized accounts and pages tied to Endless Mayfly were on their platform and removed them.[40]

These manipulators almost started a war. The online business and news journal for the Quartz news organization reported that the Qatari government had said state-run Qatar News Agency had been hacked in the spring of 2017. The attackers then planted a news story with fake quotes attributed to Qatar's emir, Tamim bin Hamad al-Thani. Adeptly stoking global tensions, the hackers falsely quoted the emir disparaging US president Trump. The attackers then ramped up their efforts, this time attributing the emir with praise for Iran, the Muslim Brotherhood, and Hamas. Having been posted to *Quartz*'s news website, the quotations naturally appeared legitimate, and so other media outlets republished them broadly. Things quickly began to get out of hand for Qatar, who was condemned by other nations, worried that perhaps they would be invaded by their neighbors.[41] All due to a hack that allowed fake news to be planted.

How do you know whether you can trust what you see with your own eyes?

It's important to note that even for cybersecurity experts it can be a challenge to determine "whodunit" with true certainty. According to reports, digital forensics traced the source of the hack at Qatar News Agency to a Russian IP address. But even that may have been a false digital trail created by cyber operatives intended to throw everyone off track; it is possible to manipulate Internet traffic to make it look like it's originating from Russia, China, North Korea, or Iran. In many such cases to find the agents responsible, forensic teams stretched for time may end the investigation there, leaving those truly responsible free to continue their malicious operations.

USING PROPAGANDA

Leveraging Gray-Market Services for Promotion

Gray-market services are defined as tools, products, and services built for commercial or nonprofit purpose, with good intention and considered legal to deploy, that are then used by bad-faith actors to promote misinformation, propaganda, and manipulation campaigns.[42] Social-media platforms and anonymization tools like virtual private networks can help create armies of fake personas controlled by automation programs called *bots* to post favorable or unfavorable posts and comments. It just takes a few legitimate accounts to repost and amplify the campaign. Trend Micro explains how in *The Fake News Machine: How Propagandists Abuse the Internet and Manipulate the Public*:

> Our research focused on the legitimate (abused) and gray-market services used to promote and distribute fake news. The pricing models are generally simple: a fixed amount of money results in a fixed amount of actions and manipulations performed on a social-media site (likes, favorites, etc.). Some of these services guarantee the quality of these actions as well (i.e., they will use humans instead of bots, etc.).
>
> The services available in these markets extend beyond spreading fake news and often include the creation of the news stories and marketing these to the target users. Comments sections are also vulnerable to being manipulated.[43]

I have seen several cases of gray-marketeering firsthand at my firm, Fortalice Solutions: An individual or organization purchases gray-market services to promote a site beyond its true popularity, to gain followers and likes on social media, and to create posts that ruin the reputation of a company or person. While conducting research for this book, I performed a Google search for "how to buy fake reviews" and received 394,000,000 results in less than one minute. It has recently been reported that opponents to vaccination, known as "anti-vaxxers," have targeted doctors and health-care organization with fake bad reviews.[44]

The marketplaces for gray services promoting fake social-media follows, news pieces, and government and business reviews are sometimes out in the open but are often listed on the dark web. Want to buy a press release or something that looks like news? On both the open and dark webs you can find any number of offers to conduct these gray-market services, many of which require payment using cryptocurrency such as Bitcoin. Many of the service providers charge less than US$500. Some even offer to help create a "citizen"-written government petition, with promises to promote the petition and manipulate the process![45]

Paying Progovernment Opinion Manipulators

If you need support for your government regime, you can pay someone to support you and amplify support all around you. They can fool even the most educated and discerning voters into thinking that a referendum or candidate is popularly supported and the one to vote for. Consider the case of the AK Trolls.

In 2013, Turkish president Recep Tayyip Erdoğan of Turkey found himself the target of mass protests that had largely been orchestrated using social media. Yet strangely, in 2013 the beleaguered Erdoğan's own Justice and Development Party—or the AKP—had amassed roughly six thousand social-media admirers. They referred to them as *volunteers*, but it's hard to follow the money and determine whether any were paid or they were all working for free. In any case, by 2014 the group of "volunteers" had become so overly energetic in producing pro-AKP posts and commentary that they began to be referred to as the "AK Trolls."

Misinformation campaigns were one of the AK Trolls' favorite tactics: They would create impersonation accounts—such as the fake Twitter account for celebrated musician Erkan Oğur—and then use the falsified accounts to post negative tweets about Turkish intelligence. The trolls then would report the account to the government, as they did to Oğur. This practice continues to evolve in propaganda campaigns targeting Turkish citizens through Erdoğan's establishment in 2016 of the New Turkey Digital Office.[46]

And consider the action Ukraine took to fight back against such mass trolling: In response to Russia's continued meddling in its affairs, Ukraine launched its own Internet army of supporters and publicly stated that the state's Ministry of Information Policy had designed a unit at i-army.org to counter Russian bots and misinformation campaigns.[47] The site solicits volunteers and uses the Twitter handle @i_army_org, which as of October 2019 has amassed almost thirty-nine thousand followers. Most of the tweets focus on their negative opinion of Russia.

Developing Fake Companies and Fake Personas

Fake company names and fake personas have been used to perpetrate fraud since the early days of online commerce. In some schemes, fraudsters would dupe hardworking people out of their cash and their credit-card and payment-card information and not send them the goods they bought. Other fraud schemes sold gray-market and black-market goods from what looked like legitimate companies. These techniques have evolved to more technically elegant and more sinister schemes.

In March 2019, Facebook and Instagram sued three people and four companies in China whom they accused of creating a network of fraudsters to design and sell fraudulent websites, company names, and social-media accounts, likes, and followers. The accused used website addresses that were close variations of known and trusted companies—like myfacebook.cc. This fraudulent practice is known as *typosquatting* or *cybersquatting*. Other victims of the scheme named in the lawsuit included Amazon, Apple, Google, and Twitter. For an idea of how vast and complex the scam was, according to the lawsuit, in the first nine months of 2018, Facebook and Instagram had to dismantle more than *2.1 billion* fraudulent accounts.[48]

Setting up a fictional company or nonprofit organization has never been easier and cheaper than it is today. Domain names are inexpensive, and social-media accounts are free. It only takes planning, patience, and creativity. As we have seen in the Russian meddling in US elections and elsewhere, Internet trolls created fake personas and fake grassroots groups and from their comfortable chairs in Russia pretended to be residents of Anywhere, USA, posting from accounts using hashtags as rallying points. End a comment with #MAGA, and you've just created a rally point for Trump supporters. Use #BlueLivesMatter in the post, and now you might have real people in law enforcement reposting and retweeting your messages. Post for both sides of any argument using two fake personas, and now you may have assembled a digital mob with clashing viewpoints.

Sock puppets, as these fake personas and fake companies are known, can be used for good—to disguise law-enforcement officers trying to bust a child-trafficking ring or to protect citizens wanting to report on human-rights abuses from their government. But fake personas can also mask Internet trolls launching massive campaigns to manipulate or misinform, leaving us to wonder, *Who can I believe? What's really true?*

Where do the fake personas and fake companies congregate? Everywhere that people are. Fake profiles on LinkedIn have proven very successful: In 2015, one such fake persona, Jennifer White, worked for a fake company, according to her LinkedIn account. She had fake colleagues and fake friends in her network. She had an attractive picture and reached out to people. Infosecurity professionals fell for it before someone spotted and called out the fake.[49] It's hard to know the motive of the actors behind the fake persona, as the account was shut down before any damage was done.

We have even had this happen at my company, Fortalice. In 2018, another LinkedIn "Fortalice" account was created, and a fake security and intelligence analyst linked to this fake Fortalice page began to reach out to individuals connected to our employees. We are a fast-growing company, but luckily for us, we had monitoring turned on, and this fake analyst hit our radar. We reported it to LinkedIn and warned anyone that we knew connected to the analyst that the account was fraudulent. The account vanished within hours. Was the scammer using our name for nefarious intent? Hard to say, but in the few hours the fake persona existed, she had sent a generic LinkedIn invite out to many of my personal connections.

Dell SecureWorks found a well-designed and carefully thought-out set of fake personas that they traced back to Iran. The operatives in Iran went further than the average fraudster, creating several fakes personas with long résumés listing the names of real global companies within the security sector. They had a set of fake personas that were considered midlevel to senior in their careers and a set of fake personas that were more junior-level. These junior-level fake personas connected to the more-senior fake personas, who endorsed them for key skills.

Impersonation at the company and persona level, even for global companies and celebrities, is often overlooked and rampant online. You may be surprised to hear that anyone can register an account with your likeness and a variation of your name—and it's perfectly legal. This is particularly useful in a manipulation or misinformation campaign when you need a company or person with celebrity power to endorse your point of view or spread misinformation. If you can't get the real one to do it, why not get a fake to do it?

In 2018, Twitter bots were created to mimic and impersonate stars tweeting about the Academy Awards, harnessing the power of celebrity fandom. The fraudsters duped fans with these illegitimate accounts, masquerading as Hollywood celebrities, using intentionally similar names, like @JordanPeele__ and @GalGadot__. The tweets would include a link to a scam site promising a free gift card in exchange for personal information. It's hard to know whether the operators were working for unscrupulous marketing firms or were merely fraudsters wanting to trick users into sending them money or their personal information. The scam links promising free gift cards and other enticements received more 277,000 clicks before Twitter found and deleted them. Many of the bots were tied back to Russians. When asked about the activity, Twitter was unable to provide real assurance that they were capable of preventing this type of scam from working again. A Twitter spokesperson said the company was "proactively implementing a number of signals to prevent these types of accounts from engaging with others in a deceptive manner."[50]

Russia has built a fabulous global network of fake personas, fake companies, fake nonprofits, and fake local grassroots groups around the world. We know from the Mueller report, journalists, and global researchers that Russia created the Internet Research Agency and hid behind it. One Instagram meme the New Knowledge report links to the IRA shows a fist clutching puppet strings reaches down to puppet-people with televisions for their heads, all captioned, "The People Believe What the Media Tells Them They Believe: George Orwell."[51] It's a neat way to introduce doubt at a time when Americans are reading about all sorts of Russian deceptions in the Mueller report. If you want to spread the truth, a lie, or, really, any message, a meme is worth a million words and can efficiently distort our ability to distinguish truth from fiction.

Open-Source Intelligence and Cyber-Footprint Surveillance of Foes

It's the stuff of great spy movies: A person sits on a park bench, reading the paper. It's a sunny day, with a light breeze, and cool enough to wear only a jacket. The person doesn't seem to have a care in the world as they peruse the travel section. Their smart watch buzzes, alerting them to a new incoming message. Once the message has been read, the person gets up, smooths out their jacket, folds the paper under their arm, and begins walking. They left something behind—a thumb drive with intel planted on it, and, just for insurance, the thumb drive has a bonus tracker so the geocoded location and network information will beacon home the moment the thumb drive is in use.

A second person sits down on the park bench, talking annoyingly loudly on their phone. Lots of hand gestures later, they walk away. Nobody noticed the thumb drive being retrieved. The drive has months of surveillance meticulously tabulated into spreadsheets: names, dates, locations, overheard conversations, tasks undertaken, phone calls, pictures, and more. An effective ground game takes years of recruiting and months of surveillance to establish, and now it may take only a few days to sift through to find what a spy team is after. This new spy work is conducted with tools, many of them free, and smart and creative operatives.

Open-source intelligence is the art of finding information that might be buried to the untrained eye but is available to be surveilled and collected. Developing a cyber footprint of a foe would follow this basic, foundational framework that is customizable for each occasion: With a name—legal name, nickname, or name used at school and work—plus a clear profile picture—preferably without sunglasses, hoodie, or a hat—the case can begin. Once you feel you have a good *target package* for the individual in question—legal records, school records, property records—you can fan out to look at the people in their circle of trust and build profiles on each of them and create a link-analysis report. All of this is done using mostly free tools, a creative mind, and a few clicks of a mouse. To give you an idea of what it may take to complete a target package, when we track down the cyber footprint of clients wanting to know their exposure, what the world can see about them, and how to clean it up, we can conduct a "level-1" search, roughly forty hours, including generating a report with findings and recommendations.

DIGITAL-AGE DICTATORS

You may have spies in your midst right now and not even know it. They might be at your teen's prom, at your block parties, at your workplace. You may think you have a keen eye for someone up to no good, but these spies hide in plain sight. Dictators and their spies have an interesting new tool they can use in their manipulation, misinformation, and propaganda campaigns—something you would expect to find in a James Bond movie. The spies are in every country and on every corner. They collect intelligence transmitted from the scene in real time. They can gather information, facts, photos, and videos faster than using a remote satellite. These spies are ubiquitous, work 24–7, and are almost free. When one spy is found out, another spy fills in for them almost instantaneously.

How did dictators amass these massive armies of spies? Simple: The spies are not human. They are bot-powered fake personas that can multiply at will and mix in with the general population. Powered by algorithms and reams of third-party marketing information, these bots are great at spotting the right targets for human interaction and delivery of dictatorship agenda items.

This technique of deploying bots as spies helps make hackers working for the manipulators much more productive.

It's a spring day in Washington, D.C., sunny but cold, and the streets are still damp from last night's rain. A few blocks away from the sightseeing crowds is a deli, popular among workers for one of the three-letter agencies that make up the D.C. government complex.

Inside the deli, Reagan-era pop music filters through the sound system as hungry diners line up, necks strained upward to read the menu. Several punch in the Wi-Fi login password on their phones, accessing the "Free Wi-Fi" advertised on the front door. Some of the patrons wear military uniforms, some are dressed in business attire, and others, students and tourists, are more casual.

In the corner, a black hat, or unethical hacker, is setting up shop for the day. He's not dressed in a dark hoodie, hunched over his laptop. He has on business-casual attire, the workday uniform of most government employees. He sips casually from a paper cup of coffee, seemingly immersed in the report he's writing. He's even practicing bad operational security by leaving his department's badge displayed for everyone to see.

Except it's all an act. An act to blend in. The badge is a forgery but looks like the real thing. Days earlier, he'd grabbed the image of a real badge, by pretending to hold his phone out and intently reading a note but really snapping a picture of someone's else's badge.

He's now setting up a rogue Wi-Fi hotspot, giving it the same name as the deli's Wi-Fi, and, yes, the same password. A recording device helps him capture conversations that he'll listen to later, and he's managed to redirect all Internet traffic from the deli's free Wi-Fi over to his, to decide whom to snoop on and whom to target later.

Soon he sees what he's looking for flash on his screen—an interdepartmental memo! Someone at the deli logged in to read e-mails, using this unsecure Wi-Fi. The department memo has a classification of "Sensitive but Unclassified" and happens to mention the name of a classified program. The memo also has fifteen other names listed for distribution.

The unethical hacker settles in for a prosperous fact-hunting mission.

This is a fictional account.

5

Hackers in the Trenches

Do you like solving tough problems? Frustrated at the political process, regardless of country? Do you believe the political elite and reporters are not doing their jobs? If you know how to hide online and want to work for great pay and flexible hours, then this is the job for you!

WHO ARE THESE PEOPLE?

If I were writing a job description to recruit someone for a manipulation or propaganda campaign, the job listing would read something like the above. My list of required skills would also include

- demonstrated ability to know how to hide,
- understanding of the limitations of proxy servers and VPNs,
- access to a variety of equipment and devices to spin up more than one operation at a time,
- ability to understand social engineering to guess passwords for account takeovers,
- and at least one well-defined sock puppet that's well populated on a variety of social-media platforms.

Optional and desired skills include

- ability to create deepfake materials—such as videos, documents, news headlines, screenshots of social-media posts, and pictures,
- and skills pertinent to building fake personas that can engage media, politicians, and members of special-interest groups.

The people that conduct the misinformation and manipulation campaigns have different motives and skill sets, but they *must* be creative and problem solvers. The technical expertise varies, and many of the technical skills can be acquired through online courses, universities' online videos, and even just trial and error. Another tactic is attending security conferences where white hats (the good guys) attend: It is not uncommon for a black hat to attend but then use the information gleaned for both ethical and unethical purposes.

If you know where to look, there are also sets of scripts and automation available for free that someone with little or no skill can execute for junior-league hacks. Our team at Fortalice Solutions has observed on the dark web low-cost tutorials that an aspiring cybercriminal can purchase to learn how to conduct an attack. Typical tutorials are PDF files that have screenshots with an arrow and a set of instructions. Other tutorials might include how-to videos. It just depends upon the hacker selling their wares and where the sale is conducted.

The Usual Suspects

A *hacker* used to be somebody who proactively hacked something to make sure it was resilient to points of failure, including digital intrusions or cyberattacks. Today, say the word *hacker*, and the person using the word most likely is referring to a person or persons exploiting unauthorized access to a mobile device, social-media account, e-mail, or company's network or cloud storage. An unethical or black-hat hacker can act alone, as part of a cybercriminal syndicate, or as part of a nation-state-sponsored trained group of elite operatives. Although each black-hat or unethical hacker is unique, here are a few profiles I have built over my years managing forensics cases.

Military Trained/Nation-States

Governments around the globe train soldiers in cybersecurity skills. Some units are trained specifically to protect and defend. Other units learn how to infiltrate enemy systems when the need arises. Intelligence agencies teach an elite unit how to use the Internet, technology, and profiling techniques to gather intelligence. The training is custom-built and delivered to units. Units receive training and may conduct capture-the-flag (CTF) exercises to promote teamwork, unity, and healthy competition. Since the training is custom to units, each unit typically has a digital calling card known as their TTPs—or their set of tactics, techniques, and procedures. When conducting incident response, we have observed that some military-trained operatives will also "moonlight" on their own time to earn extra income outside of their normal day job. That makes it hard to discern whether or not the action was a state-sponsored campaign as part of their day job or something they did on their own for personal and private gain.

Cybercriminal Syndicates

Cybercriminal syndicates can range from decentralized and disorganized to highly organized and effective conglomerates. Syndicates often coalesce around a particular specialty. For example, one dark-web marketplace sells different fake personas for hire, and another marketplace sells website vulnerabilities and exploits that can be used to force your way into databases leveraging their crimeware kits. The syndicates typically have a specialty, and everyone in it is paid for performance. Over the years we have observed that these syndicates run just like a commercial enterprise with a designated CEO and human-resources and marketing personnel, with the exception that everything they do is illegal or in a gray area of the law.

Hacktivists

Hacktivists are activists that hack for a cause. These types have been around since the early days of the Internet. You may be familiar with some of the more recent hacking collectives, such as Anonymous or LulzSec (a mashup of words *laugh* and *security*). Although these two groups are not as active as they once were—what with the FBI rounding up some of their membership, such as LulzSec cofounder Hector Xavier Monsegur, also known as "Sabu"—different groups and individual hacktivists around the globe support their chosen social issues by conducting a mixed bag of activities, such as hack-and-dump campaigns of companies within industries they disagree with; but they have also taken down websites known to traffic in child pornography.[1] As it relates to elections, hacktivists pose a real threat. They can take websites offline, post misinformation campaigns, steal inter-campaign correspondence, dump voter-registration data, and more. Their motives are rarely financial but typically focus on exposing something they believe to be criminal, elitist, or untrue or uncovering secrets that could impact the greater good. For example, on March 27, 2016, hackers calling their collective Anonymous Philippines did an account takeover of the Philippines' Commission on Elections (COMELEC) website and then proceeded to replace the text with their dire warnings.[2] Their cause? They said they wanted to highlight the lax security for the vote-counting machines at the polls.

Another collective of hacktivists, LulzSec Pilipinas, posted an online link to an election-related data dump of the COMELEC database. This incident is considered the largest data breach in the Philippines ever to take place; an estimated fifty-five million registered voters had their data dumped on the Internet.[3] The database was not hidden on the dark web; it was conveniently located at a website that says it all in the name: *wehaveyourdata*. The database and that website have thankfully been removed from the Internet, perhaps by the web-hosting sites. Forensics indicates that the website was hosted in Russia.

Script Kiddie

A *script kiddie* refers to a newcomer to hacking, a kid using scripts to hack. The newcomer is often younger in both age and experience and typically uses free or relatively inexpensive scripts to do their hacking. Although script kiddies did not seem to play a big role in past manipulation campaigns, with the increasing availability of tool options available these newcomers could decide to get involved in politics through hack-and-dump and manipulation campaigns.

THE HACKER'S TOOLKIT

When you create something like this for good, you know it can be used by the bad side too.

—Benjamin Delpy, Mimikatz Creator[4]

Let's look at a hypothetical hack and review the different techniques and tools used to pull it off. Caveat: This is not a book about how to hack or launch a manipulation campaign, so some specific details are omitted; the following is merely illustrative of how the hack might work.

Scenario: Samantha has been hired to hack into the Republican National Committee to search for salacious information to sell to the highest bidders and potentially embarrass the RNC and the president. Samantha fires up her virtual machine, turns on her VPN and proxy-server software, and signs in as a sock puppet she named "Bob Mastery." She researches the RNC leadership and learns the head of communications is a new mother named Lisa Smith. Still masquerading as "Bob Mastery," Samantha conducts an online search of Lisa Smith, and up pops Smith's Babies"R"Us registry. Samantha sees that Lisa registered for a Wi-Fi–enabled babycam. Bingo! Samantha checks her dark-web sources for the default password to the babycam and starts playing around with combinations of Lisa Smith's work and personal e-mail addresses and the password she found on the dark web for the babycam. Within hours, she has access to the babycam video monitor. Samantha has downloaded the babycam app to her phone, allowing her to move the camera around to get a good look around the nursery.

Samantha is not peeking in to see the adorable baby; she's listening to any RNC campaign information, writing down important details—including names, conversations, and meetings planned—and hoping to overhear any conversation involving the president of the United States about a discrete matter. Samantha hears Lisa Smith's husband ask what the new home Wi-Fi password is, as well as the home e-mail account, because Lisa Smith had recently changed both "just to be cautious."

Armed with this new information, Samantha is on the Wi-Fi network and in the family's personal accounts. She resends e-mails Lisa Smith previously sent to key

RNC contacts, donors, and key White House staffers with the apology, "Sorry if this is a duplicate." Then she adds an attachment that looks like a campaign flyer but is actually a *honey doc*, a booby-trapped document allowing her to track the user on the other end.

Highly skilled cybercriminals are constantly evolving and developing new techniques, sharing these strategies, known vulnerabilities, and tools. They have their own places online—some in the open and some hidden in the dark web—where they communicate, collaborate, and coordinate attacks. They also package and market stolen goods, such as pictures, names and addresses, and financial information, and trade and sell them.

To better understand the hacker's toolkit, imagine yourself shoulder surfing while you watch unethical hackers conducting their tradecraft, looking for a way to break in to systems and steal information, and you watch ethical hackers thwart their attempts. Hackers use a variety of techniques to hide their digital tracks. They may compromise an unprotected device or computer and use that to launch attacks or use *virtual private networks* and *proxy servers* to disguise their work. Because cybercrime laws vary and are different in every nation, these hackers know that if they are caught they will rarely face jail time.

Cybercriminals still rely on the now-old-fashioned technique of sending a convincing e-mail to their victims to trick them into clicking on a link that then provides the attackers access to data and accounts. If that doesn't work, there are now other low-cost and highly scalable options, such as using real-technology products and tools available in the workplace to allow them to hide in plain view. Leveraging techniques such as launching PowerShell, Windows Management tools, and something called the *secure file-transfer protocol*, many cybercriminals can create a shield to hide their nefarious activity. They attack using these everyday tools, which often means that security software, such as antivirus and antimalware software, does not notice that the attackers are in their midst. Once in, the attackers can often take over credentials of real users and grant themselves new levels of access.

So how do hackers actually pull it off? What follows is not an exhaustive list of hacking techniques; after all, this is not a book to teach you how to commit a cybercrime! My intention is to provide the nontechnical reader a peek behind the curtain so they know what they're up against. As the security industry likes to say, "Everything is hackable."

Private Social-Media Groups

The manipulation campaigns easiest to spot and shut down are the ones run in the open. However, social-media platforms such as Facebook, Snapchat, and Telegram offer private-group functions. Private groups allow people that are in a trusted circle to communicate just among themselves. While the groups are small, they are more likely to trust what is posted there, including disinformation. During the tragic August 2019 El Paso shooting, private group chats were posting messages that were not accurate. Some sent screenshots of the news leads, which were false, over to BuzzFeed News.[5] The usage of private groups is hard to monitor, which means this could be the next playground for the manipulators: to infiltrate private user groups and promote a manipulation campaign and then let the user group get upset about it and post on the open social-media platforms.

Bots

Think of the last time you were on a website and "Mary," a customer-service rep, popped up asking if you needed assistance. Many of the customer-service reps are actually computer-generated bots that can answer simple questions and commands, such as "What time do you open?" or "Check my balance." Creating a bot farm is easy to do with today's machine technology. You can create or buy fake personas on platforms and then teach them rules that are automated until you need a human to take the interactions to the next level.

Russia's Internet Research Agency allegedly used 150,000 bots in the run-up to the 2016 Brexit vote and the US general elections, to spread misinformation and "undermine democracy and the rule of law," according to a January 2018 report from the US Senate Foreign Relations Committee.[6] The bots were designed for each country—each country's political issues, candidates for office, and dividing lines around social issues. The bots were customized to do microtargeting, interacting seamlessly with humans on Twitter, Facebook, Instagram, WhatsApp, and Snapchat.

Let us look at what it takes to create a bot. Creating a bot on Twitter currently requires five steps:

1. Apply for a developer account: These are free, and you apply for them via Twitter.
2. Twitter offers a free add-on app that lets you set up basic automation functions.
3. You will need to do a little programming to make your bot work, so you need to write some code. You can also go online and use someone else's code; for example, there are code bases for bots on Google.
4. Link your Twitter app to the code you have developed.
5. Program the bot: Tell your bot what to do using the code you wrote or are leveraging from someplace else; for example, *For every new follower on Twitter, automatically send a message that says "Hello! Thanks for following me. I love memes, don't you?"*

Now you are ready to use your bot!

If you do not want to make your own, you can use legitimate marketing services, such as MonsterSocial, Jarvee, or FollowingLike. The bots you hire, by paying these companies a usage fee, will follow your rules and can work across multiple social-media platforms. You can post comments on other accounts and come across as a human engaging another human, and you can post content on your own accounts, repost, follow, unfollow, and engage accounts by sending a private direct message. The costs are relatively inexpensive, ranging from monthly fees of US$10 to $30.

Sock Puppets

Fake personas, or what is often referred to as *sock puppets*, go a level deeper than a bot. They may be completely fictional or based on real people who are deceased or whose identifying information has been stolen in a data breach. Sometimes sock puppets are created with made-up names or from free tools that generate a fake name and the basics of an identity. Often these tools will let someone choose the country their fake personas are from and generate a new name. Hackers round out these personas with stock photos and personal details, such as religious or spiritual ideals, politics, musical interests, and more. There are tools that allow you to create a new identity complete with a name, address, and credit card. One site advertises their free product, inviting users to "generate *full fake identities* with random First and Last Name, Address, Social Security Number, Credit Card, Phone Number, and more!"

Another tool boasts that its services are "To protect your real information from being leaked." Creating a fake persona does not mean you have bad motives; you may have good reason to act. These tools were meant to help people create fake information so they could protect their information on social media, but there is the possibility the tools can be misused. In one of Fortalice Solutions' client cases, a woman was being stalked by believable personas online, but a deeper look led us to operations that allow a user to create a fake persona that looks completely legitimate. On the surface, the services are not nefarious. But used by the wrong people with bad intentions, the services could be misused. An example of a sock puppet or fake persona used during the Russian manipulation campaign is mentioned in the Mueller report. He refers to Unit 74455, a second team in the GRU—Russia's military-intelligence agency—that not only created a fake news organization, DCLeaks, but also created a sock puppet called Guccifer 2.0. (This is a nod to a hacker who used the pseudonym Guccifer and once broke in to the accounts of former US secretary of state Colin Powell and others connected to President George W. Bush and dumped the findings.) The Guccifer 2.0 sock puppet was used to publish the documents stolen via the spearfishing operation to hack and dump Hillary Clinton's presidential campaign.[7]

Spear-Phishing

Spear-phishing is a popular technique used by black hats and white hats alike: An e-mail is set up to look like it originates from a friend or colleague of the person targeted. The e-mail can be infected, using a link, photo, or video to hide behind.

When the user engages with the e-mail by clicking on the link, photo, or video, the spear-phishing e-mail may be able to download something to the device that allows an attacker access to the user's other e-mails, the device, and anything to which that e-mail account or device connects.

As we will see in detail in the next chapter, Russian operatives used spear-phishing to send a fake e-mail to convince John Podesta, Hillary Clinton's campaign chairman, that he needed to reset his password. Once he clicked on the infected link, they gained access to his e-mails and used their hack to build other hacks to take over fifty computers connected to the DNC and Clinton campaign.

Social Engineering

Leveraging something an attacker knows about an intended victim, such as where they bank or that their grandchild is currently backpacking in Europe, a hacker can target that person with tricks, lies, and manipulation into doing something such as opening an attachment or wiring money to someone thought to be in trouble. It's a fraud. In the Podesta e-mail hack, operatives used this technique to devise more convincing messages. Using psychological manipulation, or *social engineering*, can yield big dividends for a hacker.

Rootkits

Remember that mischievous friend who always knew how to pick a lock with a credit card or safety pin? Today, if you need to pick a lock in the digital realm, use a *rootkit.* Think of a rootkit as the attacker's method to get at the heart of an operating system—or the root. Rootkits can be a program or several programs that allow an attacker access to a main system. Old-timers who worked in computer support before systems were connected to the Internet may have set up a support backdoor, to be able to provide service when something broke. Decades ago, most systems were islands unto themselves and not interconnected using the Internet. Anyone in security will tell you that those old-school backdoors were fundamentally insecure and would not be a good practice in today's hyperconnected world. You cannot build a backdoor bouncer that can distinguish a trustworthy support person from a black-hat hacker. I worry greatly about the support backdoors that may be hidden on election machines around the world. Chances are, if the machine is older, the design for support may just include a backdoor, which means a rootkit will work quite nicely for a black-hat hacker targeting the system.

One favorite method of black hats is to send a poisoned link in a text message, social-media message, or e-mail. The message will look innocent on its face, reading something along the lines of, "We believe someone suspicious logged in to your account. If it wasn't you, click here *helpful-link-name-but-really-hiding-malware*." Rootkits provide easy access and are often used to gain a foothold into a database, a network, and eventually all the systems and data that matter most.

Malware

Malicious software, or *malware*, includes, but is not limited to, spyware, keyloggers, ransomware, and computer viruses. Malware is designed to search and destroy. It can lock up all a hacker target's files, which they won't get back unless they pay money to the attacker via ransomware. Malware can steal files and send information to the attacker through spyware.

Keyloggers

What's the secret password? If you won't tell me, I'll just take it from you. *Keyloggers* work exactly the way they sound: Every keystroke you type in is "logged" or collected and captured to access later. In past forensics cases, I have seen keyloggers used to collect log-ins, credit-card data, personal messages, phone numbers, Internet searches, and more. The favorite tactic to install a keylogger tends to be what I call *scareware*. Hackers send you a pop-up message that says something like, "You may have a virus; please click here to remove it" or "We see a suspicious log-in; if it is not you, click here." Behind the scenes, the keylogger—a type of malware—is installed. According to the Mueller report, the GRU team Fancy Bear used the ethical hacking tool X-Agent, a keylogger, to spy on the keystrokes and look at the screens of users. The keystrokes and screenshots were logged, recorded and then used to gather additional information on the Clinton campaign.[8]

Vulnerability Scanner

White hats check systems using *vulnerability scanners*. Much like a doctor takes your blood pressure and monitors your heart rate to scan for health concerns, a vulnerability scanner scans your network, devices, communications platforms, and websites managed to know if you have an issue that needs to be fixed. But this is the same tool nation-states, cybercriminal syndicates, and hacktivists will use to target your weakest areas. We know now that this tactic was likely used by Russian operatives prior to the 2016 elections when they "scanned" election-related systems in all fifty states.[9]

SQL Injection Attack

I call the *SQL injection attack* the "Show me the money—or in this case, the data—I'm after" attack. *Structured-query-language* injection attacks commonly target websites that may store data, including voter-registration and voter-information sites. A SQL injection attack attempts to penetrate a website to get to the treasure trove of information behind it by sending malicious code into the website's database, which provides necessary clues important to gaining access. This can be voter IDs, campaign-donor names, usernames, passwords, and other valuable data elements. As we will see, Russians hackers also used this technique to hack several state-election databases. Illinois had its election databases penetrated in such an attack in June 2016. "Because of the initial low-volume nature of the attack, the State Board of Election staff did not become aware of it at first," said the Senate Intelligence Committee report.[10] "The GRU then gained access to a database containing information on millions of registered Illinois voters and extracted data related to thousands of US voters before the malicious activity was identified."[11]

Distributed Denial of Service (DDoS)

If I do not like what I see, then, fine: I'll take you offline and embarrass you. Hacktivists have leveraged *denial-of-service attacks* for years. This tactic floods a server with traffic beyond what it can handle, similar to how a hot summer day can strain energy resources and create a brownout. After flooding a web page or network or server with so much traffic that it cannot function and goes offline, the service is unavailable. We saw a DDoS attack on October 21, 2016, when the Mirai botnet crippled part of the Internet for hours, coming in two waves—first in Europe and then the East Coast. The massive attack against Dyn, a cloud-services host provider, caused major disruptions to some of the most highly visited websites in the United States.[12]

But sometimes the DDoS is actually a ruse. A technology team rushes to put out that fire, and while they are focused on the DDoS, attackers come in unobserved through another means. There have been reports about sites around the globe hit by DDoS attacks that were actually decoys. For example, in May 2017, in Knox County, Tennessee, the election website was hit in the midst of election returns, striking fear in the hearts of Tennessee voters, the precinct judges, the board of elections, and Tennessee political leaders. Cyber operatives flooded the election website just before results were to be published, while the media were demanding answers. Forensics shows that the DDoS traffic was cunning and well orchestrated, originating in sixty-five countries to throw off investigators. While amid the chaos the technology team struggled to bring the election-results page and its supporting servers back to life, a malicious probe looking for vulnerabilities was simultaneously conducted. That traffic was later traced back to the United Kingdom and Ukraine. Think of that probe as a burglar who has free reign of your house, including blue-prints, and now knows where the dogs, your security system, and security sensors are. In Tennessee, that probe allowed the hackers to create their own master key to come back. So far, they have not been back.[13]

Zombie Computer

By having a user click on a link or using other methods to hack into a computer, criminals can create a computer that seems to the owner like it's working, but the computer is actually a *zombie* that the hacker can use to initiate attacks.

Zero-Day Exploit

When a vulnerability in software or hardware becomes known but there is no immediate fix in place, a *zero-day exploit* is possible. Attackers learn of the vulnerabilities and then launch their attacks on the same day—or the zero day.

Virtual Private Networks

There's no point in a hacker's using a fake persona or a sock puppet if everything else you use points to their real identity. The first step in not getting caught is hiding the *Internet protocol address*—or IP address—that a device is talking to, using a *virtual private network*, or VPN. Tools such as NordVPN, ProtonVPN, Disconnect, and IPredator help anyone hide to retain their privacy. When enabled, a VPN creates a stealthy and secure tunnel between a device (computer, smartphone, tablet) and the Internet. The good guys use them to hide their personal traffic from cyber snoops and fraudsters, mask them from marketing firms, and in some cases report government human-rights abuses. The bad guys use them to hide their tracks and change the traffic's originating location to make it easier to get up to no good anonymously.

Anonymous Proxy Servers

Anonymous proxy servers are intermediary servers that allow users to disguise their tracks by providing privacy on the web by hiding the IP address that would otherwise tell the world the public address assigned by the user's Internet provider, which may identify the city the user lives in. These anonymous proxy servers accomplish this by rerouting all of the user's web searches through multiple public servers and addresses. The Onion Router (TOR) is a tool that increases anonymity; then a proxy service helps to hop traffic through one or more than one country to further obfuscate their tracks.

Encrypted-Messaging Apps

Encrypted-messaging apps are used for good, as they provide a layer of privacy. They can hide a reporter's tracks so they can tell the world about their country's human rights' violations without fear of being found out. However, encrypted-messaging apps hide the tracks of not only good but also of those with nefarious intent. We know that Russia and other nation-states have used encrypted-messaging platforms that allow the sender and receiver to create messages that expire. Think *Mission Impossible*, where the message self-destructs once it is read. Messages sent back and forth cannot be unlocked unless the sender and receiver provide their keys. Coordination tools that are encrypted, such as Signal, Threema, Wire, or Crypto.cat, can encrypt chats.

Password Cracking

An ethical or unethical hacker can guess a user's password—or *crack* the password—in a number of ways. One popular password-cracking tool was mentioned in the Mueller report: "Unit 26165 implanted on the DCCC and DNC networks two types of customized malware, known as 'X-Agent' and 'X-Tunnel'; Mimikatz, a credential-harvesting tool; and rar.exe, a tool used in these intrusions to compile and compress materials for exfiltration."[14] The tool Mimikatz was created as a research project by Benjamin Delpy to probe vulnerabilities in Microsoft authentication protocols and is today used to grab passwords from memory along with other important data that typically accompany passwords, such as PINs, security hashes, and more. Mimikatz can often pass one authentication to the next system, referred to technically as a *pass the hash*, which allows an attacker to look like a legitimate user as the system passes along stolen credentials.

Dark Web

A special Internet browser is required to access the *deep web*—the unindexed and unstructured part of the Internet. You'll have to know where you are going, as there is no GPS or Google search that tells you what direction to head. Within the deep web is the *dark web*, the illicit marketplaces that take advantage of the anonymity afforded and offers fake personas and disinformation services. "In 2016, the Federal Election Assistance Commission was hacked, and stolen login credentials of its staff were discovered on the dark web," reports TechRepublic staff writer Alison DeNisco Rayome.[15]

Rogue Wi-Fi Hot Spots

As we saw in our opening scenario, good cybersecurity means not using guest Wi-Fi. A hacker can come into Sally's Deli with a laptop and set up a small rogue Wi-Fi hot spot (using a device about the size of a deck of cards) with the same name (SallysDeliGuest) as the legitimate hot spot. The hacker convinces the deli's legitimate Wi-Fi to connect to the rogue hot spot, allowing all the traffic to route through the illicit hot spot. Once hackers own a user's traffic, they can see everything. It's like having a snoop peeking over your shoulder.

The hacker's toolkit evolves and improves. Many of the tactics I have described above used to be the domain of only the most elite, technically gifted minds. Now hacking has been commoditized, meaning almost anyone with the will, time, and access to the Internet can enter the game. Would you like to get an even closer look at a hacker? In conducting the research for this book, I reached out to my contacts, asking if anyone would care to share insights that perhaps had not been shared before. I caught the attention of someone walking around with a dark secret—a secret he had not planned to share with anyone. Until now.

In the next chapter, we will spend some time with an individual I will only call *Hacker X.*

It's a dreary, frigid, January day in Moscow. Hiding within in a shiny, new office building is an elite GRU unit, the central nervous system of a major coup ready for launch. The objective of this covert unit is clear: to kill the idea of fair and honest democratic elections.

The elite team comprises the best cyber operatives Russia could assemble. They work from all corners of the world in pursuit of Russia's goals to promote the motherland. Lukashev speaks up first.

"My dearest colleagues," he says, "we have much to discuss today. On the first tab, I have a list of three hundred useful idiots across the DNC, DCCC, and the Clinton campaign. On the second, I have a list of five hundred useful idiots across the Trump family businesses, the campaign people on the so-called 'Trump Train.'"

He goes on. "In purple are the highest-value targets to send targeted e-mails to first. We must be clever, as President Obama is on to us. Our objective is this: to steal passwords and gain access to computers. Stay stealthy. Watch communications. Watch traffic. Quietly inventory what we can access. When the timing is right, encrypt and zip the files, and exit the network."

Everyone nods. Lukashev then does a screen share of a process map. "Once we have documents coming in, they will be sent over to our data analysts, who will look for key words to categorize what we steal, what we decide to dump publicly . . . and what we will hold back to use as bargaining power."

The operatives nod their heads in understanding, and one responds, "Delo v shlyape," or *The matter is in the hat* or *It's in the bag.*

Half a world away, a solitary man is reviewing likes, posts, and reposts of his recent test run of a manipulation campaign. It's also a gray, wintery day but festive due to a fresh coating of snow that looks like powdered sugar. His mountaintop town looks like an Alpine village and is alive with people commuting to work and school.

He grabs a Monster Energy drink from the staff fridge and turns on his computer. He's been sharing best practices with hackers in north Macedonia, but he has some new ideas he'd like to test. He is cautious. He does not want to get caught. He's on a mission to manipulate the Americans, too.

He hits send on his latest creation. It's an old story about candidate Hillary Clinton's health, but he's added a doctored photo that looks like she's being propped up by her US Secret Service team in the same outfit she wore to the big fundraiser last night, which was above the fold of the front page of this morning's *Washington Post.*

No, he's no Russian. He's a red-blooded American. He'll be damned if he's going to let the liberal elite get her elected.

Dramatization of actual events.

6

Exclusive Interview

Anatomy of a Manipulation Campaign

HACKER X

My ask for anyone with information to share for this book caught the attention of someone who requested an introduction through a mutual connection. From the moment we first spoke, I listened with rapt fascination, a little terror, and a sense that my research had just taken a wild turn. Let's call him Hacker X.

Before our first interview, which was conducted by video conference with our mutual colleague acting as his handler, I learn that Hacker X currently works as an ethical hacker, getting paid to find security vulnerabilities for companies to fix before cybercriminals can attack. The tradecraft that he deployed leading up to the 2016 US presidential elections that I am going to reveal to you is in the gray spaces between legal constructs, codes of ethics, and court precedents. I struggled to best illustrate the mind-set of this hacker and his operations without giving away his true identity. Some of what he has told me has been omitted, as it could lead to trouble for him: If I get it wrong, he could become a target.

Hacker X describes growing up in extreme poverty, which plays nicely into a romanticized notion of a hacker; he tells of building his first computer from salvaged parts and scraps. When I ask where he got his technical training and whether he has served in the military, he dodges my questions, saying he is mostly self-taught. For fun, he plays in various heavy-metal and hardcore bands and reads and writes music. He labels himself as a fiscal conservative and a social liberal, and when I ask whom he admires, he replies, "Drudge," referring to Matt Drudge of the *Drudge Report*. "He's a master."

You may be imagining a sullen, scowling male in a hoodie, hunched over a computer—the black-clad fashionistas of *The Matrix* or the bug-eyed Mr. Robot and his friends. Without ever laying eyes on him—as his video was turned off during our first interview—I ask if he would let me guess what he looks like. He laughs heartily, thinking I'll never guess correctly. Based on our two hours speaking and my profiling skills, I hazard a guess. "You're a five-ten to six-foot twentysomething male. Earnest-looking face, perhaps—someone who could be in a J. Crew or Brooks Brothers ad or lacrosse-team picture of an Ivy League school."

I wait.

"Wow!" his handler says. "That description was stunningly accurate."

There's absolutely no machismo in Hacker X's discussion of having pulled off something stupendous. He does not talk with swagger and bravado. He marvels at what he pulled off in an aw-shucks way. Despite agreeing to talk with me, he was quite hesitant to tell me what he had actually pulled off, but I coaxed it out of him. I told him there was nothing at this point in my career that would surprise me, and I said I would withhold judgment and just listen. Once he realized I meant it, he answered all my questions in full during a series of three interviews, each lasting more than two hours. He is often twitchy, as if he's had too many Monster Energy drinks. When I ask a question that delves further than he's ready to share, he displays some vocal tics and nervous mannerisms. He punctuates nearly every complete thought with "KnowhatImean?"

I purposely ask for several days to go by between our interview sessions so that I can have the opportunity to process my own emotions and stay open-minded. I cycle through feelings of engineering awe, amazement, and downright disgust and anger. His answers haunted me then—still haunt me.

We begin the first interview on a video-conference line, each of us connecting from secured locations. I'm the only one showing myself. Hacker X pauses a lot before he answers me. He's nervous. I can tell his brain is going a mile a minute. I ask some pretty pointed questions, and I can sense he's deciding on fight, flight, or just answering the question. I cannot see him, but I sense him anxiously looking over his shoulder, as if he's wondering whether we'll be overheard. And when I ask him technical questions to pin down specifics, I can sense his concern about how much to say to me, how much tradecraft to reveal.

Slowly, a little at a time, he decides to tell me why he's speaking out. He makes it clear that he feels that getting his message out is vital. "People need to know they will always be manipulated, and they need to know how to watch for it so they can protect themselves. I have not told my story before, but I want you to tell it."

Hacker X holds no sympathy or empathy for those he manipulated, but neither does he mock them. He seems to only hold disdain for a small group, made up of "the elitist left" and the "deep state," seeing himself as the guardian of truth. I ask him to describe the elitist left and the deep state. He describes the elitist left as a covert group of people who want to transform the country into socialism; he considers them to be highly educated and wealthy, with enough monetary and political power to put their candidates into office to promote more socialism. When I ask what he meant by *the deep state*—which typically refers to a "state within a state"—his response is opaque. At times I notice he speaks in hushed tones, as if speaking the dreaded name "Voldemort," the evil wizard in J. K. Rowling's Harry Potter series whose name is never to be spoken aloud. Hacker X says the deep state is a covert group of individuals working within the government that has their own agenda. That agenda until recently was primarily driven by a desire to get Clinton elected so they could use her to further their push toward socialism in the United States. Hacker X says that he believes the members of the deep state are well funded and well connected and that they collude with each other in secret to push their agenda. People sympathetic to his worldview contacted Hacker X about taking action to protect the United States from this leftist cabal.

Hacker X never tells me the names of who approached him, only saying that it was "nobody we would know." How does one post a job looking for a hacker? "You don't," he says. "You target and recruit the people you want. I don't see it as much different from how the CIA or NSA recruit their top people." (His handler and I speculate that Hacker X and his bosses most likely found one another on the dark web.)

Hacker X tells me that, ironically, when he got the call, he initially thought he was being recruited by one of those agencies—maybe the CIA. He only describes those who approached him as "true patriots on the outside of the Beltway, the process, the machine, the establishment." Since I do not know their names, I have to refer to his bosses somehow, and over time I suggest to Hacker X that we call them "the Benefactors."

Hacker X is insistent that the Benefactors were neither part of any party's HQ nor part of any campaign. They were not opposition researchers or professional lobbyists. They were not part of any political dynasty. He describes them simply as "Americans that wanted to make sure that the country was steered in the right direction." According to Hacker X, the Benefactors have businesses that are in the public eye and actual offices in multiple locations in the United States and abroad.

Hacker X tells me that the Benefactors wanted to initiate a massive manipulation campaign with three goals: "run an online news campaign that would net them a lot of money, make sure they did not get caught, and not let the deep state get Hillary elected." The Benefactors had admired the Obama campaign and its ability to mobilize and energize voters through social media to gather, donate, and get the word out. They told him they had heard Hacker X was the best at building algorithms that could target the right message to the right people—and at hiding his tracks; they wanted to keep this operation and his existence covert. They wanted him to build this operation from the ground up, with security and privacy in mind.

"I'm sitting at a table with them, and they say to me, 'Don't you want to be part of something big? You can help us make sure the country picks the right person for the next president. Are you up for the challenge?' And I said, 'Heck, yeah—I'm ready!'" Hacker X quietly adds, "I gave up almost two years of my life serving the cause."

Not once does he mention anything about "moral values." I have no idea if Hacker X is religious; he never says anything racial, bigoted, anti-immigrant, or antigay. He does demonstrate a deep dislike for the "elites" and for Hillary Clinton, repeatedly using the phrase "destroy Hillary"; otherwise, he seems to generally love his fellow Americans and all walks of life.

I go into the first interview as a cybersecurity operative, not sure yet if I'm dealing with a potential con artist, an ideologue, or a nut job. All I know is that I trust his handler, who's assured me Hacker X is the real deal. "The Russians have been indicted, by name, for manipulating the public. How did the FBI find them but not you?" I ask Hacker X in our first interview, somewhat skeptical of his claims.

His handler immediately messages me: "Be careful—try not to spook him."

I frown to myself, and I rephrase: "Hacker X, seriously— I work hard every day to hide the tracks of our clients so hackers have a hard time getting into their companies or their personal lives. How do I know you are not completely making this up? How could you possibly do this covertly? I track criminals globally who hide their tracks, but they always make a mistake. Someone always makes a mistake. I have to ask this—and please be technical and honest with me—how did you pull this off?"

Hacker X responds, telling me he always had the mission's end in mind. He assumed that someone would find him during an investigation into the elections and ad campaigns. Assuming their operation might be found out, he built it from the start with very strict controls and mentioned he looked at spies that were found out to learn from what they did. Think *Mission Impossible* and self-destructing messages. He tells me, "I was solely responsible for hiding our operation, and I was told to build it assuming in the future someone might investigate us. When Snowden put a blanket over his head to sign in, people thought he was a weirdo, but he was accurate. He was so deeply involved with how things work, he knew there would eventually be an investigation, so he built with that in mind. I'm not paranoid; I'm well informed. Nothing is stranger than the freaking truth."

Hacker X gives me a convincing rundown of the technicalities, showing he knows his stuff. "All domains were separate and not on shared servers," Hacker X tells me. "We created rabbit holes to obfuscate our tracks. We used beyond-military-grade security. I made sure we could not be a victim to a denial-of-service attack. I purposely segmented everything from everything. I made sure there were no linkages across operations. I had a security budget that most CISOs would be envious of—everything from the code within the programs and the way they were set up. I used batch files to conduct the uploads of news stories from staging servers made to look like independent people and organizations. None of this operation was part of a public-facing organization. The organization I worked for did not know we existed. Even if a site got banned, something could be spun up to replace it. We were an unstoppable force."

He then talks about the honeydocs he deployed to gather data for his operations. Much like honeypots, honeydocs lure someone to visit a page or click on a link, and when they do, the honeydoc grabs a snapshot of information. Think of it as if, when you click on a link, someone runs by with their phone camera and takes a picture of you, your device, and information about your digital presence on that site. Hacker X designed and created communities of fake people from nothing. Each identity had a name, an age, a role of worker, student, or retiree. The counterfeit characters joined his counterfeit communities. He spins up virtual machines in the cloud: Think a computer connected to the Internet, but one that's entirely virtual and housed at a company like Google or Amazon. Every virtual machine is its own island. The virtual machines each support one fake community full of fake people, and that island of fakeness has its personal identity politics. Every entity gets its own virtual private network (VPN) instance. Think of the invisibility cloak in Harry Potter: He puts it on and can travel around, but nobody knows he's there. Just so, each virtual island Hacker X has created has its own set of VPNs for its citizens, and each citizen and island has its own separate and distinct security protocols. He creates these virtual fictional worlds to parallel our real world. As he explains to me the technology behind what he built, I have a mental image of the Wizard of Oz behind the curtain: Hacker X is the puppet master; he and only he creates every fake persona and every island, its users, its purpose, its storyboard. He creates the headlines from the real news-media headlines, and then he turns over his master plan, updated daily, to a team to scan the Internet for copy, create copy, find copy, and catalogue it.

When I ask him how he got away with the fake personas on social-media networks, he grows even more animated: "The process used to see if you were a real person is still in the Stone Ages! Provide cell phone and name? Sure! I used fake cell phone numbers and fake names. Provide SSN? Sure! I put in Elvis Presley's SSN, and it went through. Set up fake companies with fake people. They have improved it since 2016, but not much."

Hacker X made sure each fake name belonged to a domain. When he used a VPN, he would make sure the counterfeit people would always log in via the same geography—using the same topics, the same virtual machine—and he left nothing to chance. Each fake persona had its own log-in behaviors. "The controls that you would require of a bank to validate a person's identity so they cannot commit fraud under someone else's name—the social-media companies, like Facebook and Twitter, don't really do any of that. So this was easy!" He continues, "Still very easy."

Operational security, or what we in the security community call *OPSEC*, was front and center of all of Hacker X's designs. In order to prevent any security lapses, he tells me, "I was god of the whole thing. Creation, content, algorithms. I had some help with copywriting stories."

When I ask how large his staff was, he demurs and gives vague responses indicating that the operation at one point was just a few people supporting him but grew over time as his news-manipulation operation became profitable. While his news-copywriting minions worked on his grand plan, he would scour the Internet, conducting a covert-surveillance operation, guzzling down the news from traditional and nontraditional outlets. He created big-data algorithms to chunk through reams of data, showing him the best day and time to reach, say, the soccer moms or the angry white males. "I had every demographic that we wanted to keep, persuade, and motivate, down to when to post on a 24–7 cycle within fifteen-minute increments."

"The best time for the crazy lies—or the '4Chan hour'—is 11 p.m. to 2 a.m. The most potent time slot of the day was 11 a.m. for anything that was a call to action. At 7 a.m. people are just waking up; they want positive stuff—think puppies on morning-news shows. Eleven a.m., that's totally peak time. Two p.m. to 7 p.m. can be slow, so that's when you do some tests by placing random stories. It's essential to hide your tracks and do test cases. You must learn your audience by half hour. We targeted a lot of older women not working, retirees, and people underemployed. We knew we could get them out to vote. Our audience was the people the elites do not care about. They don't visit them. They don't know them. Our audience was so massive."

Once he and I walk through his virtual servers, VPN choices, enterprise architecture, data algorithms, and his approach to disseminating tasks, it's time to talk news stories. In one instance, he tells me, he made a story up and told his team to make sure it hit the headlines by that night, and they pulled it off—what he calls "The Dossie" story.

I have to probe to get him to say more. He says that his team created a misleading narrative that the FBI had started an investigation into Russian meddling in the 2016 elections solely because of the Christopher Steele dossier, a theory that has since been refuted. Hacker X truly believes that theory, by the way. But my research indicates that the investigation had started before the Steele dossier was revealed. These days, I wonder about everything I'm reading, because after studying misinformation campaigns for almost two years, I've become a skeptic of almost any report. Hacker X goes on to say that the Steele dossier was one way "they" started to undermine Trump's presidency by saying the election was "hacked" by the Russians.

When we hang up that night, I am stunned. We all know political parties from Europe, Asia, America, and elsewhere are using big-data analytics to target the direction of US politics and government with campaign messages. But I had been unaware that someone had funded an operation from scratch. It wasn't a hostile nation-state, and neither was it a power-hungry politician. It was grassroots and citizen-based. This was not your typical opposition research, James Carville and Mary Matalin–style. What Hacker X is describing to me is different, and it is disturbing. Someone was funding a mastermind operation hidden within the gray areas of the law. They were not registered lobbyists. They had created a sophisticated campaign that was hidden in plain sight. I have researched articles and law-enforcement reports, and as far as I can tell, nobody has pinpointed Hacker X and the now-defunct operation. While some might feel that what this group did was somehow illegal or immoral, Hacker X would contend they were working to distill a specific type of story to people who were dying to read it. They gave the people what they wanted, and the people clamored for more.

For our second interview, Hacker X had told me, he wanted to talk shop with a fellow practitioner, so I've invited a member from my tech team to join us. He's the best and the brightest the United States has trained, and afterward he'll tell me that the chat with Hacker X was informative—and disturbing. In this day's session, Hacker X, my colleague, and I talk for almost two hours about tradecraft. Hacker X divulges a few examples of headlines he'd created, to show me how viral something can go, but he asks me not to reveal them.

"It is all pay-to-play," he explains to us. "Actually, you know who else is great at this? It's not the Russians; it's the Macedonians. I actually contacted them to learn from them. We actually talked tradecraft. It's funny—I asked the Macedonians why they seemed so pro-Trump and asked if they were being paid by the Russians. They told me, 'We don't work for Trump or Russia. We work for money. It's all about the money.' They would post stories about all of the Democrat and Republican candidates. They didn't care about making winners or losers. It was all about earning money for clicks. However, when they checked what made them the real revenue, it was positive press on Sanders, negative press on Hillary, and positive press on Trump. So the Macedonians were somewhat anti-Hillary too, but just to make money. The Macedonians had quite the model. They would create multiple sources, make it news, have it be syndicated, and hit millions of people weekly. Sometimes they would create something with truth and then add falsehoods.

"Yeah, the Russians wanted to increase hate and create dissent," Hacker X continues. "The Macedonians, man—they are capitalists! They did it for the money! Seriously, I'm not kidding—if Hillary support would have made more money, the Macedonians would have supported her. However, they said they would post supportive content and it would flop. Macedonians got to the point where their operation would put out only pro-Trump because it made the most money."

The handler, my team member, and I discuss the fact that with the massive influx of bot traffic, it's almost impossible to discern how much is actual traffic. We wonder aloud at what point it's just bots following bots. Perhaps we've surpassed a tipping point where current analytics on social traffic are utterly meaningless.

ANATOMY OF THE MANIPULATION

Americans are stupid people, by and large. We pretty much believe whatever we're told.

—*The Wire*[1]

"I built this to stop Hillary Clinton. Nothing we did was illegal based on today's laws. The way things go viral, it can go from an account to *InfoWars* to *Breitbart* to [Glenn] Beck to [Sean] Hannity. There are psychotic crazies out there that have millions of followers. If you just target those people, they will pick it up and help it explode. Reporting and understanding of this are not accurate at all. The old stories from two years ago from archives that went viral in the past will go viral again. Every Republican in this country has probably read at least one thing from this operation. Clinton's health. Stories about Clinton Foundation, Clinton money, their associates.

We could dig up old stories, talk about how the media buried them, and package them as something new and fresh. It was a numbers game."

Hacker X continues. "Look. The bigger the lie, the more it went viral, the more it was believed. Most of the time, it was all about amplification: You can take something not even proven yet. Media wants the traffic, because they want revenue too and they want provocative. You can take a tiny thing and expand it and have it be opinion-based versus hardcore news. Most people's lives are hard, and they don't think the liberal elites care about them. When I wrote stories, I'd make sure we always had passion in the story and a call to action. Many people are like me; they don't trust the government."

I ask, "Was this a singular thing built for a singular purpose that had not been done before and, by definition, cannot be replicated?" Hacker X nods and says, "Yes, we built a model on knowing what goes viral and what doesn't. There was nothing to buy or reuse, nothing open-source about the algorithms." Having been a developer myself and managed teams of developers over the years, I know he could not have pulled this off without a little technical help and so ask who helped him accomplish the coding. Hacker X responds, "Programming teams across Europe, Asia, and the United States worked on the code."

I ask again whether anyone else was out there: "So did the Democrats have someone do the same thing for them?" Hacker X responds, "The Democrats are more tech-savvy. Republicans have been in the Stone Ages for years. Yes. Democrats do this too." He smiles and is laughing to himself. "Democrats did it too, but it is ridiculous. A unique tweet would come out from bots, and it was so obvious, people would call the bot out! The biggest thing we were battling was mainstream media. They were running propaganda for Democrats. We were combatting that. Most of this was an anti-Democrat answer to what Democrats did in the previous election."

We end interview two, and I don't sleep well for days, obsessing over what I had learned. This operation did not play by the game but had made up a new game entirely. Just as nation-states manipulate and hack on behalf of their governments' missions, this group had hacked too. They were hacking the minds of voters and making trained news anchors their unknowing tools. They had figured out what was illegal and then set up their guardrail just inside that razor-thin line. Nobody was breaking the law, but the ethics were twisted beyond recognition.

FACE-TO-FACE

These outsiders saw the giant lie at the heart of the economy, and they saw it by doing something the rest of the suckers never thought to do: they looked.

—*The Big Short*[2]

For our third interview, I convince Hacker X and his handler to meet in person, in a neutral city. I show up to our rendezvous point, and my vision beams in on one man I am sure is Hacker X. He has his back against the wall, his cap pulled way down, and he's jamming nervously to the music playing on the overhead speaker. I decide the vibe is too busy here, so I walk over and say, "Are you waiting for . . ." and I name his handler. He looks me dead on, his eyes darting left and right. He nods. I say, "Follow me." And I move us to a small alcove in the lobby of a large building. We sit down. I have brought him and his handler a gift—two cans of an IPA beer for each of them. We speak for an hour. Hacker X does not make much eye contact with me but does with his handler. He's smart, but I sense fragility, and what some may call paranoia, I call wisdom.

I know our time together is precious, so I ask him some lingering questions. "Who did you see as your competition? The other party? Opposition researchers? Traditional media? Alternative media?" His answer is simple: "Nobody. Nobody had built the news and media factory we built, with the secure platforms that made it look like we were many different types of news outlets. I tested the waters; nobody was doing this at the time." He is either blissfully and dangerously naive, or he was just way too busy at the time to check on possible competitors. I want to know if others have highly functioning operations with similar goals. We never get there. I ask, but he just shuts down each time I ask. "When I walked away, I walked away. I have not done the research. It's possible someone else is now doing what I did. I don't look for it."

He gave me an example of a test site where he could test ideas without putting the Benefactors' online entities at risk of being found out, banned, or shamed. He is vague about the Benefactors and their legitimate public-facing operations, but I will hazard a guess that they may run conservative merchandise organizations, marketing organizations, and promotion of conservative opinions and news. Hacker X's approach, his algorithms, they worked. I'm hooked. I want to know more about how he spun up news stories and sites and got them promoted.

"Some of the stories attributed to the Russians—no, that was us," he laughs. "That was my operation that created the headline or repurposed an old story with a new twist. I just planted it in places, and the Russians and others just ran with it."

I ask him if he's proud of his work or whether it dredges up negative emotions. He looks at his hands and just nods. I can tell I've triggered something. "I did do something incredible, but I don't like where it always went. Sometimes the Benefactors"—he's now calling them by the nickname I've given them—"would make me run headlines I did not want to run because the headlines were untruths and crossed the line. However, it was their business, and I was their employee, so I did it. There were terrible things that were irresponsible that were put out, but the owners wanted it to be put out."

I stop asking about the technology and the process and instead go personal to learn more about him. Those who know Hacker X only know that he's an ethical hacker who likes to play heavy-metal music and read comic books. It dawns on me that Hacker X is currently living with his head on a swivel because of his actions, scared of being found out and losing his ability to work in the security industry. I assess where to go next with my questioning. His breathing is shallow at this point. He's nervous. I wait for people to clear that quieter area. After all our time together, I feel oddly protective of his mental state. As the area clears out at our new location, he seems to relax a bit and begins joking about the music in the lobby, which has moved from some laid-back jazz to something more Mardi Gras–like. I jump back into the questioning: "Who was better at this? US political groups, trying to get their respective voting bases out to vote, or the Russians?"

"What the Russians did is a joke," he says quietly. "Nothing but bulls#*t clickbait." This is notably the first time I've heard Hacker X curse. "When people say the Russians made Americans vote a certain way, no way; they must think Americans are morons. Americans are way smarter than that. Americans don't vote based on clickbait. They vote on the issues important to them and the person they think gets their issue. It was my job to make sure they saw Trump as their man and Clinton as someone who didn't care what they thought."

"Well, wait a minute," I counter. "The Russians broke in, stole data, and then doxed the whole campaign. That may have had a say in how things went." "True," he laughs to himself. "You're right there. That probably did not help Clinton at all. She deserved it. What I'm talking about is the manipulation of news using search-engine optimization, well-placed domains, news stories, and social media. We did that. The Russians did lame clickbait going for silly headlines."

I'm scribbling notes as fast as I can before he shuts down on me. Sometimes, in my line of questioning during these hours of interviews, I lose him. He's a deep introvert. I'm an over-the-top extrovert. "Okay, I'll give you that," I concede. "Let's say the Russians on the manipulation of headlines were not as good as you; nor did you have competition. So, would you do this again?"

He looks away. "At the end . . . after we pulled it off." He means preventing Clinton from getting elected. "They made me an offer." Hacker X is talking in a shallow whisper. "I left millions on the table. I can't— I need a life. I did my part. Someone else should step up."

"What if you cannot leave?" I press. "What if you entered a pact and they call you back?" Hacker X scans the area. His handler says, "Did you just look around? Again?" Hacker X does not answer. I'd noticed they had both used a set of fake ID when entering the commercial building that we're in.

We decide to take a break. I'd hired a private limo to drive us for about forty-five minutes so we can have some privacy, making sure only my name is on the record with the car service. I sit in the back with Hacker X, whose cologne I place as Hugo Boss. We talk uninterrupted for about twenty minutes about Russia, North Korea, China, Iran, and political hacks on both sides. We discuss more generally various manipulation campaigns and big-data algorithms.

The driver cannot help himself and interrupts us during a moment when I'm letting Hacker X rest from my barrage of questions. "You know, Obama and Hillary are both supposed to be in jail." My eyebrow goes up, and I look at the handler. The driver goes on to say, "You all seem to be in the know. When is the government finally going to follow up on the thousands of sealed indictments, the FISA warrants, and stop George Soros?" The handler deftly defers the driver by saying, "Well, what are you hearing?" The driver goes on about how you "Can't trust the media . . . My friends and I were not manipulated by the Russians; we are not on social media . . . They are trying to ruin the country . . ." and when the driver pauses to slam on his breaks because we hit a terrible traffic jam, I use that pause to start my interview again,

I ask Hacker X, "Do you feel any guilt or remorse for what you pulled off?" He's swift to respond: "If you consider mainstream media is against the people. There are cases where they manipulate things via an opinion piece, and then they try to call it 'news.' I would say that's bad. Doing this is a story of just one of many. On both sides. It's already being done. Who decides if it is good or evil? I consider what I did as good, although some stories I didn't like doing. It's a very gray area nowadays on what is good and what is bad. If the government is doing it, why do they get mad if I do it? There are government-backed things that they promote."

"So, did the Russians win? Did they convince people to vote a certain way?" Hacker X does not totally agree with me that manipulation swung the electorate. "This election was won by human beings voting," he says. "I was responsible for creating a world that puts words into people's mouths. I don't regret it. Some of it was misinformation. I don't like politics anymore."

"I know I asked this before, but would you do it again? If so, what would it cost?"

Hacker X says, "I could probably influence an election at a big scale for less than a million dollars. If I needed to do it again to make sure the right candidate was elected, I would, and I could."

"The Internet used to be a beautiful thing," he adds. "It got downgraded in intelligence. Any moron can say anything. There is no question there was manipulation of the election. Years ago, the Internet was much more intelligent than it is today. This story needs to be told. People need to be warned. They will want to reverse-engineer this."

"They?" I ask.

"The Manipulators. They will scarily use this."

I don't probe to ask him to define "the Manipulators," but I assume he means the liberal opposition. He is worn out at this point. I realize how hard this has been for him. Whether you cheer or jeer at what he did, he believes he was trying to protect the world by using manipulation campaigns to combat those with the power. Whatever he wants to call these groups—the establishment, the system, the liberal elite, the deep state—in his mind they were in the wrong, and he and the Benefactors felt they needed to the right these wrongs.

I finally ask him, "I know the incentive to do this. What's the disincentive? How do we fix this? How do we stop the legitimate campaigns, hacktivists, the nation-states from manipulation schemes?" Hacker X says, "I don't know how you could battle this: The platforms are set up to make money. The social-media networks make money. The manipulators make money. To shut this down, you would have to stop everyone involved from making so much money."

Hacker X finds himself in the strange position of having done something that has been talked about all day, every day, since the 2016 elections but unable to say a thing and unable to claim credit. When I ask him in closing how he would describe the Benefactors, himself, and his staff, he finally admits, "We were ideologues." It took three meetings, over six hours, and over a thousand miles of travel to get Hacker X to acknowledge this painful truth.

It's March 2016 and a balmy twenty degrees Fahrenheit in Moscow. Although there is not much sign of spring, much has been accomplished for the GRU team in the past two months. Their smash-and-grab campaign against the Americans required an elaborate web of virtual servers in the cloud, fake personas, and freshly minted websites and e-mail addresses that were paid for in a complex cornucopia of cryptocurrencies.

The operation was hidden with currency hard to trace and with cloud instances where owners were hard to pinpoint, and the Internet traffic of the GRU was cloaked in anonymity using a VPN that had been changed and calibrated differently on a daily basis. All operating out of a shiny, new office building within a nondescript Russia nonprofit.

Their team leader, Lukashev, devised a simple but effective scheme to trick users into clicking on links in e-mails, a technique called *spear-phishing* because it's customized, targeted, and precise. This morning, he crafted a very convincing Google security notice to the chairman of the Clinton campaign, John Podesta.

"Come on! Come on, Podesta—take the bait. I can see you read the e-mail!" Lukashev is rubbing his sweaty palms on his pants. To anyone nontechnical, Lukashev's just staring at lines of code on a screen. But he's is actually watching Podesta open the e-mail in real time. The digital tracker on the deepfake Google security alert shows that Podesta has forwarded the e-mail to his IT department.

"Oh no!" Lukashev sits up. He puts his hands into prayer pose and pulls them to his chin. He stares at the screen, mind racing, as he wonders what will happen. Just then, his screen returns a message. "As they say in America, Hot damn! Thank you, Mr. Podesta, for changing your password and giving me the master key to your account."

He begins to scroll. And scroll and scroll. "Yermakov, tell those analysts to caffeine up! I'm about to steal over fifty thousand e-mails!"

Dramatization of actual events.

7

The US Elections, 2016 to 2018

Nearly eight in ten Americans are at least somewhat concerned about potential election hacking. More than 20 percent said they had little or no confidence their votes would be counted correctly.

—survey conducted October 2018 by the
University of Chicago and the Associated Press[1]

BURR: Do you have any doubt that Russia attempted to interfere in the 2016 elections?

COMEY: None.

BURR: Do you have any doubt that the Russian government was behind the intrusions in the DNC and the DCCC systems and the subsequent leaks of that information?

COMEY: No, no doubt.

BURR: Do you have any doubt that the Russian government was behind the cyber intrusion in the state voter files?

COMEY: No.

BURR: Do you have any doubt that officials of the Russian government were fully aware of these activities?

COMEY: No doubt.

BURR: Are you confident that no votes cast in the 2016 presidential election were altered?

COMEY: I'm confident. By the time— When I left as director, I had seen no indication of that whatsoever.

—Senate Intelligence Committee Chairman Richard Burr
questioning former FBI Director James Comey[2]

WHAT *REALLY* HAPPENED IN 2016?

> Vote flipping is not where the big threat is. The big threat is in activities that would disrupt the election in some ways and cast doubt in Americans' minds about the validity of the outcome.
>
> —Michael Daniel, former White House cybersecurity
> coordinator in the Obama administration[3]

Election irregularities have likely been happening since the beginning of time. Dead people voting, ballot stuffing, and more are not only the stuff of fiction novels and urban legends but ways people have actually attempted to sway votes over the last several decades. A quick scan of historical election irregularities on Wikipedia provides an exceedingly long list of countries struggling to keep their elections open, free, and secure: They include but are not limited to Italy, Iran, Sri Lanka, Romania, Ukraine, Armenia, Azerbaijani, Austria, Bulgaria, Hungary, Greece, and, yes, the United States.[4]

The narrative of what really happened in the US 2016 general elections changes as new findings from the Mueller report and the intelligence community are made public. What do we know so far about what really happened? Let's do a quick rundown of the history, because, as the wise know, those who fail to learn from history are condemned to repeat it.

Many alarms have gone off in the United States, but we've yet to heed the warnings to fix the issues today facing election security. We had our first known digital intrusion into an election campaign during the 2008 presidential election, when candidate Barrack Obama was notified that Chinese hackers had infiltrated his campaign computers as well as the computers of Republican candidate John McCain. "That campaign from China? Pure espionage," explains cybersecurity firm CrowdStrike's Shawn Henry. "They were looking for strategic advantages and to understand and be prepared for whoever won the election. Other elections have been different, where information may have been manipulated and/or widely disseminated in an attempt to influence the electorate. We've seen allegations of this around the world, including elections in France, Ukraine, the United Kingdom, Israel, and the United States. This is information weaponization."[5] What did the world do when China did this? As far as public reports indicate—nothing, other than issue a stern scolding.

What occurred in the 2016 election cycle convinced the US Department of Homeland Security to deem the election process part of the nation's "critical infrastructure," a designation the DHS has given other vital services such as banking, transportation, energy, clean air, and water. As different instances of foreign manipulation and hacking campaigns cropped up in the months before the 2016 elections, the Obama administration grew so concerned that the White House contacted the Kremlin on the equivalent of today's "red phone"—encrypted-messaging back channels—explaining that we knew what they were up to. The Obama administration warned Russia that the attacks risked setting off a broader conflict.[6] It appears that the Kremlin was indifferent.

Although intelligence and security experts have concluded, as of the writing of this book, that in the 2016 US elections no votes cast inside an election booth were "hacked" and changed, we know the election was manipulated in many ways. New reports of how vast the Russian interference was in 2016 continue to reveal new information. For example, initial reports from DHS and the FBI indicated that only a few states were probed. But a report released to the US Senate Intelligence Committee in July 2019 indicates that all fifty states were at least covertly scanned and probed by the Russians.[7]

CAMPAIGN HACKS

We know about the hack into the US Democratic National Committee—via the spear-phishing operation successfully targeting the e-mail account of Clinton campaign chair John Podesta. We know this because the treasure trove taken was partially released. (The FBI reported that the Republican Party's old web page domains were also compromised, but by the time Russian hackers accessed them, they were no longer in use and connected to obsolete e-mail accounts. That data was never released to the media or the public, and the Republican Party has not confirmed that a compromise happened.) But in the years since the hack, a fuller picture has emerged.

Here is a brief overview of what happened, according to the indictments and subsequent media reporting on the forensics efforts spearheaded by private-sector cybersecurity firm CrowdStrike. We learned from the Mueller report that Russian started their interference strategy online two and a half years before the US general elections. "By the spring of 2014, the IRA began to consolidate US operations within a single general department, known internally as the 'Translator' department."[8]

Around May 2016, various workers with several campaigns were targeted with spoofed e-mails to try to trick them into clicking on links, sometimes successfully, but the most notable one to take the bait was within the Clinton campaign, John Podesta. In March 2016 when he received the spear-phishing e-mail designed to look like a Google security notice, Podesta and his technology-support staffer had a fatal miscommunication: The staffer meant to instruct Podesta to ignore the bogus warning, but the short message was misinterpreted, and Podesta clicked on the link, where he reentered his credentials. In doing so, he handed over the digital master key to his fifty thousand e-mails, which were ultimately passed along to WikiLeaks for maximum embarrassment and damage to the campaign.

According to the Mueller indictment, "Beginning in or around June 2016, the Conspirators staged and released tens of thousands of the stolen e-mails and documents. They did so using fictitious online personas, including 'DCLeaks' and 'Guccifer 2.0.'"[9]

Others connected to Hillary Clinton also fell prey to Russian hackers when they opened up a file planted by the GRU called "clinton-favorable-rating.xlsx." Leveraging a common technique called a *vulnerability scan*, Russians used the access gained to scan the DNC networks for vulnerabilities, which they exploited to steal additional data. They hacked e-mail accounts and log-in access to networks. They put into play covert screen and log-in captures, stole data, encrypted it, and snuck out with it, deleting the log and audit files so it was like they'd never even been there.

It is true that Vladimir Putin has repeatedly denied any involvement in manipulating or misinforming the American electorate. But that is often how plausible deniability works: This particular group of civilian hackers has been known to receive tasks and a set of directives remotely, with no direct affiliation to the government regime. It's feasible that a gray directive such as, "Bring back anything you can find that could be useful," might have been their original instructions.

The Russian cyber operatives had been observed behaving as an unorganized collection of fiefdoms. The United States took the disorganization as a sign that maybe the Russians were up to something, but something with little coordination and strategy. As the United States began realizing that Russia had attacked voter-registration databases, President Obama pulled Putin to the side at the G20 Summit of leaders in China to tell the Russian president that the United States knew Russia was up to no good regarding the US elections, including the now famous quote: "Cut it out."[10]

Not long after that message was delivered, Susan Rice, the Obama administration's national security adviser, had a message hand-delivered to then–Russian ambassador to Washington, Sergey Kislyak.[11] And yet Russian interference continued. In fact, multiple different Russian cyber operatives, led separately, went after the same networks and treasure troves of information.

Dmitri Alperovitch, the Russian-born (but US-raised) cofounder of CrowdStrike, has been on the record regarding his team's investigation on behalf of the Democratic National Committee servers. He notes that he observed two groups of hackers hit the DNC infrastructure. Based on the hackers' digital tracks, Alperovitch's team gave the two groups of hackers their own code names. The group that seemed to operate as a Russian military unit was called Fancy Bear. The second unit behaved more like an autonomous and super-secret covert Russian intelligence unit and was named Cozy Bear. Forensics work indicated that the two groups operated independently and that each did not know the other was also attacking the DNC servers and information. "Cozy Bear broke into their systems the summer of 2015. Fancy Bear looks like they broke into the DNC network in April 2016, almost a year later! From what we can tell, they did not work together and did not seem to know the other one was there." Per Alperovitch, in Russia, this is not an uncommon scenario. "We consider Russian Intelligence to be some best of the best in cyber," he tells me. "They are excellent at avoiding detection, and once they gain a foothold, they do an excellent job modifying themselves to stay stealth."

When I asked Alperovitch what he considered the most damaging hit to the Clinton campaign leading up to the 2016 election, mentioning the emergence of deepfake documents and pictures, manipulation campaigns on social media, and the hack of the DNC and Clinton campaign, he answered without hesitation:

"The worst part, from my point of view," he says, "is the hack and dump."

From what I can see, the US is still totally unprepared for [it]. The Russians didn't invent the hack and dump. The credit may go to North Korea and Sony, but the Russians perfected it. Most people probably don't remember that the North Koreans stole e-mails from Sony Pictures and then dumped them to reporters and WikiLeaks. At the time, I tried to get people to focus on the hack and dump versus the election equipment discussion. This [is] the issue of our time. Most people have private things we don't want to be seen on the front pages of newspapers. Destroying reputations—that's where the real danger is.

The tough part is the stealing and releasing of real information that is damaging and truthful and then twisted a little. When I look at the DNC e-mails, there were things said that were taken out of context and misconstrued. Because there is a kernel of truth to it, it spreads like wildfire. This playbook is as old as history itself—blackmail-extortion. It's just been adapted to [the] virtual world. A lot more information on all of us is now being collected digitally that can be used to embarrass, such as texts, photos, e-mails. A small kernel of truth taken out of context can do significant reputation damage to virtually anyone. By anyone who wants to wish you harm.

A FORGED RUSSIAN MEMO

This is where the plot thickens and new-school digital meets old-school Cold War tactics. What the United States did not realize was that Russia was about to unleash an old-school Russian spy tactic—a document that was a masterful forgery.

In the early part of 2016, FBI agents were sent what was believed to be a set of documents hacked by Russia. An analysis commenced to review what Russia had stolen to determine what Russia knew. One item, which has been described as an e-mail or memo written by a Democratic operative, said that the US Department of Justice would not thoroughly investigate then–presidential candidate Hillary Clinton. The memo specifically mentioned that Attorney General Loretta Lynch would keep the investigation from going too far.[12]

Later forensics determined that this document was a planted forgery that is now considered a manipulation and misinformation campaign planted by Russian cyber operatives to create a reaction. It is believed that then–FBI director James Comey was prompted to take action upon receipt of this forged memo, in conjunction with the discovery of previously undisclosed e-mails belonging to right-hand Clinton aide Huma Abedin, on her husband's computer. Comey's next step was to notify Congress that the FBI had recently discovered new e-mails and would be reopening the investigation. "Clinton has said the disclosure, which dominated media coverage in the days leading up to the election, factored heavily into her loss."[13]

STATE VOTER-REGISTRATION WEBSITES

Before the 2016 US elections, in most states voters could register using paper registration or in person at their department of motor vehicles. Citing ballot-process improvements, new efficiencies, and cost reductions as benefits, in January 2014 the Presidential Commission on Election Administration issued a recommendation that states move to online voter registration. The move sounded like a logical one. However, in their headlong race toward automation and efficiency, with online voter-registration access election officials may have inadvertently opened up the back offices of each state to potential hacking.

The idea that voter databases could be seeded with falsified or modified data has been around for decades, but the technical know-how and motive has finally caught up with that idea. We now know that the FBI and DHS identified website vulnerabilities and other potential issues prior to the 2016 elections. According to the Mueller report, Russian GRU operatives targeted state elections by looking for website vulnerabilities, using the technique we've described earlier as an *SQL injection*. A vulnerability in the Illinois State Board of Elections website, for example, allowed the GRU access to voter-registration information, including party affiliation, for all registered Illinois voters that was stored on the site. The Russian operatives ran off with the information, undetected at the time of the intrusion.[14]

In May 2019, following the published report of Special Counsel Mueller, Florida governor Ron DeSantis admitted that two voter-registration databases in Florida had been "compromised" during the 2016 presidential-election cycle. While he declined to provide further details, DeSantis did indicate that votes were not changed and that data was not altered.[15]

Initially DHS had concerns that twenty-one states had been targeted, amounting to roughly five hundred thousand voters. However, recent reports have stated that all fifty states were at some point scanned by Russian operatives. Many of the details have been kept under wraps to avoid further vulnerabilities from surfacing.[16]

It is surmised that the hackers could have changed or deleted voter-registration data—although nobody has produced evidence that this has happened. "What it mostly looked like to us was reconnaissance," said Michael Daniel, former special assistant to the president and cybersecurity coordinator at the White House. "I would have characterized it at the time as sort of conducting the reconnaissance to do the network mapping, to do the topology mapping so that you could actually understand the network, establish a presence so you could come back later and actually execute an operation."[17]

The threat is ongoing. "For example, on August 24, 2018, cybersecurity officials detected multiple attempts to illegally access the State of Vermont's Online Voter Registration Application (OLVR), which serves as the state's resident voter–registration database, according to DHS reporting. The malicious activity included one Cross-Site Scripting attempt, seven Structured Query Language

(SQL) injection attempts, and one attempted Denial-of-Service (DoS) attack. All attempts were unsuccessful."[18]

Do we know how the Russians pulled off such a feat? Most likely the exact details are provided in the redacted sections of the Mueller report. In the case of Florida, Russian operatives disguised themselves as election-equipment vendors and set up a trap for election officials—who fell for it. In an indictment of Russian operatives, Mueller described their technique (the election-equipment company names were anonymized, labeled Vendor 1, and so on): "In or around November 2016 and prior to the 2016 US presidential election, KOVALEV and his coconspirators used an e-mail account designed to look like a Vendor 1 e-mail address to send over one hundred spear-phishing e-mails to organizations and personnel involved in administering elections in numerous Florida counties. The spear-phishing e-mails contained malware that the conspirators embedded into Word documents bearing Vendor 1's logo."[19] The remaining details have not been provided to the public. This is typical practice during an ongoing investigation, protecting the victim from additional attacks. Often in such cases the victim still has several months of work to do in order to remedy security vulnerabilities.

THE MANIPULATION CAMPAIGN

Elected officials and campaigns are no strangers to political espionage, but the relentless attacks during the 2016 cycle were unprecedented. Social-media companies played a new role in the hacking of the privacy and trust of Americans—the packaging and selling of social-media behaviors to third parties. Fake personas managed by bots targeted every argument and issues on both sides of the aisle, stirring up anger and igniting arguments on topics to the point that dialogue broke down into shouting matches and physical violence.

Since 2016 and through the present day, each time social-media and big-tech executives visit Capitol Hill to provide testimony, we learn new and interesting manipulation tactics that all sorts of players, not just the Russians, used to influence voters. Ballpark figures indicate that hundreds of millions of people were manipulated by online ads addressing social issues. The estimates only continue to increase as Facebook and other sites search and remove fake personas and groups.[20]

Acting general counsel for Twitter Sean Edgett indicated that 2,752 Twitter accounts associated with the Russian IRA had been shut down. If you've guessed that this number has only grown since Twitter executives first provided data after learning of online manipulations, you would be correct: The first number they gave the public was 201. As I have said, over my twenty years in this profession, the damage announced in the earliest days of a data breach or compromise is usually underestimated. As research into Russian election interference continues, the number of people impacted by online manipulation always grows. Clearly those ads crafted by the Russian IRA resonated enough to be shared, promoted, and commented on by almost half of Facebook's American user base.[21]

Former FBI director James Comey summed it up well:

> The reason this is such a big deal is—we have this big, messy, wonderful country where we fight with each other all the time, but nobody tells us what to think, what to fight about, what to vote for, except other Americans, and that's wonderful and often painful. But we're talking about a foreign government that, using technical intrusion, lots of other methods, tried to shape the way we think, we vote, we act. That is a big deal. And people need to recognize it. It's not about Republicans or Democrats. They're coming after America, which I hope we all love equally. They want to undermine our credibility in the face of the world. They think that this great experiment of ours is a threat to them, and so they're going to try to run it down and dirty it up as much as possible. That's what this is about. And they will be back, because we remain—as difficult as we can be with each other, we remain that shining city on the hill, and they don't like it.[22]

VOTER SUPPRESSION

It is a form of voter suppression to convince people their vote does not matter. Low voter turnout globally has been trending in many countries the last couple of decades, with the United States leading the way.[23] Turnout in the 2014 European Union elections hit a historic low, falling below 43 percent. Yet perhaps that has proven the tipping point: In a surprising development, voter turnout in 2019 EU elections trended higher, hitting 50 percent.[24] Could this be the beginning of a trend for EU voters to turn out for elections? It's hard to know how much ongoing foreign meddling is encouraging people to stay home or get out and vote. In fact, there is enough ongoing foreign meddling that a Wikipedia page is dedicated to reporting on the issue: As of this writing, the page reports concerns of unknown foreign operatives influencing a 2018 abortion referendum in Ireland, and that same year Taiwan accused China of election meddling.[25]

Many factors contributed to the low voter turnout in 2016 US elections—the lowest turnout in two decades.[26] Media and polls theorize why so many voters failed to cast a ballot on Election Day: Voter fatigue kept a lot of eligible voters home. Others were challenged at the polls by long lines, malfunctioning equipment, or not showing up on voter-registration rolls due to system glitches. Scams such as "Text your vote" were more prevalent than ever in this last election cycle. And some voters were disenchanted by the manipulation campaigns undertaken by Russian cyber operatives and extreme political operatives on all issues and in both of the mainstream political parties. Additionally, theories abound that the Clinton campaign documents leaked to WikiLeaks disenchanted voters who previously had been uninterested in voting for Trump. Other theories blame FBI Director Comey's public announcement that he was reopening the Clinton investigation. The Mueller report claims that the fake identities and personas used by Russian cyber operatives stoked fears and concerns within minority groups, with the explicit intention of suppressing the vote. The indictment also indicates that the fake personas started online falsehoods that the Democratic Party was committing voter fraud.[27]

Pew Research conducted a poll asking voters why they did not vote in the 2016 presidential election. The top three responses were telling: 25 percent did not like the candidates or the issues, 15 percent thought their vote would not make a difference, and 14 percent said they were too busy to vote. For comparison purposes, in 2012 *not liking the candidates* was the response of 13 percent of nonvoters.[28]

ENCORE: MIDTERM ELECTION OF 2018

"We continue to see a pervasive messaging campaign by Russia to try to weaken and divide the United States," acknowledged director of national intelligence Dan Coats.[29]

On September 12, in the weeks leading up to the 2018 US midterm elections, President Trump issued an executive order outlining a process to hold foreign governments accountable for meddling in US elections, called the "Executive Order on Imposing Certain Sanctions in the Event of Foreign Interference in a United States Election."[30] Did that deter foreign elements from meddling? No. Headlines and intelligence reports on the Hill indicate that we did not see Russian- or other foreign-government interference as extensive as the 2016 election meddling.[31]

So what changed? Perhaps it was because 2018 was a midterm election and less was at stake. To nation-states, it is a known fact that US voter interest and turnout are lower in nonpresidential election cycles; therefore, meddling in midterm elections would not be as lucrative as meddling in the presidential-election cycles. Russia and other international actors knew that the United Kingdom, France, and the United States were onto their hack-and-dump and manipulation campaigns. Also, companies like Facebook—with much public fanfare—created election-fusion centers where dedicated staff played online watchdog to cyber operatives attempting to manipulate voters in the lead-up to the elections.

The United States also went on the offense, aligning roughly eighty of the nation's finest military cyber operatives within US Cyber Command and the NSA and began a psyops game to rival Putin's. The US team started by contacting Russian operatives by their real names, signaling they truly knew each of them, by true identity, and exactly what they were doing. The United States warned them that if the operatives stopped their manipulations immediately, action would not be taken against them. The mind games were played so effectively that many of the Russian operatives believed they had a mole in their own operation. Next, the US team cut off their access to the Internet.[32] The proactive strike took the Russia IRA and other elite units by surprise. (If you're wondering where Putin got the idea to create his own Internet and to test unplugging it from the globe,[33] I suggest you look no further than this exceptionally successful operation.)

But while the 2018 US elections remained relatively safe from manipulation, misinformation, and hacking campaigns, there were some signs that the manipulator's playbook was still being used.

VOTER-REGISTRATION-DATABASE ISSUES

One poorly designed feature in a computer system in California opened the entire state's voter rolls to manipulation. When in 2018 a new "motor voter" program went online that would enable California voters register while visiting the department of motor vehicles, bugs and glitches began coming to light almost immediately. First, it was discovered that the central DMV network was trying to communicate with Internet servers in Croatia. California does not need to be connected to Croatia, so a hack of some sort was suspected. Not much else is known about the Croatia connection, but officials say no data was compromised. Numerous other problems with the rollout shook Californians' faith in the technology and voter-system integrity: Voters found that the system had assigned them the wrong party preferences, non-California citizens were suddenly registered to vote, and some people who were registered did not recall having ever registered.[34]

All in all, it is estimated that perhaps more than one hundred thousand errors were made in voter registrations before California's June 2018 primary.[35] As other states move their voting and voter-registration systems online, these types of hacking vulnerabilities are becoming more and more common.[36] In fact, it's understood that in all the Russian-induced chaos of the 2016 election, Russia had the technical capability to do even far more damage to voter-registration systems than they did.[37] And states find themselves without the technical expertise to respond adequately.

FAKE ADS

In response to the revelations of fake ads circulating in the run-up to the 2016 elections, many social-media companies committed to better highlighting which ads in a user's feed were political and to better disclosing the groups behind the ads, as well as to blocking ads created by fake groups or fake personas. Facebook's newsroom announced they would be "Shining a Light on Ads with Political Content." which links to an archive of ads Facebook has been paid to post.[38] As of this writing, Facebook has distributed 5,378,580 ads about "social issues, elections or issues of importance (since May 2018)," worth US$857,602,821.[39]

This is an important step in the right direction. However, this tool is not sufficient to completely unmask the fake-ad creators or to highlight fake ads and warn people they have been manipulated. In the several weeks before the 2018 US midterm elections, a time when early voting was already underway, Facebook was unable to always verify the entities buying ad space. One enterprising reporter at Vice News under false pretenses bought political ads for an unlikely duo of advertisers—ISIS and Vice President Mike Pence; only weeks before Vice publicized its findings, Facebook had reported they had shut down ads from an Iranian manipulation campaign.[40] All of the social-media companies saw influence campaigns morphing and modifying their techniques to hide in plain sight. In response, the manipulation operatives began to use more cloaking and anonymity techniques, such as VPNs, virtual machines, using third parties to create and run the ads, and paying for ads using Canadian or US currencies.

SOCIAL MEDIA MANIPULATION CONTINUES

A FBI criminal complaint filed in Virginia on September 28, 2018, describes a Russian manipulation campaign targeting the 2018 US midterms. The trolls accused Special Counsel Robert Mueller of being "a puppet" and praised President Donald Trump for his meeting with North Korean leader Kim Jong-un, saying he "deserves a Nobel Peace Prize." Elena Khusyaynova, a forty-four-year-old Russian, was named as the finance manager behind this campaign, code-named "Project Lakhta." The interference continued into the 2018 midterms, with a budget that had ballooned to more than $10 million by July 2018, and some portions of the techniques and approaches designed within that program continue to be used.[41]

Not to be outdone, Iran got into the action, using real persons to create fake accounts and then create fake personas to pull off manipulation campaigns in the lead-up to the US midterms. The Iranian trolls sent out messages that were conservative, nonconservative, anti-Israel, and pro-Palestine. In some cases, the operatives created fake accounts impersonating Republican political candidates, such as Marla Livengood and Jineea Butler. In some cases, the Iranian operatives managed to get fake letters to the editor published! All was going well until they were caught. Facebook shut down fifty-one fake Facebook accounts, and Twitter shut down 2,800 accounts.[42]

Despite heightened awareness of election meddling through social media, the American public had little confidence that tech companies would be able to stop it, according to a group report by Pew Research: "A large majority of the public (76 percent)—including sizable shares in both parties—say technology companies like Facebook, Google, and Twitter have a responsibility to prevent misuse of their platforms to influence the midterms. However, just a third (33 percent) say they are very or somewhat confident that the technology companies will achieve this objective; 66 percent say they are not too or not at all confident."[43]

HOW DO WE SAFEGUARD OUR ELECTIONS?

The race to secure elections, globally, is underway.

Today entire countries rely solely on electronic voting machines: Since 2000 Brazil has employed EVMs and in 2010 had 135 million electronic voters, and India had

380 million electronic voters in its parliamentarian election of 2004.[44] Countries like Belgium use voting computers for some citizens to cast their ballot,[45] and many nations use electronic means to aggregate votes, whether to count paper ballots or send the result from local polling stations to a central electoral authority that does a final count. Estonians vote online through an "i-voting" system.[46] Estonian officials say they have certified the safety and soundness of their system. Only time will tell.

It is easy to see why electronic voting seems the wave of the future and how the United States might aspire to model its own voting system after these countries': It's faster and cheaper, and it's more accessible for those with disabilities. But before we race toward electronic voting as the sole system we use, consider the campaign hacks and voter-website breaches detailed above. Countries like the Netherlands and Germany observed the emerging threats and have removed computer systems from different points of their process to avoid a data breach.[47]

Voting systems are more vulnerable than ever. The Brennan Center for Justice estimates that in the United States forty-one states used electronic voting machines for the 2016 midterms that were ten years old or older.[48] CSO did an online search and found thousands of work e-mails and plaintext passwords for voting-machine vendor employees.[49] You need not be a sophisticated hacker to sow election chaos: Just look for e-mails and passwords. It's as if someone taped the master key to every lock and labeled it "Master key—*please do not use*."

Further, machines equipped with Wi-Fi and remote access can still be electronically hacked using an eavesdropping device known as an *IMSI-catcher*, or a "Stingray." This device allows an individual to set up a fake cell tower that intercepts data by tricking devices into thinking that the tower is legitimate.

The Center for American Progress evaluated election security and reported that not one state was awarded an A rating. In fact, five states failed outright! Ten states do not provide any cybersecurity training. Yes, that's correct: One-fifth of the states in the nation do not train their election officials regarding these issues.[50]

But there are two things every American voter can be sure of: Eventually, every vote you cast in a US election will be electronic, and one of those elections will be hacked. No doubt about it. But Jill Stein's campaign request for a recount in Wisconsin after the 2016 election reminds us all why we need the ability to have some backup mechanism in place; otherwise, a recount wouldn't be possible. My biggest concern is that citizens will not trust election results and that the election process will lose legitimacy.

To combat these voting irregularities, it is critical that the states go back to the basics. The ability to audit an outcome is vital to responding to questions about results. States should provide postelection audits. An offensive operation should be run against each voting vendor and their voting booths, websites, and databases. White-hat hackers should attack every component as if they were the adversary and then close the gaps.

Some have called for greater federal oversight and moving toward a more restrictive security model, but states own the voting process. Providing year-round briefings from DHS, FBI, CIA, and NSA would prove very helpful over time. Also, we should remember the benefits of decentralization: Sometimes there is security in obscurity. Each state in our country, plus the District of Columbia, runs its own election operations, including voter databases. A hostile nation-state could not feasibly wipe out each system with one wave of their magic wand.

Despite the ongoing voting-integrity issues, there is hope. All fifty states took the 2016 elections as a wake-up call and have since strived to improve their security postures. Colorado and Rhode Island have mandated postelection audits; Alabama now requires election officials to take in-depth cybersecurity-awareness training; and New York has created a state Election Support Center responsible for cybersecurity-awareness training and technical support.[51]

The good news is that our government has begun to take the issue of cyber hacking and voting integrity very seriously. Prior to the 2018 midterm elections, the Department of Homeland Security offered state election officials "cyber-hygiene scans" to remotely search for vulnerabilities in election systems. DHS also conducted threat briefings and onsite reviews, as well as released a memo of best practices—guidance for how best to secure their voter databases.

A separate area of concern is the communications, contacts, and digital campaigns of candidates that are being broken into and doxed. While the media focuses on securing the votes and the voter databases of upcoming elections, there is not a lot of attention being paid to whether or not campaigns are taking seriously the threats targeting their campaigns. In the summer of 2018, Microsoft executive Tom Burt revealed that phishing attacks had targeted three US congressional midterm campaigns.[52] Additionally, former senator from Missouri Claire McCaskill and current senator from New Hampshire Jeanne Shaheen revealed that they have had to fend off attempted hacks into their systems. Nothing would hit closer to home for a candidate than if their election was hacked and they lost—or won. With the onslaught of breaches, candidates should be laser focused on cybersecurity.

WHAT'S THE GLOBAL ELECTION-SECURITY FIX?

As we move forward, creating new systems to collect our votes, we need to protect the one we already have. Defending democracy against election meddling is an undertaking of critical importance, requiring a top-down approach. As such, bodies like the United Nations must push for action. First, an international cyber coordinator must be established—perhaps within the UN or NATO—to coordinate the sharing of intelligence with allies, of deterrence measures, and of counterattacks. The cyber coordinator should also send media warnings to voters and conduct state-by-state assessments of voting systems, issuing bills of health.

Each country must create a "fusion center" through which all personnel physically deploy key subject matter experts to work on voter-system-security issues in real time. This fusion center should include professionals from that country's government, law-enforcement agencies, and intelligence bodies, along with Silicon Valley engineers. The center should employ a "red phone" process whereby the fusion center and individual regions have a direct line throughout early voting cycles and on Election Day.

Additionally, each country's government must create an easy way for organizations and individuals to report suspicious activity, involving everything from ballots to voting machines to the fusion center. In short, "See something, say something." Reports could then be analyzed to quickly determine whether the activity under consideration is normal or constitutes a malicious trend.

Some will inevitably balk at these proposals, asserting that any country's government is too bulky to effectively take on an agile cyber opponent. But the truth is that we've already created organizations that have effectively responded to complex crises in the past, ranging from terrorism to natural disasters. And make no mistake—this is a crisis.

The end goal of voter interference isn't just to undermine the outcome of the electoral contest. No, it's to completely destroy confidence in the world's democratic institutions. Because none of us will be spared the effects of this dangerous act, preventing meddling is the shared and immediate responsibility of everyone—Silicon Valley, lawmakers, elected officials, and private citizens.

WHAT CAN YOU DO TO SECURE YOUR OWN VOTE?

You can take matters into your own hands to make sure your vote counts. In the United States, I recommend the following steps:

1. If you check your state's election website and something seems strange, report it to your state board of elections immediately.
2. If you see what you believe to be a fake persona pushing fake ad messages to influence voters, report it.
   - Facebook: https://www.facebook.com/business/help/162606073801742
   - Twitter: https://help.twitter.com/en/safety-and-security/reporting-twitter-ads
   - Instagram: https://help.instagram.com/118613625676963
   - YouTube: https://support.google.com/adspolicy/answer/6014595?hl=en
3. Check your voter status before you go to the polls. Voters in thirty-seven states and the District of Columbia can register to vote online; and visit Vote.org to find out how to check on your registration.
4. Pay close attention to how you cast your ballot while in the booth, and take your time during the review process before you finalize your vote.
5. As of this writing, unless you are serving in the US military overseas or are a resident of West Virginia, you cannot vote electronically on your phone, so avoid falling victim to text-messaging and e-mail scams that say you can.

6. Trust the system. It's flawed and imperfect, but it's the only one we have. If you stay home and don't vote, then the foreign operatives, manipulators, and cybercriminals win.

7. For citizens outside the United States, the above tips are still useful in your country's elections, but make sure you research and know how to reach the election officials for your region.

The administrative assistant knocks on the door of her boss, Hans-Georg Maassen, head of the German domestic intelligence service—the BfV. "Sir, I have a covert analyst who says he needs to see you. He's from the intel unit focused on Russia. . . . He says the topic is Spain." Maassen frowns to himself. *What the bloody hell would Spain have to do with Russia?* The uniformed analyst stands at the door, a notebook under his arm. Maassen waves him into the room. "Have a seat."

"Sir, this won't take long. I'm afraid Russia is meddling with Spain and the Catalonia region. I have a few pictures from my intelligence gathering to show you. We may want to alert Spain's foreign minister, Alfonso Dastis. I have intercepted communications between the Russians and Julian Assange in the Ecuadorian embassy in London. He's throwing support behind the Separatists. Further, Internet trolls in Russia are stoking tensions; the bots have suddenly become outsiders cheering on Catalans to secede. The amount of traffic I'm tracking is mind-boggling. Would you like to see my research? What should we do? The vote is weeks away."

* * *

Salvador can see the statue of Jesus from his tidy home in Donostia/San Sebastián on the Bay of Biscay. Salvador grew up in the picturesque Catalan region. As most from Donostia, he speaks Basque, the native language; but he's also fluent in Spanish, Portuguese, French, and German. It is a source of pride that kings have tried in vain to impose the Spanish language and laws on the region but the Catalans have not budged.

Salvador is reading the news online, drinking a cappuccino and smoking, when his cell phone rings. He's puzzled and answers "Kaixo?"—Basque for *hello*. It is his good friend, Montserrat. Almost shouting, Monserrat says, "Kaixo, lagun!"—Basque for *hello, my friend*—and then launches into the reason for the call. "Have you read the news?"

"Yes, I've just started to look at the economy," replies Salvador, puzzled still. Monstserrat says, "This is the year we will seek and gain independence! It's going to happen. There is a grassroots campaign on social media. Everyone is talking about it, and the vote will go in our favor. We will become our own separate region—separate from Spain!"

Weeks later . . .

Salvador and Montserrat spoke their minds and voted, and now they watch the news together with their families to see Catalonia's parliament vote. "Why is it taking so long to get an answer?" asks Salvador's wife, Ainhoa. "Come on now!" The news media has reporters stationed inside and outside of the parliamentary building. Outside, the Separtists alternately sing and chant while waving the Estelada flag, a key symbol of the Catalan independence movement. "Here they come! We'll have our answer," says Montserrat's wife, Amaya. They all gather around the television. Salvador and Montserrat are on the couch, their kids are on their laps, and the wives are perched on the armrests.

The announcer says, "The Parliament has voted, and the vote is seventy to ten—I repeat, seventy to ten! This region declares its independence from Spain! The people of Catalonia have spoken: *This is our mandate!* I enter into the record the Catalan declaration of independence. This resolution is passed." The Catalans pulled it off.

Or did they?

While the Catalans voted to leave Spain, Spain overturned their vote, but the international community had refused to recognize it anyway, so Catalonia remains a part of Spain—for now.

I wish I could report that this story is fiction, but only the characters are imaginary. Russia has been accused of meddling on social media and enlisting the aid of Julian Assange, although nothing has been provided publicly to confirm these allegations.

This is a dramatized version of real events.

8

America Isn't the Only Target

GLOBAL HACKING

Although it might seem as if the global playbook to hijack the truth was created for the 2016 US elections, it has been in the works for years. In 2013, the World Economic Forum posted its top ten trends for their watch list; included was online "misinformation." According to reports, manipulation and misinformation campaigns meddling in social issues, political topics, and elections in the Netherlands, Catalonia, United States, France, and Germany and the United Kingdom's Brexit referendum were attributed to Russian cyber operatives 80 percent of the time. The remaining cyber operatives tie back to China, Iran, jihadist groups, and then political-activist groups. Some interference, like the cyberattack on Ukraine, occurred before 2016; others, like Russian troll armies promoting propaganda in Swedish elections, occurred after.[1] Let's look at some of the intrusions more closely.

FRANCE

In the aftermath of the 2016 US presidential election, all eyes turned to the 2017 French election. Russia seemed to be on the verge of a new relationship with France, with two pro-Russian candidates running for office: Marine Le Pen—a right-leaning former member of European Parliament—and François Fillon. However, Russian political aspirations to have an improved alliance with France were dashed with the rise in popularity of then-candidate Emmanuel Macron. Russia responded by using fake personas and website hacks to promote Le Pen and to discredit the left-leaning frontrunner, Macron.

Several studies have documented the Russian attempts to discredit the French media. The Oxford Internet Institute, part of the University of Oxford in the United Kingdom, reported that, during this period, one in four links posted and reposted on Twitter in France promoted fake news articles that, *not* coincidentally, supported pro-Russia candidates.[2] Fake news stories challenged traditional media stories, leaving readers wondering what sources to believe. The articles typically were aimed at French-speaking readers, with the aim of popularizing pro-Russian government initiatives.

In a more comprehensive study, UK-based consultancy Bakamo reviewed nearly ten million online links and social-media posts related to politics and elections across eight hundred websites in the six-month lead-up to the French election. They found that one in five of these stories promoted "alternative" or "disruptive" narratives—and 30 percent of these seemed under Russian influence. Some of the tactics included "cloaking articles as if they were published by legitimate sites, reporting nonscientific polls, pulling articles out of historical context, and simple hoaxes."[3]

One line of stories circulated by Russian trolls posted an item on a French message board with a legitimate following, called Medipart.fr, alleging that Macron was hiding offshore funds. Further, the trolls set up fake websites, accusing traditional media of blocking out coverage on the offshore accounts—in essence, accusing them of helping Macron hide the misdeeds—in an attempt to discredit any reportage that might discredit the Macron story. That might have made sense, except there was no proof the left-leaning candidate had offshore accounts. Fake news websites copied the look and feel of mainstream, respected news organizations and further pushed negative narratives about Macron, including fabrications that he was secretly funded by Saudi Arabia.

On May 5, 2017, the Macron campaign was hacked. The criminals stole communications, e-mails, and documents totaling roughly nine gigabytes of data. The documents were then altered, and the cybercriminals began posting their misinformation campaign of fake documents using an IP address in Latvia. The documents claimed on anonymous Internet forum 4chan that Macron had an offshore account and was hiding ill-gotten gains offshore; the misinformation was amplified by pro-Trump Twitter accounts using #MacronGate and #MacronCashCache.[4]

Even further than the uncovered manipulation of news sources, Japanese security firm Trend Micro reports that espionage attempts were made to hack the Macron election campaign by creating faux, lookalike sites intended to trick staffers into providing their password credentials.[5]

Days before the French went to vote, Macron announced in May 2017 that his campaign offices had been hacked.[6] The final play was a dump of twenty thousand stolen e-mails that were released hours before the election; many of these leaked documents disclosed falsehoods about Macron, which were later proven to be fake. The hashtag #MacronLeaks trended right before the election on Twitter, as well as a site on WikiLeaks that was actively promoting the disinformation.[7]

It is clear that a misinformation campaign was active, designed to disrupt the outcome and the trust in the validity of the French elections. Yet this chapter in the manipulator's playbook failed, and Macron pulled off a victory. How? Because the country united in combatting these manipulation campaigns, meaning the French were able to avert a redux of the 2016 US election.

For one, France has implemented a mandatory media blackout in the hours leading up to its elections. Also, French media did not support the fake stories, and citizens reported the stories as fake. Further, Macron's campaign had prepared for the misuse of documents and had transparently and publicly admitted being hacked. Leading up to the election cycle, Facebook had to remove nearly seventy thousand suspicious accounts in the weeks before the French went to the polls. But this was only done *after* Facebook was pressured by the public and the French government to do so.[8]

Following several concerning manipulation campaigns, the French government passed a new law in 2018 to combat them.[9] The law requires social-media networks to be more transparent by providing information on ad purchases. In an interesting twist, any social-media platform exceeding a certain number of hits in a day must have legal representation in France and is required to reveal the algorithms behind their popularity. The law also leverages an 1881 law protecting freedom of press and creates a legal-injunction process to assist with removing and stopping fake news stories from circulating.[10]

And the story continues. Since the election, France has seen an uprising known as the "Yellow-vest movement," which seemingly began as a movement in opposition to carbon taxes but has spread to protests and even riots for improved worker conditions. Are these protests genuine or a result of a Russian manipulation campaign to foment worker angst? Cybersecurity and intelligence experts are not sure.[11]

GERMANY

It is no secret that Germany does not approve of Russia's ongoing war in Ukraine. It is not a stretch of the imagination to say that Russia's president Vladimir Putin and chancellor of Germany Angela Merkel are probably not trading holiday greeting cards at the moment, and neither would they choose to hang out as buddies. If you are not a friend of Russia's ambitions and/or Russia's political leaders, then prepare to be targeted by misinformation and manipulation campaigns.

In August 2015, Germany discovered that their networks in parliament had been hacked. Forensics indicate that Russian cyber operatives, apparently part of the Fancy Bear hacking gang, were responsible.[12] If this sounds familiar, it's because it is: Although no data or documents dumps from that hack have been reported, it's eerily similar to the hack-and-dump campaign waged against the Clinton campaign. But even after responding to this cyberattack, Germany couldn't let down its guard: In January 2016, the "Lisa case" ran rampant. Twice.

In January 16, a thirteen-year-old Russian-German girl referred to as "Lisa F." was reported missing by her parents. When she returned home over a day later, she alleged she had been held against her will and repeatedly raped by Middle Eastern immigrants. The account was appalling and frightening. And also turned out to be completely false.[13]

But as soon as the allegations were made, the Lisa story was pushed by Russian media, where it was then picked up by other media before eventually going viral. Initial reports had the relatives of the young woman lamenting the lack of action taken by German police: *These men were on the loose; who knows where they could be and what they would do next!* The tragedy tugged at the heartstrings of parents everywhere. However, the investigation found issues with the young woman's story: German police told the media that, according to cellular records, the woman had slept at a friend's house the night in question and that she had since retracted her claim of rape.[14] And yet the story persisted.

So how did the Russians deploy a story designed to stoke immigration fears?[15] First, Russian news network First Russian TV broadcasted the fake story, along with RT, Sputnik, and RT Deutsch. Then the story was distributed via social media. Groups coordinated demonstrations on Facebook. Russia had reporters in Germany cover the demonstrations. Finally, Russian foreign minister Sergej Lavrov spoke publicly about the case and criticized German police, alleging a cover-up.[16]

The situation got so out of hand that both the German Federal Intelligence Service and the Federal Foreign Office began checking Russian sources of manipulation of German public opinion.[17] Eventually, German news media were able to convince viewers that the abduction and rape reports were fraudulent.

BREXIT

In November 2017, UK prime minister Theresa May accused the Russian government of meddling in global elections and disseminating fake news.[18] US and UK investigations into the factors influencing citizens to vote to leave the European Union in the Brexit vote have discovered that Russia launched pro-Brexit manipulation campaigns. One report, produced by US Democrats on the Senate Foreign Relations Committee—*Putin's Asymmetric Assault on Democracy in Russia and Europe: Implications for US National Security*—references University of Edinburgh research that found that roughly four hundred Russian-run Twitter accounts known to promote manipulation campaigns during the 2016 US election had also been conducting manipulation-campaign activity surrounding Brexit. Swansea University in Wales and the University of California at Berkeley coauthored a research report indicating that 156,252 Russian accounts tweeted about #Brexit and that in the last forty-eight hours leading up to the Brexit vote these accounts had posted over forty-five thousand pro-Brexit messages.[19]

Research firm 89up found that between January and June of 2016 Russia Today and Sputnik had published over 261 media articles that were anti–European Union.[20]

A postmortem analysis of social-media activity shows that in the weeks leading up to the Brexit referendum, "not only were there twice as many Brexit supporters on Instagram, but they were also five times more active than 'Remain' activists." On polling day, pro-Leave tweets numbered in the hundreds of thousands and have since been pinpointed to foreign accounts.[21] One report indicates that on the day of the Brexit vote, June 23, 2016, Russia had over 3,800 fake Twitter accounts promoting Brexit and using pro-Brexit hashtags such as #ReasonsToLeaveEU. In fact, data from Twitter shows both Russian and Iranian bots and fake accounts sent more than ten million tweets in an effort to manipulate Western perspectives on specific social and political topics, including Brexit.[22]

SPAIN

Parts of Spain believe that they are taxed the most and benefit the least from being a part of a unified Spain. One such part of Spain is the Catalan region, whose residents are a mix of hip, high-tech professionals along with families, Basques and Spaniards, and farmers and textile workers, whose earnings account for 19 percent of Spain's gross domestic product.[23] A call for Catalan independence has grown in the past two decades, culminating in a 2017 independence referendum. In the lead-up to the vote, the Catalonian referendum was an incredibly active news story circulating on social media, which is not surprising. However, it's who was behind many of those posts that is troubling. A closer look into who was popularizing the topic online revealed it was not only citizens of Spain: social-media posts often originated from elsewhere—not just Russia but also Venezuela.

For months leading up to the vote, the separatist movement in Catalonia seemed to grow daily. The voices on social media showed a groundswell of support to leave Spain and become an independent region. On October 27, 2017, the parliament of Catalonia voted overwhelmingly in favor of independence, with a final vote of seventy to ten. The cheers and applause of the separatists were silenced less than an hour later when the senate of Spain in Madrid voted to enact Article 155 of Spain's constitution—a provision that allows Spain to suspend Catalonia's independence vote.[24] The government of Catalonia was disbanded, and Spanish prime minister Mariano Rajoy scheduled snap elections for citizens to pick new politicians, to be held in two months' time. Despite Catalonia's vote, the world largely stood behind a unified Spain, with the EU Commission, the EU Council, Germany, Italy, the United States, France, and the United Kingdom all voicing support.[25]

In the weeks following the referendum, as Spain's leaders asked themselves what had happened, a clandestine meeting was convened between an unlikely pair, in an unlikely place. On November 9, 2017, only weeks after the failed attempt to secede and weeks before the snap elections, Catalan entrepreneur and publisher Oriol Soler met with headline maker and WikiLeaks founder Julian Assange.[26] It is alleged that the topic of discussion was the separatist movement.

Perhaps it was, and perhaps it was not, but the meeting was enough for NATO Intelligence to sound the alarm. On November 20, 2017, NATO announced their team monitoring Russia had found that Russian online networks had shifted their focus to Catalonia. The Alliance's Strategic Communication Center of Excellence (StratCom) had investigated the bots they were tracking on social media that typically focused on stoking the emotions around Ukraine and Syria and Russian's involvement. These accounts, curiously, were focused on Catalan independence, and they were posting a high volume of messages.[27]

Is Russia a friend of Catalonia? Likely not. Their goal is to undermine what the West thinks it can believe in. Russia wants to undermine the free press, democracy, anyone unfriendly to Russia's desire to undermine any country or politician that is unfriendly to Russia's interests globally, the European Union, the UN, and NATO. Ultimately, though, Russia wants to manipulate its own citizens into believing that the world is a mess and that Russia is not.

Regardless of what you think about Catalonia's independence from Spain, know that Russia wins by stoking the discontent of Catalan separatists and helping pass a referendum that the greater part of Spain and the better part of the West dislike, which then backs a democratically elected government into overturning the results of a free election. By comparison, the free West certainly looks chaotic compared to their rigidly controlled state back east in Russia.

In their behind-the-scenes attempts to influence the Catalan referendum, Russia enhanced its social-media manipulation campaign by having reporters and anchors from Russian government-backed media promote misinformation. They ran one story that twelve countries had voiced support in favor of a separate and independent Catalan state. Once published, Russian bots pushed the stories out more widely on the Web.[28] During elections in Spain, bots promoted Catalan separatist movement.

ITALY

In Italy's early 2018 elections, Russian-driven social-media accounts and automated bots, to stoke anti-immigrant fear, posted and reposted true news stories that highlighted the threat of illegal immigration.[29] This issue created a movement of Italian voters that mobilized and voted for the two populist and anti-immigrant candidates in great numbers. By hiding behind actual news stories and not posting fake content, the Russian trolls' actions were not as easy to detect.[30] In the spring of 2016, hackers had attacked Italy's Ministry of Foreign Affairs. The *Guardian* reports that Russia was suspected and had actually gained access to the foreign ministry's unclassified e-mail systems for roughly four months before they were detected. Not much else has been reported about this attack other than the issuance of public assurances that classified communications were not compromised during the hack and that since the foreign minister at that time, Paolo Gentiloni, did not use e-mail, he was not compromised.[31]

Another manipulation and misinformation campaign meant to influence views on immigration swept Italy in November 2017. A news story was picked up by French media alleging that a nine-year-old Muslim girl had been hospitalized in Padua after being assaulted by her thirty-five-year-old husband. Matteo Salvini, leader of Italy's anti-immigration party Lega, posted the false story to social media. That's all the manipulation campaign needed, and Italians became outraged despite police insistence that the story was false. News organizations retracted the story, and eventually Salvini deleted it from his social-media accounts.[32]

One manipulation campaign targeting Italy came in the guise of a masterfully designed but completely fake poll: The data were falsely attributed to the BBC, the *Daily Star* of Lebanon, and *Der Spiegel*, legitimizing results in the eyes of readers. In this poll, Italy's Five Star Movement—a populist party known for anti-immigrant stances—was said to be on track to receive almost half of all votes in an upcoming election, despite the fact that all other legitimate polls showed a trend of less than 30 percent of the votes would go their way.[33]

TAIWAN

Behind the scenes a battle is being waged to subvert the independence of Taiwan and manipulate its citizens, without using a tank, gun, or soldier. China has enlisted academics and journalists in its attempt to legitimize propaganda that targets elected Taiwanese officials in an overt effort to discredit the administration of Tsai Ing-wen.[34] Cybersecurity researchers, think tanks, and government groups have found the digital footprints of Chinese cyber operatives at data-crime scenes and on social media, and they warn that China's cyber-warfare techniques continue to advance.[35]

The Chinese-directed manipulation campaigns are designed with efficiency in mind by using bots. At content farms prolific writers are handed topics to create propaganda laced with the truth, making the propaganda both believable and difficult to detect.[36] Chinese cyber operatives have online posed as Taiwanese citizens speaking both for and against Taiwan's center-left Democratic Progressive Party and its conservative Kuomintang party.[37] Sound familiar?

Additionally, China-backed Internet trolls use fake personas, bots, and content farms to stoke the fears and anxieties of the Taiwanese on a number of societal issues, such as pension reform and global warming.[38] One manipulation campaign promoted the idea that President Tsai had plans to dismantle and ban Buddhist traditions in Taiwan, such as incense burning.[39]

GLOBAL RESPONSES

In response to the onslaught of cyber-based espionage, countries have begun establishing new defensive processes and in some cases enacting new laws in an attempt to protect themselves from disinformation—and hold the perpetrators accountable. As of this writing, the European Union has discussed laws and sanctions pertaining to cyber manipulation, France has enacted a law to combat fake news,[40] the Parliament of the United Kingdom has established a board of inquiry to investigate election meddling, Finland has established the Security Strategy for Society in efforts to inform and engage its citizens to combat the threats, the German Bundestag has passed a law to combat hate speech used in manipulation campaigns, and Italy has created a user-friendly online platform that helps its citizens report fake news. The Netherlands has proactively created a framework to combat manipulation campaigns and fake news, running their offensive operation out of the Office of the Coordinator for Counterterrorism and their Ministry of Justice and Security.[41]

In November of 2017, the European Union announced it would be establishing a high-level group of experts to address false, inaccurate, or misleading information promoted for profit or harm. The group was charged with designing and developing a framework to thwart the dissemination of fake news, as well as ensure that EU citizens have tools at the ready to verify information. The group evaluated the magnitude of the issue of manipulation campaigns, how they are promoted, how they impact citizens' views, and whether or not they create mistrust in traditional-media news outlets.[42]

The group first convened in early 2018 and published its findings in March of 2018, calling manipulation and misinformation campaigns a global and complex threat. For the most part, they found, laws fail to consider the fabrication and distribution of misinformation to be illegal, and there remains a vast unclear area to seek justice through legal precedent. They also found that current manipulation and misinformation campaigns trap and confuse citizens so they do not know what to believe.[43]

The report notes that these misinformation campaigns use techniques including falsified information, creation of forged and fake documents, creation and promotion of fake grassroots groups, hijacking of legitimate grassroots groups by interlopers, and automated amplification to press their agenda. The manipulation playbook, the group acknowledges, goes well beyond politics and the discrediting of democracy to include demeaning and dividing citizens on issues such as health care, finance, and education. The authors recommend abandoning the term *fake news*, because it has become a catchall phrase itself misused to discredit legitimate news that someone disagrees with.[44]

The report also takes to task big tech and calls for social-media platforms to evolve and their companies to expand their thinking concerning their responsibilities both on and off their platforms. The report encourages social-media companies to freely provide tools that empower citizens and journalists to vet information and flag disinformation. By masking how their algorithms promote one item above another, or give users more of what they want, social-media companies are "opaque—sometimes by design."[45]

Certain social-media companies have conceptually agreed that widespread sharing of what we understand about cybersecurity threats and greater transparency when lapses occur will help stall manipulation campaigns. Some changes already being made are promising: In January of 2017, Germany enacted the Network Enforcement Act, which mandates that social-media platforms monitor for fake news and adhere to strict standards to block or remove it within twenty-four hours of identification. Noncompliance can result in a fine of up to fifty million euros.[46] And in March 2019 the European Union set up the Rapid Alert System (RAS) to enable spontaneous dismantling of misinformation, in coordination with EU international partners, including the G7 and the twenty-nine countries making up NATO.[47] The RAS engages social-media networks and online platforms in these efforts to thwart disinformation campaigns. The Poynter Institute's International Fact-Checking Network has created a European branch of independent fact-checkers covering fourteen member nations and has launched a website in eleven EU languages.[48]

Will it be enough?

It's November 6, 2020, three days since the 2020 US presidential election, a seminal event in world history. The night of the election, November 3, reports of voter irregularities started filling social-media streams, with voters complaining they did not exist on voter rolls and telling news reporters they were not allowed to vote.

Many reported receiving text messages while standing in long lines telling them they could vote using their phone. Not realizing this was part of a botnet operation to manipulate voters, many "voted" via text and stepped out of line. Others pointed to messages on Snap, WhatsApp, Facebook, Twitter, Instagram, TikTok, and YouTube with doctored clips of "news reports" saying that voting was rigged where they lived and said, *Why even bother voting?*

President Trump was declared the winner, but the Democratic candidate would not concede due to the reports of irregularities. The US Park Police and the Metropolitan Police in Washington, D.C., held an emergency meeting, knowing trouble was brewing. They were summoned to the White House's Situation Room to put together a security plan.

Within hours, all around the United States, people were taking to the streets, at first chanting and picketing peacefully, but soon followed by waves of angry rioting, while police in full SWAT gear attempted to corral the crowds. One woman in full clown-face makeup with tear drops drawn on her cheeks held a sign reading, "US Elections Are a Clown Show." Others carried signs saying "President Putin Won" or "The World Is Doomed." One protestor dressed as Jesus—complete with a flowing robe, long reddish-brown hair—waved a sign declaring, "Jesus Saves. Jesus for President. WWJD <3?"

In the days that follow, reporters learn that encrypted messaging services had organized the protestors. The entire eighteen acres of the White House complex is under siege, with reporters staked out outside the iconic Press Briefing room in West Wing. In the Situation Room, people are coming and going. President Trump is watching cable news while simultaneously tweeting disparaging comments about the female demonstrator dressed as a clown—still out there—who's just given an interview to CNN, explaining she is "crying" because her vote did not count.

The US Navy ensign swiftly answers a ringing phone. A voice says, "This is the White House Operator. I have a call for President Trump. It's an urgent call from the United Nations secretary-general, António Guterres." Ensign Parker scans the room, looking for the right person to summon instead of the president, motioning over the deputy chief of staff and whispering in his ear. He looks puzzled and then annoyed. DCoS looks at the mayhem reflected on the TV screens around the room. The chyron ticker-taping across the bottom of the news feed reads like a conspiracy-theorist blog post come to life: "Deep Fakes," "Secret Group Sends Group Texts" "Voters Duped," "Voters Deleted," and "Bots Hack Voter Database."

"Mr. President, you have a call from the United Nations secretary-general, António Guterres. Do you want to take it privately?" The president frowns to himself, then puts down his Android phone and smiles. "No, no, no—put him on the speakerphone; we might as well all hear what he wants. I think I already know."

DCoS nods, and Ensign Parker puts the UN secretary-general on speaker and moves efficiently, effortlessly, past everyone, back to her station.

President Trump says with a smile and in his best conversational Portuguese, "Saudações para você"—*Greetings to you.*

"Saudações para você, President Trump. I understand that I am on the speakerphone, no?"

"Yes, it's okay—the team here needs to hear what you have to say," the president says.

There's a pause, partially due to the complexity of processing the software being used by the White House Communications Agency securing the conversation. It's also due to Mr. Guterres's hesitation; he inhales, holds the breath, and exhales as he delivers what he knows will not be welcome news. "President Trump," he says, "I am so sorry to hear what is happening with your elections. We have just had an emergency meeting, and the United Nations has loaded up an airplane to send over to Washington a team to inspect the US election processes and results."

There's an audible gasp in the Situation Room by one of the staffers. "Why on earth would you do that?" President Trump demands icily.

"Because the world is concerned that the leader the American people chose may or may not be the one seated at the inauguration," counters the secretary-general. "We have to know for sure. I am sorry for this unfortunate situation."

The president wraps up the phone call with niceties and then looks at the room. "Okay, people, we have work to do." The chief of staff rushes to the table and begins to plan with the staff what to do when the delegation arrives and what to say to the media.

This is fiction . . . for now.

9

The Next Target

What Attacks Can We Expect in 2020 and Beyond?

Make no mistake: The threat just keeps escalating, and we're going to have to up our game to stay ahead of it.

> —FBI Director Christopher Wray, testifying before Congress
> Appropriations subcommittee on FBI's preparations
> for the 2020 presidential elections, May 7, 2019[1]

They're doing it as we sit here.

> —Robert Mueller, testifying before Congress, July 24, 2019,
> on whether Russians are likely to meddle in future US elections[2]

ELECTION OF THE NEXT US PRESIDENT

As we have shown, elections globally are under attack—it's never been easier or cheaper for nontechnical people to launch a cyberattack or manipulation campaign. Malware and phishing attacks targeting election processes and political candidates were detected in 2018 and 2019 elections in countries such as Russia, Turkey, Colombia, Azerbaijan, and even Mali.[3] "It looks like the 2020 presidential primary is going to be the next battleground to divide and confuse Americans," said Brett Horvath, one of the founders of Guardians.ai, which protects elections from manipulation and information warfare. "As it relates to information warfare in the 2020 cycle, we're not on the verge of it—we're already in the third inning. . . . We can conclusively state that a large group of suspicious accounts that were active in one of the largest influence operations of the 2018 cycle is now engaged in sustained and ongoing activity for the 2020 cycle."[4]

Although much has been done in the United States to secure elections on all fronts, the attacks against the 2020 election will most likely reveal that cyber operatives have developed new tactics. Clint Watts, a fellow at the Foreign Policy Research Institute and at the Center for Cyber and Homeland Security at George Washington University, tells me, "We are very open where we have issues with election security in 2020. We need to really watch those known weak spots. If the contest ends up being close, there will be claims of election fraud, and it will come down to societal trust. Can we have a fair election that is believed by anybody? There are hackers much more skilled than the Russians that could create massive chaos without even changing a vote but creating distrust. I am apprehensive emotions will be manipulated, causing violence, like someone showing up with a gun and threatening people at the polls."[5]

Richard A. Clarke's fear when I asked him his predictions for 2020 is eerily similar. "My biggest concern is that the Russians will either successfully penetrate voter rolls, or *claim* they have, in the key swing counties within battleground states," he tells me. "This time around there will likely be ten battleground states. Some counties are 'red,' and some are 'blue'; these will be the swing counties. What if the Russians delete red voters off in one county and blue voters off in another? The claim they did this would create chaos, aimed at having the electorate distrust the vote." He adds, "What if they do an attack in the middle? What if the precincts send up one vote count to their central reporting authority but the numbers change because the Russians or someone else changes them as to what gets reported publicly? The press will report one outcome due to the twenty-four-hour news cycle. The local people running the election will realize that is not what they reported. That would be chaotic. Remember, the Russians are less about Trump and more about distrust in the election process and democracy. Any evidence of disruption or tampering will create issues with the electorate."[6]

These predictions by my colleagues are sobering. Here are my own predictions for 2020: Cyber operatives will use a variety of techniques leading up to the elections to play their manipulation games. Let's take a look at the mayhem and strategies they could deploy.

MANIPULATING VOTER-REGISTRATION ROLLS

Cyber operatives will predictably target each country's elections, not just in the United States. In the United States in 2020 they will target states' board-of-elections websites, scanning for any and all vulnerabilities. Cyber operatives of nation-states will lie in wait to see which states have failed to patch their web pages or missed a tough-to-spot vulnerability. They will look for any side door to get into voter-information databases, looking for potential information and clues. If cyber operatives do access voter-registration databases, anything is possible, from selling the information, to posting it online, to deleting or changing records, and then claiming responsibility. It only takes a few thousand votes in some districts to swing an election for one candidate versus another. Strategically placed campaigns convincing swing-state voters that the system is rigged could disincentivize them to stay home.

TAKING VOTER INFORMATION OFFLINE

Another technique that would be debilitating and effective would be to launch distributed denial-of-service attacks against each US state's voter websites. These attacks could render the websites inoperable, preventing people from accessing basic but necessary information: voting locations and hours, forms for registering to vote, and requesting an absentee ballot. We mentioned earlier that this type of attack occurred just weeks before the last US presidential-election cycle, disrupting the Internet in the United States for several hours.

SMASH, GRAB, AND DOX CAMPAIGNS

Spear-phishing campaigns by cyber operatives that target large donors, political-party headquarters, campaign managers, and political candidates and their families will be incredibly popular and will not be limited to e-mail. We know that in 2008 then–Republican vice presidential nominee Sarah Palin had her e-mails hacked and dumped on the Internet. We already reviewed in detail how John Podesta's e-mail account was hacked in 2016 and how the campaign of France's President Macron was targeted. I expect the coming global elections may be less about candidates' e-mails and more about private chats that take place on Snapchat, Twitter, Facebook Messenger, and Instagram. Just because those are newer platforms and you have not heard about their being targets of dox campaigns does not mean they are safer platforms; they are likely the next place cybercriminals and manipulators will target to steal internal campaign communications.

LOOSE LIPS SINK SHIPS

The new "loose lips" are recycled and weak passwords. A decade of data breaches has put many of the world's passwords in the domain of cyber operatives. You may be visualizing a cyber operative manually typing out passwords at the keyboard, like a thief with his ear to a bank vault, trying to guess the combination. Automation has taken password cracking to new lofty levels.

Expect to see the 2020 campaigns and the electoral process targeted by "password-stuffing" bots. These bots will be programmed to target certain candidates' e-mail accounts or social-media platforms and attempt to log in using every password, or some variation, that's been stolen as part of a data breach. Humans, after all, are creatures of habit and tend to leverage similar passwords over and over, making only minor tweaks, such as capitalizing or adding a number or special character. For example, they may use "PanthersDivisionChamps2019" and then in another place use "Panthers-Champs2020." Attackers also know that many platforms allow cross-authentication to other apps, which means one password could provide the master key to all.

How prevalent are password-stuffing bots? Internet company Akamai indicates that botnets launch almost three hundred thousand log-in attempts an hour, with the top three launch locations being the United States, Russia, and Vietnam.[7] Fighting back is tough. The attackers building password-stuffing bots are creating increasingly more sophisticated and stealthy designs. Often it takes specialized tools and a very strong password-management policy and system to combat this. My prediction is that passwords in the political process will be cracked using both social-engineering methods and credential stuffing. If you work on a political campaign, consider yourself forewarned.

ARTIFICIAL INTELLIGENCE (AI)

In 2020, campaigns could be subjected to cyberattacks launched not by cyber operatives but by artificial intelligence. Computer programs created with AI to target ideologies or anyone in the political public eye could take on a life of their own. Although a human would have to create the AI and train it by feeding it data, as the AI becomes contextually more aware and sophisticated, it could potentially attack political parties, campaigns, political-action groups, and more without any human launching the attack.

DISCREDITING VOTING MACHINES

The United States allows states to manage their elections, and the states turn to for-profit companies to purchase their election software and voting booths. The United States has fretted about actual voter fraud for decades, but if someone were to simply discredit the voter-registration databases or the votes cast themselves, that could cause serious problems in determining the winner of the presidential election and other races. Cyber operatives can sow mayhem simply by making US citizens doubt the voting machines and the manufacturers. By posting deepfake videos, deepfake photos, and deepfake news, they could launch a misinformation campaign of epic proportions to cast a shadow on a race's outcome.

Ethical hackers have shown us the vulnerabilities that need to be fixed to secure votes, and the Department of Homeland Security, states, and election-equipment providers are racing to fix them. Imagine a misinformation campaign, complete with doctored photos or videos, claiming voting machines have been rigged to vote "Democrat" or "Republican." Other fake news stories will interview supposed voters who said that they cast their vote one way and watched the machine repeatedly pick the other candidate. These stories will be amplified on social media, claiming that "mainstream media" will not cover the story. The social-media accounts will be seeded with fake followers to make them look legitimate; remember, we have shown that fake followers can be purchased for a modest price.

The goal of these cyber operatives will be to make sure voters are bombarded with lots of political noise, claims of hacking the election, and counterclaims that those claims are falsehoods. Voters will run to the Internet for answers and will walk away even more confused. The cyber operatives have a term for this: *cognitive hacking*, or the hacking of how you and I think. There are multiple motivations for creating a misinformation campaign about rigged voting machines: The manipulators can get rich with clickbait headlines and ads, nation-states can sow discord and distrust, and political operatives might just be able to get their person elected or ensure the wrong person is not elected. We cannot and we will not let them win.

MEMES

One word on everybody's lips today, *meme*, can be traced back to 1976 book *The Selfish Gene*, written by British scientist Richard Dawkins. He coined the term *meme* and defined it as "a unit of cultural transmission."[8] The use of Internet memes in manipulation campaigns unquestionably gained momentum in 2016 and does not show any signs of slowing down. Internet memes are hard to trace, do not look like an ad, and can be easily and quickly shared in private user groups on social media and by other digital means. Although social-media companies are committed to tackling political ads, they are having a tough time tracking down memes and determining whether or not they are ads, manipulation campaigns, or free speech. A lot of work has been done, but we clearly have more work to do.

As a mother of three and CEO of a company where some of the staff are millennials and the interns are from Gen Z, I am personally immersed in the meme culture. My staff and kids often respond to questions I may ask or provide me a status update not in text but in memes. Want to try your hand at making your own meme? It's easy to do: You can download an app to your phone, or you can also try one of the many meme generators found online. One free option is the Imgflip meme generator found at https://imgflip.com/memegenerator. As always, do your homework, and pick the meme generator that's the best fit for you, and always check the user reviews and ratings for privacy and security.

One meme making the rounds before the 2020 presidential campaign attempted to discredit former Democratic presidential candidate Kamala Harris by claiming she was not a citizen—playing off the knowledge that her parents are Jamaican and

Indian immigrants. The meme was first posted by an anonymous account on Twitter in 2017 and in May 2018 was found on the social platform Reddit on the message board r/The_Donald.[9] Reddit is a rogue community policed by its own, where deepfake-creation software had its origins.[10]

Users picked up the Harris "birther" meme and began to post it on 4Chan and Pinterest. Gaining steam, it was then posted on Twitter as well as Gab and Voat, gaining additional momentum when CNN anchor Chris Cuomo—himself very active on Twitter, with over one million followers—said on air that Harris should prove her US citizenship. Cuomo eventually apologized, but his reference was enough to give the fake story life.[11]

One targeted meme was specifically designed to test Facebook's foreign-meddling alert system but eluded detection, Bloomberg reported. In the month leading up to European parliamentary elections at the end of May 2019, a group called Bits of Freedom reportedly created a political meme focused on the German far-right political party known as AfD and the center-right Christian Democrats. Wanting to see if they would trip the sensors for political ads that Facebook had put in place after 2016 global election meddling, Bits of Freedom used a Dutch Facebook account and Dutch bank account and then pointed their political ad, an Internet meme, at voting-age German residents eighteen years of age who lived in Bielefeld. While the group was setting up their post in Facebook, which was clearly set up by a Dutch account but targeting Germans, the Facebook algorithm helpfully suggested that the ad should target people with interests in "nationalism" and the "military." The meme managed to rack up two thousand people engagements, sixty-two reactions, and sixteen comments from German Facebook users. Thankfully, it was just a test, but the test still got past the moderators, the sorting programs, and even the media.[12]

MERCHANDISE

While trolling American voters, to ensure their online presences had a look of legitimacy, the Russian teams created and sold merchandise propping up various politically charged social issues that they promoted on their social-media accounts. In one case they sold, "I Support American Law Enforcement" T-shirts.[13] They also posed as Black Lives Matter supporters and produced merchandise with slogans such as "Young, gifted and black," "Melanin and muscles," and "Our sons matter," which they sold on the "Blacktivist" Facebook page. They did not sell a lot of them—roughly a hundred—but the point wasn't to make money in T-shirt sales but to simply promote the illusion that they were social activists acting in good faith and to get their message out in yet another forum, keeping contentious conversations alive. Pocketing some money on the side was a bonus.[14] We only learned about these merchandise-selling techniques long after the damage was already done.[15]

LEVERAGING WHITE HOUSE PETITIONS

As evidence that Russians do not own the global playbook of manipulation, one need to look no further than the White House website, which allows US citizens to speak up by posting their own petitions. The "We the People" website, at https://petitions .whitehouse.gov/, was created in 2011 by the Obama administration. The process currently states that any single petition that accumulates one hundred thousand signatures or more within thirty days will go into a queue for White House review and an official response.

Politico reports that petitioners with the appearance of legitimate citizens seeking to name the left-wing, antifascist militant group Antifa as a terrorist organization was actually a manipulation campaign. The petition surpassed the one hundred thousand signatures required by the White House in less than five days. Politico spoke with the person behind the petition, who goes by the code name Microchip and said the focus of registering the petition was to have conservatives stop fighting with each other to focus on a common enemy.[16]

ISSUE TROLLS

According to American news organization Axios, Russia has a goal to spread misinformation around health care issues, not just about vaccinations, ahead of the 2020 election. The *New York Times* found that the *Russian Times* is peddling a manipulation campaign to discourage implementation of 5G cellular technology, stating it is linked to deadly or chronic health concerns, such as cancer, Alzheimer's, and other health issues.[17]

DEEPFAKES

> While synthetically generated videos are still easily detectable by most humans, that window is closing rapidly. I'd predict we see visually undetectable deepfakes in less than twelve months. Society is going to start distrusting every piece of content they see.
>
> —Jeffrey McGregor, chief executive officer at Truepic,
> a San Diego–based startup developing image-verification technology[18]

While the trolling targeting the 2016 elections were about amplification of news and events, 2020 will be about not being able to believe what you read, see, or hear with your own eyes and ears. You may see a news video from a trusted news source and not be confident that what was broadcast is actually news. You may see a document that was reportedly written by an official that holds a deep, dark secret, but you may not be certain of its true origins. You may see a post on an elected official's Twitter account saying something terrible, but you may not know for sure whether or not it was posted by the account holder. Why? Deepfakes.

Deepfakes are AI-generated forgeries that are so convincing you cannot believe your eyes. In the case of deepfake videos, someone can place the face and other body parts of one person onto the moving video form of another person. With this technology, for example, you could put person A's face over person B's, making it look like it was person A running the race, jumping out of the plane—or appearing in the porn film. The *Washington Post* reports that Hollywood star Scarlett Johansson became the victim of deepfake video technology when a video of her face was edited into pornographic film footage, labeled "leaked" material, and spread online, where it was viewed over 1.5 million times.

We have seen a quantum leap in the ease of creating deepfake videos. This technology is increasingly simple to obtain: In January 2018, one Reddit contributor provided the community with an easy-to-use app that could be freely downloaded. In fact, one app called Deep Nude appeared to take pictures of clothed women and render them naked in seconds. The results were so startling real that it sparked public outrage and the app has since been deactivated, but the threat is disturbing.[19]

"The combination of photo-real synthesis of facial imagery with a voice impersonator or a voice-synthesis system would enable the generation of made-up video content that could potentially be used to defame people or to spread so-called 'fake news,'" notes Michael Zollhöfer, visiting assistant professor at Stanford University. "Currently, the modified videos still exhibit many artifacts, which makes most forgeries easy to spot. It is hard to predict at what point in time such 'fake' videos will be indistinguishable from real content for our human eyes."[20]

Disturbingly, this technology has been used to alter videos of world leaders, wreaking havoc. On May 23, 2019, deepfake technology finally caught the attention of the US Congress when an amateur deepfake video circulated featuring House Speaker Nancy Pelosi. In the video, her voice and mannerisms were slightly altered by slowing them down, making it appear as if she were medically impaired. The video went viral on some news sites and was trending on Facebook until deemed a deepfake. One version of the slowed-down video was viewed on Facebook more than one million times and had more than thirty thousand shares.[21] "Now is the time for social-media companies to put in place policies to protect users from misinformation, not in 2021 after viral deepfakes have polluted the 2020 elections," warned US House Intelligence Committee Chair Adam Schiff. "By then it will be too late."[22]

Creating a deepfake is surprisingly easy and inexpensive to do, as I demonstrated in a May 2019 segment on the *Today Show*.[23] The more time you have to run computations to edit and refine your video, the more convincing the end product will be. Deepfakes can be created at a basic level with free software and a home gaming computer. Although viewing a deepfake on a large 4K television would make it easy to spot, many people consume their news on small smartphone screens where it is harder to discern the telltale signs of a fake.

CASE STUDY: A POLITICAL DEEPFAKE

Florida senator Marco Rubio had a tweet falsely attributed to him that was part of a manipulation campaign. Thankfully Senator Rubio took to Twitter to debunk the tweet's origins. The manipulation campaign was subtle and deceptive: The anonymous manipulators, allegedly from Russia, created an image of a tweet designed to look like it came from Senator Rubio's account. In the fake tweet, it shows Senator Rubio accusing British intelligence of using deepfakes to influence 2020 elections. Senator Rubio never tweeted that accusation, and yet his account was not hacked. Senator Rubio spotted it and said it was a deepfake forgery made to look like he had tweeted it.[24]

On his Twitter account on June 19, 2019, Senator Rubio wrote the following: "Want to know what a #Putin disinformation campaign looks like? The image below is a fake. No such tweet exists. But #Russia created this realistic looking image & then had it posted online in blogs & fringe news sites. And this is minor compared to what lies ahead for us."[25] Massachusetts senator Elizabeth Warren was the subject a doctored photo, in which the manipulators planted a blackface doll in her office photo.[26] This type of dirty politics has been around for decades, but it's only now that the fakes are being distributed at the speed of the Internet. How do you unsee something that affects your judgment?

GENERATIVE ADVERSARIAL NETWORKS

How will we differentiate truth as we know it when we know we can no longer trust what we see? Technology companies keep producing technical options that far outpace our abilities to create laws and put consumer protections in place. Look at the images at this *Wired* website: https://bit.ly/2Kte3wx. It's part of their article, "Is This Photo Real? AI Gets Better at Faking Images." Can you detect what all the images have in common? They're all computer generated.[27] None of what you see is real. These people don't exist. These cars never rolled off an assembly line. These kittens are no one's pets. Each image was generated by artificial intelligence, relying on millions of stock images to create something from nothing. This process is known as *generative adversarial networks*. GANs, as they are called, are trained to manufacture a category of images, such as renderings of people, vehicles, buildings, and other animate and inanimate objects. At Alphabet Inc., Google's parent company, an AI lab called DeepMind leverages a database of fourteen million images to generate original content.

The difficulty in detecting these fake personas is a real problem. On April 22, 2018, our clients, colleagues, and brand-new employees at Fortalice Solutions were contacted by a Fortalice Solutions analyst named Emily Thawe. Her professional background was that of a young woman making her way in the field. Her photo was pleasant and professional. Only Emily was a fake. I individually messaged each person she connected to that was connected to us, I contacted LinkedIn about the forgery, and then I made a public announcement that she was not an employee and a fake. A reverse lookup of her face led us to believe that Emily Thawe was a fake persona, with content managed by bots; on closer analysis, her face seemed altered. The account vanished quickly.

In June 2019, the Associated Press reported a similar scheme making the rounds. Katie Jones sure seemed plugged into Washington's political scene. The thirty-something redhead boasted a job at a top think tank and a who's-who network of pundits and experts, from the centrist Brookings Institution to the right-wing Heritage Foundation. She was connected to a deputy assistant secretary of state, a senior aide to a senator, and economist Paul Winfree, who is being considered for a seat on the Federal Reserve.[28]

But Katie Jones doesn't exist, the Associated Press has determined. Instead, the persona was only one of a vast army of phantom profiles lurking on the professional-networking site LinkedIn. And several experts contacted by the AP said Jones's profile picture appeared to have been created by a computer program.[29]

FAKE-NEWS BOTS

Fake-news bots are designed to push an agenda to the forefront of social media without getting found out and shut down. A fake-news bot can be used to push marketing campaigns, to bully a person or company, or to hijack how you think about your country's elections. The bot is designed to push topics to go viral without triggering obvious violations of the user guidelines of a social-media platform.

While researching this book, I noticed a few patterns common to fake-news bots: Often the bots are set up around the same date and time, lead back to the same geography, and sometimes even have the same e-mail addresses tied to the social-media accounts in common. One set of fake-news bots may begin by posting real but outdated news and word their post to make it seem as if the news is current. The next set of bots reposts the old news. A third set of bots can then start to comment for and against the news posts. Yet a fourth set of bots then begins to interject fake news stories into the communications. The bots controlling these accounts and independently tweeting based on hashtags and topics—liking other news stories, posting retweets, and in some cases sending a direct message on platforms—appear to be very human.

The technology for fake-news bots continues to evolve and will be hard to shut down. Yet some in the academic community are designing and testing tools that can discern the subtle differences between a human and a bot. One promising platform using machine learning, developed through a joint collaboration between the University of Eastern Finland (UEF) and Linnaeus University in Sweden, can detect automatically generated tweets in any language. This is a good start, but more needs to be done. UEF professor Mikko Laitinen notes that nearly 25 percent of all tweets posted are from bots; furthermore, he estimates, bots represent between 5 to 10 percent of all Twitter users.[30]

WHAT SHOULD WE BE DOING NOW TO SAFEGUARD AGAINST MANIPULATION CAMPAIGNS?

Our adversaries and strategic competitors probably already are looking to the 2020 US elections as an opportunity to advance their interests. More broadly, US adversaries and strategic competitors almost certainly will use online-influence operations to try to weaken democratic institutions, undermine US alliances and partnerships, and shape policy outcomes in the United States and elsewhere. We expect our adversaries and strategic competitors to refine their capabilities and add new tactics as they learn from each other's experiences, suggesting the threat landscape could look very different in 2020 and future elections.

—Dan Coats, former director of National Intelligence[31]

Is the global manipulator's playbook in frequent use even after the big reveal of names, Bitcoin wallet numbers, and more in the Mueller report? Yes. In fact, it's still being used very effectively and has only added more tactics to its pages since the 2016 elections.

In the days following the 2020 elections, we are likely to see seeds of doubt sown as to whether election booths were hacked, voter-registration rolls were accurate, and perhaps where illicit campaign donations and off-the-books lobbying came from. These misinformation and manipulation campaigns will create voter malaise and impact whether or not people vote in presidential elections to come.

So what can we do to stop it?

Democratic countries around the world will have to fight the battle together. As a country, we must understand that the efforts to secure our elections must be shared among the private sector and the more than 1,200 government organizations dedicated to national security. We covered a lot of ground between the 2016 presidential elections and the 2018 midterms in defense of the sanctity of our vote, but there is more work to be done. My biggest fear is that Internet trolls have already been successful in using social media to pit citizen against citizen, either influencing how people vote or disenfranchising people from voting at all. There are disturbing opportunities for security breakdowns on state websites that provide location information, in voter-registration databases, of election-booth equipment, and in how people receive news and information in our digital age. We know that social-media companies have been actively engaged in shutting down fake personas and fake ads, but we also know that many Americans were already influenced by those ads before they were caught.

The media has done a great job of informing Americans what's at stake, but there is more to be done, such as creating an easy place for media consumers to report election-security issues for investigation. Media outlets should also consider implementing a behind-the-scenes, unique watermark to "verify" all of their news photos and videos. If the photo or video is altered in any way, it will void the watermark and the video or photo would no longer be vouched for. This will help combat deepfakes.

It will be incredibly difficult for the United States to mobilize and unify against the enemy: The United States has not passed one bipartisan bill regarding election security in Congress since the 2002 Help Americans Vote act, with the exception of funding appropriated to help states bolster their election security.[32] So how can we expect the world to come together to combat election meddling when we cannot agree on laws and enforcement for our own US elections?

The Honest Ads Act, introduced in the Senate in 2017, was meant to force transparency about the origins of social-media ads as a part of blocking misinformation campaigns. To close the gap in voting-booth security, the Secure Elections Act and the House's PAVE Act, also introduced in 2017, were meant to establish a bare-minimum security standard for voting machines, ranging from paper backups to audits. To date, neither of these bills has passed both chambers of Congress.

Meanwhile, ethical hackers have documented concerning security issues in current voting-machine technology: tech support provided remotely that potentially allows hackers access to reprogram software, modems that transmit voter reports on election night across hackable Internet connections, and memory cards used to transfer and store voting data.

An overarching challenge facing the security of global elections is the war for talent. There's a huge labor challenge, and the public sector is competing for the same workers as the private sector—but without Silicon Valley's glamour and perks. I know our states' civil servants and the election officials of our allies are diligent and vigilant, but they have a monumental, daunting task ahead of them in rooting out fake personas and misinformation campaigns.

Americans and global citizens should know that, in the face of the considerable challenges, some encouraging efforts are underway. For instance, US Cyber Command launched "the first known overseas cyber-operation" to target and undermine Russian attempts to spread disinformation and meddle in US elections.[33] And although it's no silver bullet, there is also the nonpartisan US Elections Infrastructure Information Sharing and Analysis Center: EI-ISAC is federally funded and provides states with a place to call twenty-four hours a day to address the cybersecurity needs of elections operations. The team there is not staffed or equipped to handle every issue that may arise, but they provide free advice and can serve as a clearinghouse for questions about who to contact to address a specific incident. In some cases, the EI-ISAC can also provide states with suggestions for security tools and employee training.[34]

Securing safe elections for 2020 is a team sport, and we all must play a role. Silicon Valley, the news media, voting citizens, candidates, political parties, global election entities, and the US government must coordinate and communicate regardless of political ideology.

WHAT CAN CONGRESS OR YOUR
COUNTRY'S ELECTED OFFICIALS DO?

Congress can offer a lot in the fight against cyberattacks. I recommend four program areas for consideration:

1. Election security
   - Continue to push the agenda to improve our election security. Lots of great work has been completed to date, but securing our elections is a journey, not a destination.
2. National security of the private and public sectors
   - Hold hearings on Capitol Hill with academia, private-sector cybersecurity experts, and researchers that track manipulation campaigns, asking subject-matter experts to identify their biggest concerns.
   - Provide budget increases to help recruit and retain cybersecurity and intelligence staff at critical government departments and agencies, including the FBI.
   - Continue to push to ensure that all elements of an election—the ecosystem of websites, databases, software, and voting machines—continue to improve their overall cybersecurity measures.
   - The global information sharing regarding threats, vulnerabilities, and manipulation campaigns must continue to be a priority, and Congress should inspect the overall processes for outcomes.
   - Emergency communications systems must be put in place to quickly alert the likely targets of an imminent attack.
3. Consumer-privacy bill of rights
   - Push forward a standard for international data sharing, recommending punishments and settlements when cybercriminals are harbored in other countries.
   - Create a consumer-privacy bill of rights in response to the regular data breaches that hit our nation's organizations. Congress may want to time the enactment of the bill of rights in coordination with the California Consumer Privacy Act, a sweeping privacy law that went into effect January 2020.
   - Make plans to eliminate the use of Social Security number or add layers of additional identification to better secure citizens' credit and access to health insurance and their information stored with government agencies.
4. Going on the offensive at home while coordinating defense abroad
   - In many cases, private-sector security companies, intelligence agencies, and law enforcement know who is behind a cybercrime but are powerless to seek justice through the US or international legal systems. Unless our adversaries suffer consequences, there is little incentive for them to cease their attacks on US interests.

- We must send a strong signal to global hostile actors that the United States is determined to assume an aggressive offensive stance. We can do this by being transparent about our US might without compromising sensitive programs and citizen privacy and demonstrate our will to invoke our capabilities when necessary.

WHAT CAN GOVERNMENT DO AGAINST ALL FORMS OF CYBERATTACK?

As we approach 2020, the United States should expect to see an increasing trend in successful cyberattacks. Our infrastructure is sometimes the most vulnerable where we least expect it. Past attacks provided a barrage of alarming wake-up calls. The slowdown and widespread unavailability of the Internet in the United States and parts of the EU in the October 2016 Mirai Botnet DDoS attack reminded us of the fragility of the Internet infrastructure we rely upon.[35]

As previously mentioned in this book, in 2013 the official Twitter account of the Associated Press was hijacked by a group calling themselves the Syrian Electronic Army. The SEA spooked financial markets by spreading the false story that President Obama had been injured. Cyber-manipulation campaigns for 2020 and beyond will be sponsored by nation-states as well as by criminal and hacktivist groups.

While an increasing number of nation-states with more-advanced cybersecurity capabilities continues to threaten destabilization across the globe, there is also the added possibility that a relatively unsophisticated bad-faith actor will be successful within the cyber domain. The reasons for this are twofold: First, the increasing availability of automated hacking tools in the public domain enables individuals or groups with only basic skills or even modest financial means to buy their way in to successful cyber-manipulation campaigns. Second, the increasing availability of on-demand, elastic-computing infrastructure enables attackers to design and deploy complex and effective attack infrastructures with ease: By way of explanation, consider when cybercriminals attacked Dyn to deploy botnets, weaponize *Internet-of-things devices*—IoT devices are things like Internet thermostats, baby webcams, and security monitors—and automatically register and deploy hundreds of unique attacks on Internet domains within minutes.

Congress may ask, *Which groups will attack the United States, and which tools, tactics, and procedures will they use more of?*

All of the above: ransomware, destructionware, cryptocurrency-mining that siphons processing power from victims' machines, social-engineering e-mails, malware-infected links on websites, botnets powered by hacking-as-a-service operations, DDoS attacks via weaponized IOT devices, and more.

Whether the bad-faith actor is Iran, Russia, North Korea, or China—or some future adversary not yet on our radar—the US Congress must continue to dedicate resources to answering the following question: *What attacks are we facing that we cannot detect?* It is this question that is quickly drowned out by the noise of large public-data breaches, publicized DDoS attacks, or even broadly discussed hacktivist activities, like WikiLeaks's.

Fundamentally, the United States must address cybersecurity with the same level of concern appropriate to the next Manhattan Project, harnessing a combination of government resources, national lab research, private-sector-industry expertise, and collaboration with educational institutions. What we know now is this: that we don't yet have the solution to solving the cybersecurity problem. And we will never find the solution without dedicating ourselves to a bold, new approach for reducing the risk to the national and economic security of the United States.

Cyberspace is now recognized as the fifth war-fighting domain—alongside land, air, water, and space—and requires offensive and defensive capabilities as well as dedicated, effective resources and strategy to protect and defend against adversaries. A safe and secure homeland and a thriving economy require a definitive cybersecurity strategy to protect the systems underpinning US national-security interests, our commerce, and our way of life.

However, the strategies pursued to date have failed to deter nation-state actors or prevent nation-states, cybercriminals, and hacktivists from compromising key American systems and data. A critical first step in developing a protective strategy is to understand how the top nation-states fund, resource, plan, and target the United States and other democratic governments with dynamic, evolving cyber operations.

Given the fact that the average data breach takes 197 days to detect, according to a recent IBM study, it is highly likely that unethical cybercriminals can enter a vital system, such as a military network, government network, or private-sector network, do whatever they want, and be long gone before they are detected.[36] Their paths leave a wake of critical service disruption or leaked data that is sometimes exposed, sold as commodities, held for ransom, or manipulated. Most cybercriminals are dynamic and evolve their tradecraft often to develop new attack methods and remain undetected.

The United States, our allies, and our businesses need to heed the warning that many cybercriminal syndicates are hosted not only by the countries most often making the headlines; and in some circumstances, the cybercriminals are not aligned with a specific country at all. My team at Fortalice Solutions has also seen attacks happen against US government and private-sector interests carried out by other countries, including a recent attack on a retail company that was launched from Kosovo. Examples of other countries suspected of espionage include, but are not limited to, Argentina, Lebanon, Vietnam, and Belarus.

The most effective cybersecurity strategy to combat manipulation campaigns is an aggressive offensive posture that blends cyber talent, actionable-threat intelligence, processes, and technology. An aggressive, proactive approach involves a solid understanding of how cybercriminals will target a company or government organization and what motivates them the most. We must quickly evaluate the effectiveness of diplomatic measures, such as negotiations and sanctions, and set up a threat-hunting team that aggressively searches for adversarial activity.

For example, the White House, US federal departments and agencies, and governments and businesses around the globe should leverage honeypots or honey traps as part of manipulation and misinformation campaigns. *Honeypots* are a technique used by the "good guys" to understand the tactics, approaches, and sometimes the motives of cyberattackers. If the UN wants to know more about the persons trying to attack their networks, they set up a simple misinformation honeypot, such as a computer named "UN schedule," and then leave it defenseless—like connecting it to the Internet with outdated software. This lures attackers, who will begin assessing and analyzing the device, how to get in, who it belongs to, and whether they can break in without getting caught. Their activity leaves behind a trail that investigators can then analyze.

Cryptography can be used in a similar way to create misinformation campaigns, luring in nation-states and other political operatives in search of an advantage. The technology approach, known as *honey encryption*, allows an attacker to steal what looks like legitimate data. When an attacker steals the encrypted data and then tries to hack into the encryption by guessing a key and they are wrong, the key tells them they were correct and provides incorrect information to them. The attacker thinks they've won the cryptography game, takes the data, and operates off of the misinformation.

As George Washington wrote from Mount Vernon in 1799, "offensive operations, often times, is the surest, if not the only (in some cases) means of defence."[37] The new playbook to counter the manipulators should include feeding our adversaries a dose of their own medicine.

It's 4:30 in the afternoon on November 6, 2028. Marty Eberson sits in a coffee shop in downtown Boise, a cup of tea cooling in front of him. Occasionally he picks up his phone and stares at the screen. With the press of one key he can vote for the next president, but he hesitates.

Marty is eighty-eight years old. He's voted in every election since he was old enough to vote. But this year . . . this year he struggles to see the point. In 2016 Russia influenced the election. In 2020 China, Russia, and Iran all ran social-media campaigns to divide our nation and manipulate the vote. Then 2024 rolls around, and China has figured out how to hack the new online-only voting site. Actual votes are swept away, changed, or created by foreign countries.

He remembers the days when you could trust election results, when you pulled a lever and your vote made a difference. Now he sees fighting in the streets, shootings, hate groups egged on by propaganda attacking each other. The influence has moved beyond elections and into our workplaces, our neighborhoods, and the activities of everyday life.

Marty shrugs and thinks to himself, *What's the point?* He shuts his phone off, pays for his tea, and leaves.

* * *

It's 2029, and America's steel market is firing on all cylinders. New technology has made steel production and fabrication safe, affordable, and more environmentally friendly than ever before. It's a new golden age, and exports are in high demand.

On February 2, the market starts out as on any other day, but by 10 a.m. EST, publicly traded US steel stocks begin to plummet. Market traders watch in disbelief as steel-company market caps shrink throughout the day.

The dive in steel begins to pull down other stocks in the transportation and construction sectors. The press and politicians place calls to CEOs at steel companies, demanding to know what's going on, but the CEOs have no answer. The market hits an all-time low at the closing bell. Over $1 trillion in global wealth is wiped out in a day, and consumers are left with severely weakened 401(K) portfolios.

Forensics are done after the fact. Months later, after the damage is done, it's discovered that the technology purported to make our lives easier actually created the free fall. The manipulation playbook used to influence the US and UK elections was so successful that it was redesigned and enhanced to target industries where Russia wants to even the playing field. Bots, originating from Belarus and Kazakhstan, logged in to bogus social-media personas and accounts and posted news stories about polluted water, mysterious deaths, and company cover-ups related to the US steel industry. The news stories were from credible news outlets and included interviews of experts with brilliant credentials as well as company whistleblowers.

Bots pushed these news stories, tagging legitimate news organizations and leveraging trending hashtags in their posts. As the posts swirled around social media, real people with real accounts commented, added emojis, and shared their views. Market models powered by artificial intelligence that surf the Web looking for leading indicators began to be overwhelmed with the negative press and began processing "sell" orders on steel. As steel fell, the interconnected and dependent sectors began to falter as well.

* * *

On the other side of the country, a realtor named Marcie surveys the old stock exchange and makes notes on her phone about its condition. It's empty now, and the building is up for sale. All the monitors are dark, some smashed in by an angry mob on the day the exchange closed. All the traders have left. She shakes her head, knowing that the prospects for a new tenant in a New York City enveloped by chaos are poor.

So many people have decided, *If you can't trust the market, if it can be manipulated by a few keys tapped in some basement in Iran, then why invest?* The economy is depressed, so people are hoarding their money. The risk of the exchange being hacked is too daunting. With the Social Security system failing, nobody is willing to take that risk.

* * *

It's 2030. In San Francisco a wealthy Russian businessman named Dimitri, who has made a billion dollars by influencing votes on sanctions in the US Congress, sits in his luxury hotel room. He works at his computer, an AI holograph projected on the wall. He's e-mailing a high-level official in Moscow, discussing the final takeover of the weakened United States with the cooperation of the current US president. Russia got her elected.

He's not worried about somebody finding his e-mails, because everything is so easily hacked these days; he can just deny that he ever wrote them. He sends off the final message. A moment later the lights in his room flickers and then go dim. A few minutes later he hears sirens and shouting in the streets.

The attack on the country's grid is starting. In a few hours, the whole country will be dark.

This is fiction.

10

Your Worst Nightmare

The Death of Democracy

WHERE WE ARE TODAY

All of this [voter suppression] is about making sure that your vote doesn't count but also that you know your vote doesn't count so that you're less likely to vote next time and to breed cynicism and a sense of submission in the voting public.

—Dan Pfeiffer on *Pod Save America*[1]

Vote flipping is not where the big threat is. The big threat is in activities that would disrupt the election in some ways and cast doubt in Americans' minds about the validity of the outcome.

—Michael Daniel, former White House cybersecurity
coordinator in the Obama administration[2]

Although misinformation and manipulation campaigns targeting voters have received media attention globally, democracy is still in danger of being greatly damaged by these campaigns. In fact, 83 percent of Europeans believe that the complexity and frequency of misinformation and manipulation campaigns threaten modern life and democracy.[3] In the United States, almost seven out of ten of Americans said their confidence in government has been shaken by fake news.[4] The manipulator's playbook that can hijack an election, smear a company or person, and leave global citizens not knowing what to believe, is escalating in aggression. With the deployment of artificial intelligence—machine learning—any sophisticated group—and, increasingly, as the software gets more sophisticated, many unsophisticated groups—can conduct a digital walk-in and take on the persona of a company, an individual, or a government official either through account takeovers or sneaking in by creating fake accounts that look like the legitimate person or organization. It's hard to discern the real from the fake. All it takes is a well-thought-out campaign, some bots to pose as humans, and some marketing know-how and you have a reputation-damaging playbook that can be used over and over, easily modified on the fly at speed and scale.

Today some of the largest and most powerful tech companies in the world, such as Google, Facebook, and Twitter, have transformed our society. But while cybersecurity has focused on safeguarding data, hardware, and software, the trust and interplay among users of social media have been hacked through profiling, artificial intelligence, and bots, allowing a small army to act as if they are thousands upon thousands strong. Remember the saying from the now-epic *New Yorker* cartoon: "On the Internet, nobody knows you're a dog"?[5] Now we can add, "or a bot."

In 2013, YouTube executives were dismayed to realize that their site was receiving as much traffic "from bots masquerading as people as from real human visitors," according to a report in the *New York Times*.[6] Experts fear the potential fallout on our democracy. "A small number of very active bots can actually significantly shift public opinion," says Tauhid Zaman, associate professor of operations management at MIT Sloan School of Management. "And despite social-media companies' efforts, there are still large numbers of bots out there, constantly tweeting and retweeting, trying to influence real people who vote."[7]

This means that, increasingly, fringe views will be overrepresented electorally. This means, also, that voters, repeatedly disenfranchised, will become apathetic. Unless you have a money machine behind you to combat the manipulation or curry favor with the state-sponsored manipulators, you can't win. The adage used to be that the campaign with the best message that incents voter turnout wins. This is no longer true. The adage is now, *Keep your head down, and don't incite the trolls.*

WE ARE STILL A PEOPLE DIVIDED

Are these misinformation and manipulation campaigns really to blame for dividing us? Yes, according to political scholar Kathleen Jamieson Hall, author of *Cyberwar: How Russian Hackers and Trolls Helped Elect a President: What We Don't, Can't, and Do Know.*[8] Consider that out of all the fake personas created at Russian troll factories, just six of their accounts generated content that was shared a staggering 340 million times. As we saw earlier in chapter 3, the Facebook page for a fake group, Blacktivist, purposely stoked racial discord by pushing out horrific videos of police violence against African Americans and generating discussions through provocative statements against law enforcement. This fake page, manned by Russians, had more hits than the page of the legitimate group Black Lives Matter.

Shutting down public discourse and stoking the fires of disagreement has been a proven tactic to divide nations. A 2017 Pew study on the partisan divide found that the gap among Americans on the political left and right has increased since 1994 from 15 percentage points to 36 points.[9] In a 2018 poll by *USA Today* and Suffolk University, out of one thousand registered voters surveyed via landline and cell phone during mid-December, 78 percent agreed that the country has become more divided since the 2016 presidential election cycle.[10]

And despite the exposure, these manipulation campaigns have not let up. As discussed earlier, Twitter and Facebook accounts designed to appear as if they belonged to real US citizens but in reality powered by Iranian trolls, using hashtags like "#lockhimup," "#impeachtrump," and "notmypresident," continue to fuel our postelection rage.

But why end there? Why settle for disrupting a political cycle? Russia and other countries, as well as covert teams with no national affiliation, have a new playbook, and when they choose to use it, we face something even scarier than a mere partisan divide.

CYBERCRIMINALS ARE ALWAYS INNOVATING

Long before elections around the world began to be affected by social-media meddling and other cybercriminal activities, Estonia had a wake-up call that should have served as a blaring Klaxon for the entire world. In 2007, Estonia was the victim of a digital assault ostensibly at the hands of Russian operatives. Triggered by a dispute with Russia over moving a Soviet-era monument from the Estonian capital, Tallinn, to the outskirts of the city, Estonia suffered what is widely believed to be one of the first cyberattacks on a nation.

Following two nights of riots protesting the monument's removal, a massive amount of Internet traffic—a denial-of-service attack—rained down upon their systems like a digital barrage of torpedoes, overwhelming servers and eventually shutting them down. This attack, which quickly was recognized as retaliatory, also used traditional military operations but was primarily a cyberattack that shut down the systems of Estonia's government and crippled banking services and news-media distribution. Russia pressed forward by paying three news websites to promote Russia's own interests through government-led talking points. It was the first known attack of its kind, but it wouldn't be the last.

If Iran, China, Russia, and North Korea were to collude to launch manipulation campaigns, any country, politician, business, or individual subject to their assaults will be powerless to defend themselves. How do you prove a narrative false that has gone viral and in the public mind space is considered true? How do you ask people to unsee or unhear fake videos that have been doctored to appear real? There is no need to hack actual voting machines if you can just hack the mind-set of the voting public. What will define the truth in the coming years with the abuses of these technologies?

OUR TECH COMPANIES ARE FAILING TO PROTECT US

If you've built a chaos factory, you can't dodge responsibility for the chaos. Taking responsibility means having the courage to think things through.

—Tim Cook, CEO of Apple, commencement Speech at Stanford University[11]

What's gone from the Internet, after all, isn't "truth" but trust: the sense that the people and things we encounter are what they represent themselves to be. Years of metrics-driven growth, lucrative manipulative systems, and unregulated platform marketplaces have created an environment where it makes more sense to be fake online—to be disingenuous and cynical, to lie and cheat, to misrepresent and distort—than it does to be real. Fixing that would require cultural and political reform in Silicon Valley and around the world, but it's our only choice. Otherwise we'll all end up on the bot Internet of fake people, fake clicks, fake sites, and fake computers, where the only real thing is the ads.

—Max Read[12]

For better or worse, Silicon Valley companies direct our daily lives. If you think that's an overstatement, ask yourself how you looked up today's weather forecast. Did you listen to local radio or local TV, or did you consult a weather app or ask Siri, Alexa, or Google? If you used anything that was not local media, Silicon Valley steered you to the forecast they deem most appropriate. Need some sort of service performed at work or home, such as cleaning, painting, or repair? Looking for the best person to complete the job? Do you ask your coworkers and neighbors, or do you consult the Internet? It's very likely you conducted your search using Google or checking Google Maps. If you did, you're in great company, as estimates indicate that an astounding 90 percent of all searches globally originate or leverage Google's platform.[13]

In a June 2019 exposé, the *Wall Street Journal* reported that many of the local businesses and services with an online presence are completely fake. Cybercriminals and manipulators go where the action is, and they are now going local on Google. You would think that Google could spot a fake pretty easily, but the company has said they're struggling to shut down these entities, despite having assembled the brightest and best data scientists and big-data algorithm engineers in the world. If Google can't stop the deceit, than who can? According to the *Wall Street Journal* report, online-advertising specialists estimate that approximately eleven million businesses operating on Google Maps are fake.[14] A fake business listing could be used not only to defraud people of money but also to provide fake grassroots operations an air of legitimacy. Fake Facebook pages—like Heart of Texas, the prosecession troll page that egged Texans into an ugly anti-immigration mob—may appear to be the real deal if bolstered by a fake business listing.

In the aftermath of the 2016 US presidential election, Capitol Hill grilled Silicon Valley over how many fake personas pushed fake ads during the lead-up to the vote. Researchers preparing reports for Congress observed how reluctant tech companies were to comply with the investigations. "It is unclear whether these answers were the result of faulty or lacking analysis or a more deliberate evasion," one Oxford University report noted. Facebook initially underestimated that the Russian efforts were reaching only ten million Facebook users, only later to be forced to conclude that their initial estimates had missed the mark and that the operatives, in essence, had reached one hundred and twenty-six million Americans.[15]

Protections against these fake personas are weak. Up until the aftermath investigations of 2016, creating a fake persona and using it to buy ads was almost effortless, costing only pennies on the dollar using cryptocurrency. It was hard to spot a fake, and tech companies were doing little to ensure ad buyers were who they said they were. In September 2017, while investigating how hard or easy it would be to purchase fake ads on social media, *Forbes* was able to successfully game the Facebook system. According to the reporters, "Our fake page was the very definition of a red flag. Aside from the sketchy page, we also targeted minorities in our adverts and backdated every post to months before the page was actually created to make it look legitimate. The very existence of the latter feature (which has now been removed) suggests Facebook doesn't—or at least didn't—take fake pages, posts, or adverts very seriously."[16]

BUYING FALSE PERSONAS

What's the best way to make sure people believe you are a legitimate person or organization pushing an agenda? Often we cannot ask for credentials or identification, so the best measure we have to measure "legitimacy" is (1) how many followers an account has and (2) how many "likes" that account has. For a small fee, phony accounts can be made to look more legitimate by purchasing a valid phone number to tie them to. How easy and inexpensive is this to do? While researching phone-verified accounts for purchase, I performed a quick search for "PVA Facebook," and the following came back on the first entry:

> *Buy Facebook Pva Accounts—Buy Facebook Accounts*
> *pvaaccountss.com/buy-facebook-pva-accounts*
> *50 FB PVA Accounts; USA PHONE NUMBER VERIFIED + GMAIL/YAHOO QUALITY MAIL VERIFIED; 5 DAYS GUARANTEE FOR ANY PROBLEM . . .*

I had my pick of vendors, options, and money-back guarantees. This is all in plain sight, within easy access. No need to traffic in buying fake personas on the dark web; just pay a service you find operating in plain sight to do it for you.

THE PLAYBOOK THAT CAN DAMAGE *YOUR* REPUTATION

In the near future, manipulation campaigns can and will be directed at more than just elections. I mentioned earlier in this book Putin's desire to cast doubt on the

American energy industry by amplifying both truths and untruths about fracking. This is just one way cyber operatives can turn to the manipulator's playbook to target a person, industry, or company to weaken and eventually ruin them.

At Fortalice Solutions, we have helped countless companies and individuals repair their reputations over the years. Oftentimes the damage had been caused by a disgruntled employee, spurned lover, or unhappy customer. The FBI's Internet Crime Complaint Center received approximately fifteen thousand reports of reputation-destroying extortion campaigns in 2017 alone.

At Fortalice we have noticed a disturbing trend in campaigns that can damage personal or workplace reputations. The playbook looks as follows:

1. A damaging review is published to Yelp!, Facebook, or Google, telling people to not use your services.
2. Fake business listings boosted with paid advertisements are designed and placed on Google Maps under names similar to your company's name, and search traffic is directed to the fake listings, which use the phone numbers of your competitors.
3. Search-engine optimization drives search traffic to the negative reviews and to your competitors.
4. Bots are activated to monitor your attempts to clear your good name.
5. New content using deepfake documents, such as a forged arrest warrant, are posted; deepfake video or audio is created that portrays you in the act of saying or doing something unscrupulous.

This is not fictional; this is really happening. We have worked several cases at Fortalice Solutions where hackers have seriously damaged a business or individual. Although they are not one of our clients, we tracked the extortion-attack case of travel agency Cheapair. Hackers e-mailed the company, threatening to "destroy personal or company reputation online." Cheapair could avoid destruction, the e-mail warned, if they paid 1.5 Bitcoins—which at the time was trading at the rough value of US$10,000. The extorters planned to spam search-engine results, essentially tricking the search-engine algorithm into returning inappropriate, or even offensive, results whenever someone performed a search in connection with Cheapair. And once the spamming had started, the extorters warned, even they couldn't undo it.[17]

For the victim of this kind of extortion, the mental scars last a lifetime and the cleanup is tedious and onerous.

The best defense is a good offense: Set up Google alerts to e-mail you daily with any mentions of your name and your company. If you have a spat with a customer, employee, or loved one, set up a Google alert with their names and your names in the search alert. Hopefully you will never encounter this sort of problem, but knowing early on that a campaign is underway puts you in a better position to combat it. Often, ignoring the threat, taunt, and misinformation may make the aggressor move on, but if it's a sophisticated campaign, it can take on a life of its own.

FIGHTING DEEPFAKE TECHNOLOGY

As Google, Microsoft, Facebook, Twitter, and other big-tech and social-media companies attempt to shut down access to fake personas, fake affinity groups, and fake political-ad campaigns, technology continues to struggle with quickly identifying and shutting down fake websites, deepfake videos, bogus research organizations, fraudulent or fake fundraisers, and other bad-faith operations online.[18] Private-sector, US military, research, and government organizations are racing to build strong algorithms to spot fakes by feeding computers examples of real videos and deepfake videos. However, public policy leaves a gray area for manipulators to play in: Are fakes considered protected free speech? If so, when? The world has not answered those questions, and neither have the US-based big-tech companies and social-media platforms. These players must do more to recognize and fight the problem and not hide behind the curtain of "free speech." We need to improve the ability to check an authoritative source to discern between deepfakes and legitimate information.

Cell phone, video, and audio-recording and camera companies could use digital watermarks so that their apps and programs brand their video or audio to be "original." Perhaps Virginia can lead the way: In 2019, that state passed an amendment to its 2014 revenge-porn law, updating a ban on nonconsensual pornography to include doctored videos, photos, and deepfakes. This provides victims of revenge-porn a means of holding their aggressors accountable. The amendment follows bills introduced in US Congress by Senator Ben Sasse (R-NE) and Representative Yvette Clarke (D-NY) that would regulate deepfakes. Other states, including Texas and New York, have either passed or proposed legislation dealing with deepfakes or digital replicas.[19]

FUTURE DIRECTIONS IN MANIPULATION CAMPAIGNS AND THE CYBERATTACKS BEHIND THEM

Anyone can be a high-value target for manipulators, from an elected official to your own grandmother, or from an Oscar winner to a major corporation. I realized years ago when I worked at the White House that if we took incremental steps in our cybersecurity strategies to fend off threats, we would fall behind and lose the battle. Based on what has happened to date with cybercrime tactics and social-media-manipulation campaigns, I am convinced that if we continue to focus on small steps, we are doomed to failure.

Here's the reality of what we face in combatting the globally employed tactics of these manipulators:

- Our current strategy does not work, and the path I am suggesting we take is not going to be easy.
- The manipulation campaigns are profitable ventures and self-funding.

- The financial models of big-tech and social-media companies rely on maintaining the status quo.
- News organizations, political campaigns, and social-media companies must change to address the threat.
- Global politicians struggle to keep pace with the emerging technologies behind the threat to legislate and provide oversight.

Manipulation campaigns are effective only when the cybersecurity plan to combat them is weak. Having the technological ability to thwart a hack-and-dump attack costs money. The revenue model of social-media companies is based on interactions of any kind, leaving them little incentive to stop a manipulation campaign before it starts. Rather, stopping this kind of threat requires an unconventional overhaul: One study says that Americans check their phones up to eighty times per day.[20] Password-vault company LastPass reports that in 2017 the average business user accessed roughly 191 different online accounts throughout the course of a calendar year.[21] You may be astonished at how much big tech and Silicon Valley leave it up to you to drive your own protection from manipulation campaigns and your own cybersecurity. This is the fundamental reason why every day, cybersecurity fails to protect you from manipulation campaigns: Everyone is counting on the user to do the heavy lifting to ensure they are not manipulated.

As a cybersecurity and intelligence services expert, I view this as a travesty. It is essential that big tech, social-media companies, and cybersecurity reevaluate how they view the problem. The new path for combatting manipulation campaigns through better cybersecurity should be driven by a core principle: "Design for humans."

What does this mean?

Have you ever installed childproof or safety locks in your house to protect toddlers or pets? Even with the locks, you still tell your kids, "Don't touch this" or train your pets; but just in case they have selective hearing and move toward the danger anyway, you design safety guards into your house with them in mind.

This is what cybersecurity should look like: education campaigns to alert users to fraud and manipulation campaigns, reinforced by guards in place to make it harder, less lucrative, and more painful for bad-faith actors to target their platform's users.

MAKING EVOLUTIONARY CHANGE

As with any change, things evolve over time. To make evolutionary change and protect against manipulation and misinformation campaigns, we need to start with the following:

- understanding and incorporating the knowledge of human nature and the human psyche into the cybersecurity profession and across all digital-news and social-media platforms,

- and innovating new, unique cybersecurity technologies and policies that combat manipulation and misinformation campaigns.

In my opinion, we must act now; we are headed on a dangerous course where we cannot protect our elections or the reputations of people or companies from manipulators. Failing to commit to a new cybersecurity strategy that combats the manipulation and misinformation threats could result in cyber war, where countries launch digital and physical offensive and defensive strikes against one another with the digital identities and devices of civilians potentially being targeted and becoming the real causalities.

HOW THE WORLD MUST CHANGE

To date, the global growth of hijacking elections and manipulation campaigns is still in its infancy. Many organizations from nonprofits to think tanks and governments are working to end the meddling and manipulation. However, most of that work is looking in the rear-view mirror—concerned with what we know the Russians, Iran, China, and North Korea have already done. But what if the manipulation campaigns that we know are what these countries and the operatives *want* us to know? What if they've made it easy for us to find some of the operation while leaving a more clandestine operation undiscovered? While we're dealing with the obvious threat, are we missing the subtler, more devastating one?

We need to establish a global center to focus on tracking the proliferation of cyber manipulation and cybercrime tactics so we can educate users and stop them from becoming victims. The global center would have a "red phone" concept. Just as the red phone provided a direct line of communication during the Cold War between the United States and Russia, global democracies need a red phone that rings into a central organization that can be used in times of democratic disaster. This group must bring together countries, security professionals, media, political parties and politicians, and technology experts to proactively anticipate what countries such as Russia, China, Iran, and North Korea might try next. "To make this happen requires open dialogue and government- and private-sector coordination at a level we have never seen, other than perhaps in the weeks following 9/11," agrees CrowdStrike's Shawn Henry. "If we are to beat the adversary at their game, it requires open sharing of actionable intelligence, real-time response, nonpartisanship, and 'one team.'"[22]

When it comes to security and combatting the manipulators, there are currently no international "*Good Housekeeping* seals of approval." We can't let that be the excuse for our coming up short. We must get this right and act now. We are careening toward a perilous future. This is the crisis of our time. Manipulation tactics and technology will get only more advanced, accelerated, and imperceptible, with no clear way to stop them. The only fix is for us all to be informed about, engaged in the efforts to stop, and enraged by the manipulators. It is time for the digital generation to rise up against those trying to hijack our minds and manipulate what we know to be true.

If we act now, our future could take a different course . . .

After hacks into election databases around the globe and fake personas were found manipulating political and social issues during recent elections in the United States, United Kingdom, Canada, Germany, Spain, and Italy, the world recognized that it needed to take coordinated action.

Countries agreed that an internationally recognized arbiter was necessary—one that could not be seen as favoring one country over another or as having a political agenda. The world decided that election security and manipulation campaigns impact global markets, and so the World Economic Forum was asked to set standards, a governance structure, and an overall policy on election security.

In order to combat the subterfuge around the globe, an international organization was created with resources from all countries to deploy armies of AI bots. These bots now analyze new accounts to determine if they should be shut down right away. In some cases, the AI is smart enough to determine whether an account is being created for nefarious purposes. Now, when a suspicious user attempts to open an account, they see a message: "You are not authorized to have an account."

The AI bots in the international centers are trained by elite engineers and digital anthropologists to hunt for deepfakes and altered videos and photos that promote fake news, and to remove them.

The WEF has directed the UN to invest heavily in real-time actionable intelligence. The UN maintains large mega physical centers that are globally connected, housing cybersecurity and intelligence teams from social media, governments, law enforcement, and private-sector companies. A team of data scientists, cybercriminal ring leaders, and social-media manipulators have defected from their cybercriminal syndicates, realizing that they were on the losing end, and have joined the fight to shut down cybercrime.

Each of the data scientists was allowed to choose their new citizenship and now works for a special division of the UN but reports their findings directly to the WEF. Their mission is clear—thwarting cybercrimes impacting businesses and elections and shutting down manipulation campaigns before they influence voters. Having studied the global meddling that occurred in the past, this unit can anticipate what individual cybercrime syndicates and bad actors are likely to do next.

Additionally, today all election employees are schooled repeatedly on digital hygiene, such as how to spot suspicious phone calls and links in text messages, e-mails, and websites that could be phishing attempts. Election centers in every country receive cutting-edge, comprehensive threat feeds from NATO, which also takes its direction from the WEF. When necessary, trust-but-verify processes go into effect. When in doubt, election nerve centers of each country can use the red phone to report that an attack is imminent or underway. The processes leverage machine learning to detect anomalies and alert election officials that they should manually scan ballots and do a statistical sample by counting votes by hand. Election websites, databases, and voting mechanisms are segmented away from the Internet, and critical IP addresses are protected.

Google, Facebook, Twitter, and other social-media companies have invested in and made a commitment to stopping the proliferation of fake news. Because deepfake photos and videos that look like real news are always going to be hard to detect, social media has created a "verified" flag provided to news sources and outlets that visually separates real news from suspicious stories.

Individuals have learned to spot, report, and ignore manipulation campaigns. . . . Democracy is safer. Social and political discourse is protected. Fake personas can no longer launch sophisticated, covert manipulation campaigns without someone reporting it.

This is a fictional account, for now.

It's a crisp, gorgeous election day in North Carolina. The leaves of the gingko trees are bright yellow. Around the city of Charlotte, people are heading to their polling places. Everyone of eligible age is fired up to vote. No one is still undecided; one group loves the current leader, and another cannot vote fast enough to get him out of office. Parking lots at polls have been crowded since six 6 a.m., with lines stretching out the door.

As a "battleground" state, North Carolina's electoral votes are considered crucial to any candidate's win. An hour after the polls have opened, something curious happens: Random voters appear to be missing from the registration rolls. "What do you mean *I'm not on the list*" demands an exasperated Wilma Stone. "I have my voter-registration card right here! I'm a lifelong Democrat!" The poll workers confer and then hand Wilma a paper ballot to fill out. Across town, the same thing is happening to Bob Mulligan, a registered Republican. "Sir, did you move recently? Maybe that's it." Bob shakes his head, irate. "No. Been living in the same place for over a decade."

This scene plays out all across the county, causing delays. Some voters arrive, see the long lines, and leave, intending to try again later—or maybe giving up altogether. Rumors begin circulating that someone has deleted voters from the database, and the news media hop on the story, offering live updates.

After a long day at work, you finally head over to your local precinct an hour before the polls close. You tell the volunteer your name, and she shakes her head in resignation. "I'm sorry," she says slowly. "I don't see you on my list. I'm going to have to ask you to step aside."

This is a fictional account, for now.

11

What Can You Do?

Despite all I have learned, I still feel ill-equipped to protect everyone from what's to come. The government and big tech want to do more to solve this problem for us, yet I realize that, as things stand now, sadly, they can't, and in some cases won't, protect us from the manipulators. Governments, news media, big tech, and social media have put certain countermeasures in place to shut down the manipulators, and they work, but the manipulators pivot and evolve their tactics.

Why can't big-tech and social-media companies develop a technology solution that will stop the cybercriminals and manipulators? The ecosystem of social media and how it pays for itself through advertising revenue are primary obstacles to reform. Globally, the entire ecosystem requires a reboot, starting with social-media networks and online-news domains.

To adequately counter online manipulation campaigns, existing social networks and online-news aggregators must vet posts quickly and accurately (likely not going to happen) and identify that a user is who they say they are (complexity in design); ads on social and political issues need to run without any targeting (that's probably a revenue- and deal-killer); and the social-media platforms should inform and perhaps pay us when they sell our information to marketing firms and campaigns (wouldn't that be grand?). Given that this online utopia is not likely to manifest—and neither will the laws and the courts catch up any time soon—it's up to you and me to spot and stop manipulation campaigns.

What has surprised me most in my study of these manipulators is the financial motive driving many of them. While some may have started out hoping to divide us, or to pick electoral winners or losers, what I have learned is that the manipulators have created huge revenue-generating machines. As Hacker X confirmed for me during our interview, making money was vital to the Benefactors, the Macedonians, and others. Making money for many of the cyber operatives and the manipulation-campaign bosses is often a primary focus and has been very lucrative.

SO, KNOWING ALL THIS, WHAT'S THE CALL TO ACTION?

We must spot manipulation campaigns and point them out to our colleagues, friends, and loved ones; we need to report manipulation campaigns to authorities on social issues, no matter how small or inconsequential the issue may seem; and we must vow to end manipulation campaigns by not spreading them ourselves— even if the headline is tantalizing and confirms our own bias on a topic—and by reporting them.

How?

I offer below some actions we can take. None of these strategies require you to purchase anything new, but they will require your dedication to the cause and some of your time. After studying fake versus real information relayed on any social issues, including whom to vote for, I have found several tips that work well for me to help spot voter influence or other manipulation campaigns. I want to enlist your aid in stopping the manipulators. Try some of the techniques and tools that I offer below.

REPORTING ELECTION ABUSES

For now, there is not one single clearinghouse to report manipulation and misinformation abuses, but here are some steps to help alert others.

1. Report the abuses to your country's election-security regulator.
2. Report abuses to your local and national news sources.
3. Flag accounts on social-media platforms.
4. Warn your circle of trust.

As of writing this book, here are some locations online where you can report manipulation and misinformation campaigns.

FACEBOOK

You can mark a post as false news on Facebook.

1. Click on the ellipses marks (. . .) next to the post you'd like to mark as false.
2. Click *Give feedback on this post.*

3. Click *False news*.
4. Click *Send*.[1]

TWITTER

On their election-integrity page, Twitter describes its approaches to combatting misinformation, which are updated from time to time. If you suspect misinformation is being spread on Twitter, from the app

1. Select *Report tweet*.
2. Select *It's misleading about voting*.
3. Then, select the option that is the best match for why the tweet is misleading.
4. Submit your report to Twitter.[2]

GOOGLE

Visit Google's Electoral Integrity Project online to report issues and keep up to date with the ways Google is combatting misinformation across its platforms.[3]

DEFLECTING NEWS STORIES
DESIGNED TO MANIPULATE

From my interview with Hacker X, you know that manipulation campaigns are launched both by foreign cyber operatives as well as those in your own country. Your fellow citizens know your culture the best and therefore might be even more effective manipulators than any campaign sponsored by a foreign government. Here are some telltale signs that what an online news story trending in your friends' feeds or on your own might be designed to manipulate:

1. Exclusive stories: Sensationalistic headline and the "news source" says it is the first to break the news.
2. Clickbait: A small image with a lead-in like "You will not believe what this candidate says about this issue!" encourages you to click.
3. Alternate news organizations: Check their story sources to see if any of their information refers to the Associated Press or Reuters or other trusted news sources, and check the original content; visit those news sources regarding that story for yourself.
4. Search-engine optimization: Manipulation campaigns have mastered driving your search traffic to the stories they are promoting; try going to trusted and vetted news sources and conducting your search within those news websites.

5. Private social-media groups: Manipulation trolls hide in plain sight in these private groups, as it's harder for big-tech and social-media companies to monitor what's shared, said, and posted within private groups.
6. Hashtags: Manipulation campaigns will hijack legitimate hashtags or make up their own to help make a story benefitting their purposes go viral; keep in mind that #MAGA was (and continues to be) a favorite of Internet trolls from Russia and Iran.
7. Memes: Your mind-set is being hijacked by memes; look for the source of the meme where possible, and do not be taken in by the one-liners of memes displaying falsified information.
8. Fake personas and hijacked personas: Do your research before deciding who to listen to and whom to believe; that person posing as someone living in your area could be a nation-state persona or an unscrupulous citizen trying to manipulate views of issues or candidates.

DIFFUSING DEEPFAKES

So far no tech company has released automated, easy, fast ways to spot a deepfake, but they are in development. For now, protect yourself with the following strategies:

1. Go to the real source: If you see something on social media, be sure to go to the actual news website itself to watch the video. Don't jump to conclusions without a trust-but-verify approach. Hold off sharing the media broadly until you can verify its authenticity.
2. Always truly verify the source: Was it a real news outlet that you know and trust that generated the media or one you haven't heard of? Do your homework. Are other trusted news outlets outside of social-media posts displaying this *exact* video?
3. Inspect the face: Look closely at the eyes and the mouth in the video. Artificial intelligence has a very hard time replicating natural human eye blinking or rendering the movement of lips, teeth, and tongue to match the voice. If the person in the video has long hair or dangling earrings, look closely at them, as AI does not handle movements of either very well yet. Study the ears; sometimes they will look grainy and inhuman, as AI struggles with the varying shapes of human ears.
4. Check the quality and detail: Check the video's image quality by viewing it on a large screen in high fidelity, both sped up and slowed down. Look for slight flickering around the edges of the face or if something moves in front of the face or person. Are there plausible physical differences between the image and who it's supposed to be? If the physical body of the person doesn't match the recent appearance of that person and seems to be noticeably smaller or heavier or has other major changes to their physique, you are

most likely looking at a fake. No, it's not likely that the politician just gained two hundred pounds!

5. Short clips are red flags: Deepfake videos are not technically complex to make, but they are labor intensive, and it's difficult to manufacture a believable deepfake video with a long run time; a short vignette is less time-consuming to produce.

6. Don't fall for clickbait: Things labeled "rare footage" or "never seen before" are a dead giveaway of a deepfake video. If you watch the clip and it seems incredible, then it's probably a fake.

7. Don't trust unsourced media: Where the video comes from helps determine its authenticity. Check other sources, and if nobody else is airing the video, it's probably a deepfake.

8. Check your confirmation bias: Is this a story you are prone to believe? Your viewpoint may be blinding you to the truth.

HOW CAN YOU AVOID BEING MANIPULATED?

As cybersecurity expert Clint Watts told me, "Only in today's modern age can you hate your neighbor but love someone you've never met that is posting something on social media."[4] Your active participation in consuming online media is key to protecting yourself. When encountering a new story, check that it's airing across multiple platforms—such as on the Internet, radio, and TV. Talk to your friends to fact-check the information presented. Remember that headlines that are part of a manipulation campaign often cause strong reactions. Fact-check the elements of the story using a trusted resource (identified later in this chapter). Follow more than one news source on social media so that you are presented with different reporting styles and news sources.

At this point, sadly, nobody can be believed. You cannot even believe your own eyes. You cannot believe your news feed on your social-media accounts. You have to be your own curator. Remember my class of bright high school English students whom I'd coached on how to spot a deepfake? When asked to determine which media were real and which were fakes, many of them couldn't—even after my coaching. One student earnestly told me how she verified a story: "I search for it on Google, Bing, and Yahoo!. If it comes up on the first page of all three, then it must be true." She paused and then looked me in straight in the eye, asking, "Right?"

First of all, I applaud this student. She did the right thing: Her first instinct is to fact-check using more than one source. And she's in great company; many consumers believe that the higher something appears in Google search results, the more reliable it is. However, many are surprised to learn that all of the popular search engines, including Google, have automated algorithms that source content based on advertisements and keywords, not by human curators of truth.[5]

When I began this journey to unmask the manipulators and reveal them to you, I had no idea where I'd be taken. I had assumed that nation-states, hacktivists, and domestic ideologues around the world were behind most of the more nefarious misinformation and manipulation campaigns. What I was surprised to learn during my hours of research, Internet sleuthing, and interviewing was the vast amount of money to be made as a manipulator.

When I started this journey, I thought that what most of the manipulators would have in common was the sole purpose of stoking division and driving people to act. However, almost every manipulation campaign that I've looked into has also generated great amounts of revenue, creating an alternate motive for mischief. In my discussions with Hacker X, he said more than once that he had been told to "make a lot of money, don't get caught, and don't let Clinton get elected." Online manipulations aren't solely about elections; money is always prioritized.

The manipulators fund their operation through their successful ability to manipulate; they have a virtuous cycle that works for them. They have adopted tactics that are cunning, sophisticated, and stealthy. They meddle in other countries' affairs, and they meddle locally. Their techniques work effectively to distort the truth.

We should continue to ask all globally elected officials to do more to fight the spread of misinformation, and we should continue to impress upon social-media companies and big tech that we are holding them accountable. We deserve better.

Protect yourself from manipulation: Keep up-to-date on current events and developments in cyber-manipulation techniques so that it's harder for a bad-faith actor to take advantage of you. I hope this book encourages you and inspires you to become an expert in spotting lies, reporting them, and fighting back. I can't do this alone. I need your help to protect your family and friends from falling prey to the manipulator's playbook.

RESOURCES

New and fabulous resources to help you spot and combat manipulation campaigns are created regularly. This is by no means an exhaustive list of the variety of critical resources available, and services will continue to be added, evolve, and change.

Handy Resources to Conduct Fact-Checks

FactCheck.org, https://www.factcheck.org
Snopes, https://www.snopes.com/fact-check/
Washington Post Fact Checker, https://www.washingtonpost.com/news/fact-checker/
PolitiFact, https://www.politifact.com

Tools to Spot a Fake

Education is key. The *Washington Post* has developed the Fact-Checkers Guide to Manipulated Video, which features educational videos illustrating recent examples of videos that have been edited either out of context, for satire, or to create a deepfake. Their site also allows you to report a video for fact-checking.[6]

The Observatory on Social Media is researching, developing, and deploying tools to spot fake posts, videos, and news stories.[7] They have many tools on their website that are free to use. For starters, try using educational tool Fakey to teach yourself and those in your circle of trust how to spot a fake ad or a meme spreading fake information.[8] Another great tool is Hoaxy, which creates visualizations of how fake news is spread on the Internet.[9]

Can you spot a deep fake? Test yourself?[10]

Need a deepfake face? You can find it online.[11]

HAVE AN EXPERT "SHOULDER SURFER" POINT OUT MANIPULATORS' ONLINE ADS

If you want a digital advisor looking over your shoulder as you surf the Internet, you may want to try browser plug-ins designed to fact-check, spot fake news, and highlight manipulation campaigns. As of this writing, some of the services available include NewsGuard, TrustedNews, and the Official Media Bias Fact Check.[12]

Sensitive social and political issues touching on age or gender or political-party affiliations are targeted every day by campaigns hoping to influence how you think about them. These campaigns are distributed across radio, print, and TV in the hopes of mobilizing a base of support to donate or vote. Various nonprofit groups also want to mobilize on the key issues they address to attract volunteers and donations. Facebook ads can target very specific slices of a population and be very effective in motivating those populations; even the ads running only a short time can have lasting impacts. At the end of 2017, ProPublica launched a project to determine who buys Facebook's online ads and whom the ads target. The collection of ad information is amassed from volunteers who have downloaded ProPublica's user-friendly plug-in.[13] At their ever-growing ad database you can toggle ads based on age, gender, and sociopolitical affiliation.[14] Although predominately US–focused, citizens of other countries are using ProPublica's tool too.

CHECK YOUR SOURCES

- AllSides' Media Bias Ratings helps consumers find information sourced through different perspectives at https://www.allsides.com/media-bias/media-bias-ratings.
- The Duke Reporters' Lab at Duke University maintains a database of global fact-checking sites at https://reporterslab.org/fact-checking/.

- Open Sources researches any site identifying itself as news organizations or independent news outlets to categorize the domain name as either legitimate news or fake, unreliable, or even clickbait, at https://docs.google.com/document/d/10eA5-mCZLSS4MQY5QGb5ewC3VAL6pLkT53V_81ZyitM/preview.
- FlackCheck.org, within the Annenberg Public Policy Center of the University of Pennsylvania, helps debunk political ads and deception campaigns.
- The Center for News Literacy at Stony Brook University, using funding from the John S. and James L. Knight Foundation, has created a free online course, open to anyone, titled Making Sense of the News: News Literacy Lessons for Digital Citizens, at https://www.coursera.org/learn/news-literacy.
- Truth-O-Meter is populated by the journalists writing at PolitiFact.com, who scour campaign materials, social media, interviews, speeches, and news stories and press to the determine the veracity of the claims they find there, posting them at https://www.politifact.com/truth-o-meter/. You can also request a fact-check by e-mailing truthometer@politifact.com.
- TruthOrFiction.com sorts news items, labeling them as fake news, viral stories, entertainment stories, politics, and more but also categorizes old rumors and urban legends, researching the facts and tracing back to original sources.

DON'T ALLOW THE MEDIA TO BE SILENCED

- Mapping Media Freedom tracks attacks against media and journalists at https://mappingmediafreedom.org/. Report new violations at https://mappingmedia freedom.ushahidi.io/posts/create/14.
- The Resource Centre on Media Freedom in Europe uses a platform developed by the Osservatorio Balcani e Caucaso Transeuropa as part of the European Centre for Press and Media Freedom to compile information concerning the state of media freedom and freedom of the press in Europe, at https://www.rcmediafreedom.eu/. Among several research reports they compile, annually they publish *Democracy at Risk: Threats and Attacks against Media Freedom in Europe*.[15]

CLOSE THE MANIPULATOR'S PLAYBOOK

Our relationships with each other, our social discourse, our physical safety, and global democracies are at risk. We cannot wait for super heroes to swoop in and save us (although I do believe a dose of Tony Stark's innovation and the bravery and might of the Avengers could fix this). Our elected officials have been outmaneuvered, global organizations are powerless to deflect the attacks, and big-tech and social-media fixes lag behind the evolving tactics of the manipulators. It is up to us. Join me, and together we can and we will close the manipulator's playbook.

Acknowledgments

Behind every success stands a group of amazing people. My husband and kids have cheered me on, and although much of this book was written while on the road for work, when I was at home, they would wake in the mornings to find me at the kitchen table, already about two to three hours into my research and writing. My sweet family would often be greeted with, "Good morning—guess what I learned!" and they never acted like they were tired of hearing it.

A big shout-out to my high school English and creative-writing teacher, Nancy Brown. Her tough-love grading and encouragement sparked my love of writing. A heartfelt thanks to my book agent, Joelle Delbourgo, who pushed me to reframe my approach for this project and worked hard to get this book to the right publisher. Also big thanks to my editor, Melissa Schorr, who challenged me every day to present the facts to you in story mode. Her thoughtful edits taught me so much about how to communicate this issue, and the lessons learned will stay with me whenever I teach about cybersecurity in the future. I want to thank Nancy Boysen, who helped me shape my concerns into a book outline and inspired me to weave in the fictional vignettes for each chapter. Thanks also go to my team at Fortalice Solutions, who provided their analysis and opinion along the way, and to my security colleagues who took the time to share their insights from the front lines of cybersecurity. Finally, thanks, Rowman & Littlefield, for your support.

Notes

FOREWORD

1. Joseph Dunford and the US Marine Corps, *United States Marine Corps Service Campaign Plan: 2014–2022* ([Washington, DC]: US Marine Corps, 2014), 8, https://www.usmcu.edu/Portals/218/CAOCL/files/2014%20Marine%20Corps%20Service%20Campaign%20Plan%20for%202014-2022%20FINAL%20(MS).pdf.

2. In October 2016, the Mirai botnet was used to conduct a series of distributed denial-of-service attacks that temporarily wiped out Internet access across swaths of Europe and North America. See Lily Hay Newman, "What We Know about Friday's Massive East Coast Internet Outage," *Wired*, October 21, 2016, https://www.wired.com/2016/10/internet-outage-ddos-dns-dyn/; and also see *Wikipedia*, s.v. "2016 Dyn cyberattack," last edited October 31, 2019, https://en.wikipedia.org/wiki/2016_Dyn_cyberattack.

INTRODUCTION

1. "Word of the Year 2016 Is . . ." Oxford Dictionaries, accessed October 7, 2019, https://languages.oup.com/word-of-the-year/word-of-the-year-2016. And see Sabrina Tanquerel, "Quand l'exigence de vérité devient secondaire . . ." *The Conversation*, February 12, 2017, http://theconversation.com/quand-lexigence-de-verite-devient-secondaire-70718.

2. Sanja Kelly, Mai Truong, Adrian Shahbaz, Madeline Earp, and Jessica White, "Key Findings," in *Freedom on the Net 2017: Manipulating Social Media to Undermine Democracy* (Washington, DC: Freedom House, 2018), https://freedomhouse.org/report/freedom-net/freedom-net-2017.

3. Cynthia McFadden, William M. Arkin, and Kevin Monahan, "Russians Penetrated US Voter Systems, Top US Official Says," NBC News, February 7, 2018, https://www.nbcnews.com/politics/elections/russians-penetrated-u-s-voter-systems-says-top-u-s-n845721.

4. Kim Zetter, "The Crisis of Election Security," *New York Times Magazine*, September 26, 2018, https://www.nytimes.com/2018/09/26/magazine/election-security-crisis-midterms.html; Associated Press, "Federal Government Tells 21 States Election Systems Targeted by Hackers," September 22, 2017, NBC News, https://www.nbcnews.com/storyline/hacking-of-america/federal-government-tells-21-states-election-systems-targeted-hackers-n804031.

5. Dan O'Sullivan, "The RNC Files: Inside the Largest US Voter Data Leak," UpGuard (website), first reported June 19, 2017, and last updated July 17, 2019, https://www.upguard.com/breaches/the-rnc-files.

6. Daniel Howley, "Warren Buffett: 'Cyber Poses Real Risks to Humanity," Yahoo! Finance, April 30, 2019, https://finance.yahoo.com/news/warren-buffett-cyber-attacks-131445079.html.

7. Robinson Meyer, "The Grim Conclusions of the Largest-Ever Study of Fake News," *The Atlantic*, March 8, 2018, https://www.theatlantic.com/technology/archive/2018/03/largest-study-ever-fake-news-mit-twitter/555104/. In the article, Meyer paraphrases Jonathan Swift, in *The Examiner*, no. 15, November 2–9, 1710, p. 2, col. 1, https://books.google.com/books?id=KigTAAAAQAAJ&q=%22Truth+comes%22&hl=en#v=snippet&q=%22Truth%20comes%22&f=false.

8. Arkaitz Zubiaga, Maria Liakata, Rob Procter, Geraldine Wong Sak Hoi, and Peter Tolmie, "Analysing How People Orient to and Spread Rumors in Social Media by Looking at Conversational Threads," *PLOS ONE* 11, no. 3 (2016): e0150989, https://doi.org/10.1371/journal.pone.0150989.

9. Laura Hazard Owen, "Americans May Appreciate Knowing When a News Story Is Suspect, but More Than a Third Will Share That Story Anyway," Nieman Lab, June 29, 2018, https://www.niemanlab.org/2018/06/americans-may-appreciate-knowing-when-a-news-story-is-suspect-but-more-than-a-third-will-share-that-story-anyway/.

10. Kerry Flynn, "A Timeline of Everything We Know about How Russia Used Facebook, Google, and Twitter to Help Trump Win," *Mashable*, September 8, 2017, https://mashable.com/2017/09/08/facebook-elect-trump-russia-election/.

11. Mary Clare Jalonick, "Russian Influence Operations Still Stoking Tensions on Social Media, Senate Reports Say," PBS, updated December 17, 2018, https://www.pbs.org/newshour/politics/russian-influence-operations-still-active-and-ongoing-on-social-media-senate-report-says.

12. US Senate Select Committee on Intelligence, *Report of the Select Committee on Intelligence, United States Senate, on Russian Active Measures: Campaigns and Interference in the 2016 US Election*, vol. 2, Russia's Use of Social Media with Additional Views (Washington, DC: US Government Publishing Office, 2019), redacted text available at https://www.intelligence.senate.gov/sites/default/files/documents/Report_Volume1.pdf. And see Craig Timberg and Tony Romm, "New Report on Russian Disinformation, Prepared for the Senate, Shows the Operation's Scale and Sweep," *Washington Post*, December 17, 2018, http:www.washingtonpost.com/technology/2018/12/16/new-report-russian-disinformation-prepared-senate-shows-operations-scale-sweep/.

CHAPTER 1: HOW DID WE GET HERE?

1. Melissa A. Jackson, "Rahab, Comedy, and Feminist Interpretation," *Oxford Biblical Studies Online*, Focus On: Rahab, accessed October 3, 2019, https://global.oup.com/obso/focus/focus_on_rahab/.

2. Ralph D. Casey, "The Story of Propaganda," in *EM 2: The Story of Propaganda*, GI Roundtable series, pamphlet (Washington, DC: American Historical Association, 1944), archived online at https://www.historians.org/about-aha-and-membership/aha-history-and -archives/gi-roundtable-series/pamphlets/em-2-what-is-propaganda-(1944)/the-story-of -propaganda.

3. Simon Worrall, "Author Says a Whole Culture—Not a Single 'Homer'—Wrote 'Iliad,' 'Odyssey,'" *National Geographic*, January 3, 2015, https://www.nationalgeographic.com/news/ 2015/1/150104-homer-iliad-odyssey-greece-book-talk-travel-world/.

4. Aristotle, *Rhetorica*, ed. W. D. Ross, trans W. Rhys Roberts, vol. 11, *The Works of Aristotle* (Oxford: Clarendon Press, 1924); reprinted as Aristotle, *"Rhetoric" and "Poetics,"* trans. W. Rhys Roberts and Ingram Bywater (New York: Modern Library, 1954); text available online at http:// classics.mit.edu/Aristotle/rhetoric.html.

5. *Catholic Online*, s.v. "Pope Urban VIII," accessed October 3, 2019, https://www.catholic .org/encyclopedia/view.php?id=11834.

6. Ian Cooke, "Propaganda as a Weapon? Influencing International Opinion," World War I, British Library, January 29, 2014, https://www.bl.uk/world-war-one/articles/propaganda -as-a-weapon.

7. David Welch, "Persuading the People: British Propaganda in the Second World War," *History Extra*, December 9, 2016, https://www.historyextra.com/period/second-world-war/ persuading-the-people-british-propaganda-in-the-second-world-war/.

8. William Boyd, "The Secret Persuaders," *Guardian*, August 19, 2006, https://www.the guardian.com/uk/2006/aug/19/military.secondworldwar; Nicholas J. Cull, *Selling War: The British Propaganda Campaign against American "Neutrality" in World War II* (Oxford: Oxford University Press, 1995).

9. Elaine Showalter, "The Brilliance of the Women Code Breakers of World War II," Outlook, *Washington Post*, October 6, 2017, https://www.washingtonpost.com/outlook/the -brilliance-of-the-women-code-breakers-of-world-war-ii/2017/10/06/ec64ca8a-9e2c-11e7 -9c8d-cf053ff30921_story.html.

10. "Nazi Propaganda," the United States Holocaust Memorial Museum, accessed October 8, 2019, https://www.ushmm.org/collections/bibliography/nazi-propaganda; Elaine Showalter, "The Brilliance of the Women Code Breakers of World War II," Outlook, *Washington Post*, October 6, 2017, https://www.washingtonpost.com/outlook/the-brilliance-of-the-women -code-breakers-of-world-war-ii/2017/10/06/ec64ca8a-9e2c-11e7-9c8d-cf053ff30921_story .html.

11. Hubertus Knabe, "The Dark Secrets of a Surveillance State," filmed June 2014 at TEDSalon Berlin, transcript of video, 19:15, https://www.ted.com/talks/hubertus_knabe_the _dark_secrets_of_a_surveillance_state/transcript.

12. *Wikipedia*, s.v. "Stasi," last modified September 25, 2019, https://en.wikipedia.org/ wiki/Stasi.

13. In interview with Ben Popken, "Factory of Lies: Russia's Disinformation Playbook Exposed," NBC News, November 5, 2018, https://www.nbcnews.com/business/consumer/ factory-lies-russia-s-disinformation-playbook-exposed-n910316.

14. Thomas Boghardt, "Operation INFEKTION: Soviet Bloc Intelligence and Its AIDS Disinformation Campaign," Historical Perspectives, *Studies in Intelligence* 53, no. 4 (December 2009), Central Intelligence Agency, https://www.cia.gov/library/center-for-the-study-of -intelligence/csi-publications/csi-studies/studies/vol53no4/soviet-bloc-intelligence-and-its -aids.html.

15. Seth G. Jones, "Russian Meddling in the United States: The Historical Context of the Mueller Report," *CSIS Briefs*, Center for Strategic and International Studies, March 27, 2019, https://www.csis.org/analysis/russian-meddling-united-states-historical-context-mueller-report; "Report by the Chairman of the Delegation of the Committee for State Security (KGB) of the USSR, General-Colonel V. M. Chebrikov during Soviet Bloc Meeting on Western Radio," April 23, 1980, History and Public Policy Program Digital Archive, Bulgarian Interior Ministry Archive, Fond 22, Record 1, Document 124, obtained by Jordan Baev, trans. Sveta Milusheva, https://digitalarchive.wilsoncenter.org/document/121522.

16. Seth G. Jones, "Russian Meddling in the United States: The Historical Context of the Mueller Report," *CSIS Briefs*, Center for Strategic and International Studies, March 27, 2019, https://www.csis.org/analysis/russian-meddling-united-states-historical-context-mueller-report.

17. Richard A. Clarke, in discussion with the author, August 2019.

18. Ben Popken, "Factory of Lies: Russia's Disinformation Playbook Exposed," NBC News, November 5, 2018, https://www.nbcnews.com/business/consumer/factory-lies-russia-s-disinformation-playbook-exposed-n910316.

19. United States Department of State, "The USSR's AIDS Disinformation Campaign," chapter 5 in *Soviet Influence Activities: A Report on Active Measures and Propaganda, 1986–87*, 33–49 (Washington, DC: US Department of State, 1987); Ben Popken, "Factory of Lies: Russia's Disinformation Playbook Exposed," NBC News, November 5, 2018, https://www.nbcnews.com/business/consumer/factory-lies-russia-s-disinformation-playbook-exposed-n910316.

20. Richard A. Clarke, in discussion with the author, August 2019.

21. VK, or VKontakte, is a Russian-based social-networking service that looks a lot like Facebook.

22. *New York Times* reporter Adam Ellick interviewed by Terry Gross, in "Inside The Russian Disinformation Playbook: Exploit Tension, Sow Chaos," *Fresh Air*, November 15, 2018, https://www.npr.org/2018/11/15/668209008/inside-the-russian-disinformation-playbook-exploit-tension-sow-chaos.

23. Ibid.

24. Johnson is likely referring to "the Golden Cavalry of Saint George," Britain's colloquial name for government bribes. As told to Scott Shane, in "Russia Isn't the Only One Meddling in Elections. We Do It, Too," *New York Times*, February 17, 2018, https://www.nytimes.com/2018/02/17/sunday-review/russia-isnt-the-only-one-meddling-in-elections-we-do-it-too.html. And see *Wikipedia*, s.v. "Golden Cavalry of St. George," last edited September 29, 2019, https://en.wikipedia.org/wiki/Golden_Cavalry_of_St_George.

25. Scott Shane, "Russia Isn't the Only One Meddling in Elections. We Do It, Too," *New York Times*, February 17, 2018, https://www.nytimes.com/2018/02/17/sunday-review/russia-isnt-the-only-one-meddling-in-elections-we-do-it-too.html.

26. Ibid.

27. Ibid.

28. Markar Melkonian, "Meddling in Presidential Elections," *Hetq Online*, January 13, 2017, https://hetq.am/en/article/74607; Scott Shane, "Russia Isn't the Only One Meddling in Elections. We Do It, Too," *New York Times*, February 17, 2018, https://www.nytimes.com/2018/02/17/sunday-review/russia-isnt-the-only-one-meddling-in-elections-we-do-it-too.html.

29. Scott Shane, "Russia Isn't the Only One Meddling in Elections. We Do It, Too," *New York Times*, February 17, 2018, https://www.nytimes.com/2018/02/17/sunday-review/russia -isnt-the-only-one-meddling-in-elections-we-do-it-too.html.

30. Natalie Nougayrède, "In This Age of Propaganda, We Must Defend Ourselves. Here's How," Opinion, *Guardian*, January 31, 2018, https://www.theguardian.com/commentisfree/ 2018/jan/31/propaganda-defend-russia-technology.

31. "Nigerian Letter or '419' Fraud," FBI.gov, accessed October 8, 2019, https://www.fbi .gov/scams-and-safety/common-fraud-schemes/nigerian-letter-or-419-fraud. And for information about identifying and avoiding other scams and frauds, visit https://www.fbi.gov/ scams-and-safety/common-fraud-schemes.

32. Rebecca Hiscott, "10 Chain Emails That Haunted Your Youth," *Mashable*, March 12, 2014, https://mashable.com/2014/03/12/chain-emails/.

33. "Kim Jong-un Named *The Onion*'s Sexiest Man Alive for 2012," *Onion*, November 14, 2012, https://www.theonion.com/kim-jong-un-named-the-onions-sexiest-man-alive-for -2012-1819574194; Edward Wong, "Kim Jong-un Seems to Get a New Title: Heartthrob," *New York Times*, November 27, 2012, https://www.nytimes.com/2012/11/28/world/asia/ chinese-news-site-cites-onion-piece-on-kim-jong-un.html.

34. "The Perils of Speed before Accuracy," Media Watch, Australian Broadcasting Corporation, broadcast February 4, 2013, published July 11, 2018, http://www.abc.net.au/mediawatch/ transcripts/s3682970.htm.

35. The original, fake news release, "ANZ Divests from Maules Creek Project," was published without authorization by Jonathan Moylan on January 7, 2013, archived online by the Australian Broadcasting Corporation at http://www.abc.net.au/mediawatch/transcripts/ 1301_fake.pdf.

36. "Whitehaven Coal Shares Plunge after Media Hoax," Australian Broadcasting Corporation, updated January 7, 2013, http://www.abc.net.au/news/2013-01-07/whitehaven-coal -shares-plunge-after-media-hoax/4455362.

37. Nidhi Dave, "Top 3 Viral Marketing Campaigns to Take Inspiration From," *SEMrush Blog*, March 9, 2018, https://www.semrush.com/blog/viral-marketing-campaign-inspiration/.

38. "Viral Marketing," *Investopedia*, reviewed by Julia Kagan, updated March 14, 2019, https://www.investopedia.com/terms/v/viral-marketing.asp.

39. While various sources claim to be the inspiration for the expression, it became eternally associated with Andy Warhol after he printed it in the program to his premier art exhibition in 1968 at the Moderna Museet in Stockholm, Sweden. "Warhol 1968," Moderna Museet (website), accessed October 8, 2019, https://www.modernamuseet.se/stockholm/en/exhibitions/ andy-warhol-other-voices-other-rooms/with-andy-warhol-1968-text-ol/.

40. George Cando, "'Avengers: Endgame' Makes Box Office and Social Media History," *Movie TV Tech Geeks*, April 27, 2019, http://movietvtechgeeks.com/avengers-endgame-makes -box-office-and-social-media-history/.

41. Numbers are as of this writing; "Avengers: *Endgame* Cast Sings "We Didn't Start the Fire," YouTube video, 2:06, from a performance on *The Tonight Show* on April 22, 2019, posted by The Tonight Show Starring Jimmy Fallon, April 22, 2019, https://www.youtube .com/watch?v=-onk-Qm7ATw.

42. Tide, "Gronk Knows Tide PODs Are for Doing Laundry. Nothing Else," Facebook video, 0:21, January 12, 2018, https://www.facebook.com/Tide/videos/gronk-knows-that -tide-pods-are-for-doing-laundry-nothing-else/10155319188423231/.

43. David D. Kirkpatrick, Mike McIntyre, and Jeff Zeleny, "Obama's Camp Culti-vates Crop in Small Donors," *New York Times*, July 17, 2007, https://www.nytimes.com/2007/07/17/us/politics/17obama.html.

44. Simone Baribeau, "5 Ways the Obama Campaign Was Run like a Lean Startup," The Pivot, *Fast Company*, November 14, 2012, https://www.fastcompany.com/3002973/5-ways-obama-campaign-was-run-lean-startup.

45. Michael Scherer, "Inside the Secret World of the Data Crunchers Who Helped Obama Win," *Time*, November 7, 2012, http://swampland.time.com/2012/11/07/inside-the-secret-world-of-quants-and-data-crunchers-who-helped-obama-win/.

46. Simone Baribeau, "5 Ways the Obama Campaign Was Run like a Lean Startup," The Pivot, *Fast Company*, November 14, 2012, https://www.fastcompany.com/3002973/5-ways-obama-campaign-was-run-lean-startup.

47. Josh Rivera, "Why You Should Be Skeptical of 2020 Candidates: 'Astroturfing' Can Distort Public Opinion," *USA Today*, updated April 24, 2019, https://www.usatoday.com/story/opinion/2019/04/24/trust-2020-candidates-astroturfing-distort-public-opinion-column/3534379002/.

48. *Wikipedia*, s.v. "Astroturfing: History of Incidents," last edited October 5, 2019, https://en.wikipedia.org/wiki/Astroturfing#History_of_incidents.

49. Josh Rivera, "Why You Should Be Skeptical of 2020 Candidates: 'Astroturfing' Can Distort Public Opinion," *USA Today*, updated April 24, 2019, https://www.usatoday.com/story/opinion/2019/04/24/trust-2020-candidates-astroturfing-distort-public-opinion-column/3534379002/.

50. Fanny Potkin and Augustinus Beo Da Costa, "In Indonesia, Facebook and Twitter Are 'Buzzer' Battlegrounds as Elections Loom," World News, Reuters, March 12, 2019, https://www.reuters.com/article/us-indonesia-election-socialmedia-insigh/in-indonesia-facebook-and-twitter-are-buzzer-battlegrounds-as-elections-loom-idUSKBN1QU0AS.

51. Arjun Bisen, "Disinformation Is Drowning Democracy: In the New Age of Lies, Law, Not Tech, Is the Answer," *ForeignPolicy.com*, April 24, 2019, https://foreignpolicy.com/2019/04/24/disinformation-is-drowning-democracy/; Fanny Potkin and Augustinus Beo Da Costa, "In Indonesia, Facebook and Twitter Are 'Buzzer' Battlegrounds as Elections Loom," World News, Reuters, March 12, 2019, https://www.reuters.com/article/us-indonesia-election-socialmedia-insigh/in-indonesia-facebook-and-twitter-are-buzzer-battlegrounds-as-elections-loom-idUSKBN1QU0AS.

52. Tai Nalon, "Did WhatsApp Help Bolsonaro Win the Brazilian Presidency?" Opinion, *Washington Post*, November 1, 2018, https://www.washingtonpost.com/news/theworldpost/wp/2018/11/01/whatsapp-2/.

53. Janna Anderson and Lee Rainie, "The Future of Truth and Misinformation," Pew Research Center, October 19, 2017, https://www.pewinternet.org/2017/10/19/the-future-of-truth-and-misinformation-online/.

CHAPTER 2: MOTIVES AND TARGETS

1. Krutskikh made these comments while addressing an assemblage on the first day of Infoforum 2016, a Russian national information-security forum, in Moscow, Russia, February 4–5, 2016. David Ignatius, "Russia's Radical New Strategy for Information Warfare,

Washington Post, January 18, 2017, https://www.washingtonpost.com/blogs/post-partisan/ wp/2017/01/18/russias-radical-new-strategy-for-information-warfare/; "Infoforum 2016: Program," Infoforum.ru (website), accessed October 9, 2019, https://translate.googleuser content.com/translate_c?depth=1&rurl=translate.google.com&sl=auto&sp=nmt4&tl=en&u =https://infoforum.ru/conference/conference/program/cid/20%3Fformat%3Dpdf&xid=172 59,15700021,15700186,15700191,15700256,15700259,15700262,15700265,15700271& usg=ALkJrhj8Suige4LUoJWkb-23j6B-aJEqTQ, page 6, English translation from the original Russian.

2. Robert S. Mueller, *Report on the Investigation into Russian Interference in the 2016 Presidential Election* (Washington, DC: US Department of Justice, 2019), https://www.justice.gov/ storage/report.pdf, vol. 1, p. 36; the GRU is the foreign military-intelligence agency of the General Staff of the Armed Forces of the Russian Federation.

3. James Clapper, Marcel Lettre, and Michael S. Rogers, "Joint Statement for the Record to the Senate Armed Services Committee, Foreign Cyber Threats to the United States," United States Senate Committee on Armed Services (website), January 5, 2017, https://www .armed-services.senate.gov/imo/media/doc/Clapper-Lettre-Rogers_01-05-16.pdf.

4.

FRONTLINE NARRATOR: The State Department said they were simply promoting democracy, not trying to steer the outcome. But to Putin, Clinton had crossed the line, threatening his hold on power.

PETER BAKER, COAUTHOR *KREMLIN'S RISING*: No question he's looking at revenge at Hillary Clinton. There's no question that he sees Hillary Clinton as an adversary. And he wanted to— like, you know, he wanted to get her back.

Adapted from the transcript of part 1 of "Putin's Revenge," episode 2 of *Frontline*, season 2017, PBS, original air date October 25, 2017, https://www.pbs.org/wgbh/frontline/film/ putins-revenge/transcript/. View the entire episode at https://www.pbs.org/wgbh/frontline/ film/putins-revenge/.

5. US Senate Select Committee on Intelligence, *Report of the Select Committee on Intelligence, United States Senate, on Russian Active Measures Campaigns and Interference in the 2016 U.S. Election*, vol. 2, Russia's Use of Social Media with Additional Views (Washington, DC: US Government Publishing Office, 2019), redacted text available at https://www.intelligence .senate.gov/sites/default/files/documents/Report_Volume2.pdf.

6. Issie Lapowsky, "Facebook and Twitter Eye Iran in Latest Fake Account Crackdown," *Wired*, August 29, 2018, https://www.wired.com/story/facebook-twitter-eye-iran-fake-account -crackdown/.

7. Daniel Victor, "Why Are People Protesting in Hong Kong?" *New York Times*, November 13, 2019, https://www.nytimes.com/2019/11/13/world/asia/hong-kong-protests.html.

8. Transcript of interview of Vladimir Putin by Chris Wallace, for Fox News, Helsinki, Finland, July 16, 2018, "Read Vladimir Putin's Full Testy Interview with Fox News' Chris Wallace," *Daily Mail*, July 16, 2018, https://www.dailymail.co.uk/news/fb-5960759/READ -VLADIMIR-PUTINS-TESTY-INTERVIEW-FOX-NEWS-CHRIS-WALLACE.html. And watch the entire interview at https://www.youtube.com/watch?v=rHY8yG4mVzs.

9. Madeline Roache, "Russian President Putin Calls Liberalism 'Obsolete' Amid G20," *Time*, June 28, 2019, https://time.com/5616982/putin-liberalism-g20/.

10. Washington Post editorial board, "What Does Putin Fear?" Opinion, *Washington Post*, August 11, 2019, www.washingtonpost.com/opinions/global-opinions/what-does-putin-fear/ 2019/07/22/fdd23cc4-aca5-11e9-8e77-03b30bc29f64_story.html.

11. Neil Macfarquhar, "A Powerful Russian Weapon: The Spread of False Stories," *New York Times*, August 28, 2016, http://www.nytimes.com/2016/08/29/world/europe/russia-sweden-disinformation.html.

12. Sanja Kelly, Mai Truong, Adrian Shahbaz, Madeline Earp, and Jessica White, *Freedom on the Net 2017: Manipulating Social Media to Undermine Democracy* (Washington, DC: Freedom House, 2018), https://freedomhouse.org/sites/default/files/FOTN_2017_Final.pdf.

13. "New Report Reveals Growing Threat of Organised Social Media Manipulation World-Wide," press release, Oxford Internet Institute, July 20, 2018, https://www.oii.ox.ac.uk/news/releases/new-report-reveals-growing-threat-of-organised-social-media-manipulation-world-wide/. And see the report in full at Samantha Bradshaw and Philip N. Howard, "Challenging Truth and Trust: A Global Inventory of Organized Social Media Manipulation," working paper 2018.1, Oxford Internet Institute, Oxford, UK, July 20, 2018, http://comprop.oii.ox.ac.uk/wp-content/uploads/sites/93/2018/07/ct2018.pdf.

14. Originally published in 2013, the updated manual can be found at Michael Schmidt, ed., *Tallinn Manual 2.0: On the International Law Applicable to Cyber Operations*, 2nd ed. (Cambridge: Cambridge University Press, 2017).

15. Josh Gerstein, "Trump Campaign: WikiLeaks Posting Hacked DNC Emails Was Legal," Politico, updated October 26, 2017, https://www.politico.com/story/2017/10/25/trump-campaign-wikileaks-hacked-dnc-emails-244173.

16. Samantha Bradshaw and Philip N. Howard, "Executive Summary," in "Challenging Truth and Trust: A Global Inventory of Organized Social Media Manipulation," working paper 2018.1, Oxford Internet Institute, Oxford, UK, July 20, 2018, http://comprop.oii.ox.ac.uk/wp-content/uploads/sites/93/2018/07/ct2018.pdf, page 3.

17. Sanja Kelly, Mai Truong, Adrian Shahbaz, Madeline Earp, and Jessica White, *Freedom on the Net 2017: Manipulating Social Media to Undermine Democracy* (Washington, DC: Freedom House, 2018), https://freedomhouse.org/sites/default/files/FOTN_2017_Final.pdf, p. 1.

18. UK Digital Culture, Media, and Sport Committee, "Summary," in *Disinformation and 'Fake News': Interim Report Contents* (London: Parliament of the United Kingdom, 2018), https://publications.parliament.uk/pa/cm201719/cmselect/cmcumeds/363/36303.htm. Read the committee's final report at https://www.parliament.uk/business/committees/committees-a-z/commons-select/digital-culture-media-and-sport-committee/news/fake-news-report-published-17-19/.

19. Though Cambridge Analytica's website is now offline, an archived copy can be found at The Wayback Machine, under a search for "https://cambridgeanalytica.org/," at http://web.archive.org/web/20160301173820/https://cambridgeanalytica.org/.

20. *Wikipedia*, s.v. "Cambridge Analytica," last edited September 27, 2019, https://en.wikipedia.org/wiki/Cambridge_Analytica.

21. "Cambridge Analytica CEO 'Admits to Dirty Tricks,'" *The Week UK*, March 20, 2018, https://www.theweek.co.uk/92390/cambridge-analytica-ceo-admits-to-dirty-tricks.

22. James Vincent, "Academic Who Collected 50 Million Facebook Profiles: 'We Thought We Were Doing Something Normal,'" The Verge, March 21, 2018, https://www.theverge.com/2018/3/21/17146342/facebook-data-scandal-cambridge-analytica-aleksandr-kogan-scapegoat.

23. Joe Myers, "Nearly a Third of the Globe Is Now on Facebook—Chart of the Day," World Economic Forum (website), August 5, 2019, https://www.weforum.org/agenda/2019/08/facebook-users-social-media-internet/.

24. Michael Nowak and Dean Eckles, for Facebook Inc., "Determining User Personality Characteristics from Social Networking System Communications and Characteristics," Application US15/173,009, filed September 10, 2012, and archived online at https://patents .google.com/patent/US9740752B2/en.

25. Michelle Nichols, "North Korea Took $2 Billion in Cyberattacks to Fund Weapons Program: UN Report," Reuters, August 5, 2019, https://www.reuters.com/article/us-north korea-cyber-un/north-korea-took-2-billion-in-cyber-attacks-to-fund-weapons-program-u-n -report-idUSKCN1UV1ZX.

26. In October 2018, the yellow-vest movement was born in France. Fueled by taxpayers unhappy with a variety of tax increases, including ones that would impact professional car services and drivers, protestors donned the yellow vests French drivers are required to wear if their vehicle is in a crash or shuts down. The yellow-vest protestors have become vocal and visible for over a year, as of this writing, and have successfully convinced President Macron and other politicians to back down or roll back tax increases. Agence France-Presse, "France's Yellow Vests: Diminished but Not Vanquished," *France 24*, November 12, 2019, https://www .france24.com/en/20191112-france-s-yellow-vests-diminished-but-not-vanquished.

27. ICORating, *ICO Market Research: Q1, 2018* (Saint Petersburg: ICORating, 2018), https://icorating.com/pdf/2/1/g5A7etmwJSxjF9ygOlzyfsK1r30Kisn3mcjUSFcR.pdf.

28. Irin Carmon, "Donald Trump's Worst Offense? Mocking Disabled Reporter, Poll Finds," NBC News, August 11, 2016, https://www.nbcnews.com/politics/2016-election/ trump-s-worst-offense-mocking-disabled-reporter-poll-finds-n627736; Sarah Harvard, "Trump: Supporters Like Me More When I Call Media 'Enemy of the People,'" *The Independent*, November 2, 2018, https://www.independent.co.uk/news/world/americas/us-politics/ trump-media-maga-supporters-axios-media-enemy-of-the-people-fake-news-a8614556.html.

29. BBC Trending, Jessikka Aro interviewed by Will Yates, "Jessikka Aro: How Pro-Russian Trolls Tried to Destroy Me," *BBC*, October 6, 2017, https://www.bbc.com/news/ blogs-trending-41499789.

30. Jack Stubbs and Christopher Bing, "Special Report: How Iran Spreads Disinformation around the World," Reuters, November 30, 2018, https://af.reuters.com/article/ idUSKCN1NZ1FT.

31. Ibid.

32. Craig Silverman and Jane Lytvynenko, "Reddit Has Become a Battleground of Alleged Chinese Trolls," *BuzzFeed News*, updated March 14, 2019, https://www.buzzfeednews.com/ article/craigsilverman/reddit-coordinated-chinese-propaganda-trolls.

33. Shajida Khan, "China's Communist Party Raises Army of Nationalist Trolls," *Pakistan Defence*, December 30, 2017, defence.pk/pdf/threads/chinas-communist-party-raises-army-of -nationalist-trolls.536205/.

34. Bruce Sterling, "Ideological Declaration from Chinese Cyberspace Administration," *Wired*, November 9, 2018, https://www.wired.com/beyond-the-beyond/2018/11/ideological -declaration-chinese-cyberspace-administration/.

35. Joshua Philipp, "Leaked Emails Show Chinese Regime Employs 500,000 Internet Trolls," *Epoch Times*, updated July 26, 2015, https://www.theepochtimes.com/leaked-emails -show-chinese-regime-employs-500000-internet-trolls_1142634.html.

36. Gary King, Jennifer Pan, and Margaret E. Roberts, "How the Chinese Government Fabricates Social Media Posts for Strategic Distraction, Not Engaged Argument" *American Political Science Review* 111, no. 3 (August 2017): 484–501, https://www.cambridge .org/core/services/aop-cambridge-core/content/view/4662DB26E2685BAF1485F14369B

D137C/S0003055417000144a.pdf/how_the_chinese_government_fabricates_social_media _posts_for_strategic_distraction_not_engaged_argument.pdf.

37. Yuan Yang, "China's Communist Party Raises Army of Nationalist Trolls," *Financial Times*, December 29, 2017, https://www.ft.com/content/9ef9f592-e2bd-11e7-97e2 -916d4fbac0da.

38. Steven Jiang and Shen Lu, "Bad Romance? Lady Gaga Angers Her Chinese Fans with Dalai Lama Meeting," CNN, June 28, 2016, https://www.cnn.com/2016/06/28/asia/china -lady-gaga-dalai-lama/index.html.

39. John Follain, Adela Lin, and Samson Ellis, "China Ramps Up Cyberattacks on Taiwan," Politics, Bloomberg, updated September 20, 2018, https://webcache.googleusercontent .com/search?q=cache:nUxlq0eoaNYJ:https://www.bloomberg.com/news/articles/2018-09-19/ chinese-cyber-spies-target-taiwan-s-leader-before-elections+&cd=1&hl=en&ct=clnk&gl=us.

40. Chris Horton, "Taiwan's President Quits as Party Chief after Stinging Losses in Local Races," *New York Times*, November 24, 2018, https://www.nytimes.com/2018/11/24/world/ asia/taiwan-election-results.html.

41. John Follain, Adela Lin, and Samson Ellis, "China Ramps Up Cyberattacks on Taiwan," Politics, Bloomberg, updated September 20, 2018, https://webcache.googleusercontent .com/search?q=cache:nUxlq0eoaNYJ:https://www.bloomberg.com/news/articles/2018-09-19/ chinese-cyber-spies-target-taiwan-s-leader-before-elections+&cd=1&hl=en&ct=clnk&gl=us.

42. "Sally" is not her real name. Dramatization based on reporting by Simon Adler and Annie McEwan, producers, "The Curious Case of the Russian Flash Mob at the West Palm Beach Cheesecake Factory," *Radiolab*, audio episode, 40:25, with reporting help from Becca Bressler and Charles Maynes, February 20, 2018, https://www.wbez.org/shows/radiolab/the -curious-case-of-the-russian-flash-mob-at-the-west-palm-beach-cheesecake-factory/ d78104d5-a4ce-4a3e-868d-213509e4ba4b.

CHAPTER 3: HOW DO YOU KNOW
WHAT YOU THINK YOU KNOW?

1. "The Disinformation Report," New Knowledge, December 17, 2018, https://www .newknowledge.com/articles/the-disinformation-report/.

2. Casey Michel, "How the Russians Pretended to Be Texans—and Texans Believed Them," *Washington Post*, October 17, 2017, https://www.washingtonpost.com/news/democracy-post/ wp/2017/10/17/how-the-russians-pretended-to-be-texans-and-texans-believed-them/.

3. Tim Lister and Clare Sebastian, "Stoking Islamophobia and Secession in Texas—from an Office in Russia," CNN, updated October 6, 2017, https://www.cnn.com/2017/10/05/ politics/heart-of-texas-russia-event/index.html.

4. US Senate Select Committee on Intelligence, "Report of the Select Committee on Intelligence, United States Senate, on Russian Active Measures Campaigns and Interference in the 2016 US Election," Volume 1: Russian Efforts against Election Infrastructure with Additional Views (Washington, DC: US Government Publishing Office, 2019), redacted text available at https://www.intelligence.senate.gov/sites/default/files/documents/ Report_Volume1.pdf.

5. Tim Lister and Clare Sebastian, "Stoking Islamophobia and Secession in Texas—from an Office in Russia," CNN, updated October 6, 2017, https://www.cnn.com/2017/10/05/ politics/heart-of-texas-russia-event/index.html.

6. Casey Michel, "Organizers behind Armed White Supremacist Protest in Houston Revealed as Russian," *Think Progress*, October 9, 2017, https://thinkprogress.org/armed-white -supremacist-protest-organized-by-russians-d730f83ca275/.

7. Ibid.

8. US Senate Select Committee on Intelligence, "Report of the Select Committee on Intelligence, United States Senate, on Russian Active Measures Campaigns and Interference in the 2016 U.S. Election," Volume 1: Russian Efforts against Election Infrastructure with Additional Views (Washington, DC: US Government Publishing Office, 2019), redacted text available at https://www.intelligence.senate.gov/sites/default/files/documents/ Report_Volume1.pdf.

9. Ryan Lucas, "How Russia Used Facebook to Organize 2 Sets of Protesters," NPR, November 1, 2017, https://www.npr.org/2017/11/01/561427876/how-russia-used-facebook -to-organize-two-sets-of-protesters.

10. Ryan Lucas, "How Russia Used Facebook to Organize 2 Sets of Protesters," *NPR*, November 1, 2017, https://www.npr.org/2017/11/01/561427876/how-russia-used-facebook -to-organize-two-sets-of-protesters.

11. Simon Adler and Annie McEwan, producers, "The Curious Case of the Russian Flash Mob at the West Palm Beach Cheesecake Factory," *Radiolab*, audio episode, 40:25, with reporting help from Becca Bressler and Charles Maynes, February 20, 2018, https://www .wbez.org/shows/radiolab/the-curious-case-of-the-russian-flash-mob-at-the-west-palm-beach -cheesecake-factory/d78104d5-a4ce-4a3e-868d-213509e4ba4b; Frank Cerabino, "Local Trump Supporters Shrug Off Being Paid and Played by Russians," *Palm Beach Post*, updated February 23, 2018, https://www.palmbeachpost.com/news/local-trump-supporters-shrug-off -being-paid-and-played-russians/3WCytHAHy3PodLVePU1PMK/.

12. Robert S. Mueller, *Report on the Investigation into Russian Interference in the 2016 Presidential Election* (Washington, DC: US Department of Justice, 2019), https://www.justice.gov/ storage/report.pdf, vol. 1, p. 22.

13. Richard A. Clarke in conversation with the author.

14. Mary Clare Jalonick, "Russian Influence Operations Still Stoking Tensions on Social Media, Senate Reports Say," *PBS NewsHour*, updated December 17, 2018, www.pbs.org/ newshour/politics/russian-influence-operations-still-active-and-ongoing-on-social-media-senate -report-says. And read the report in full at "The Disinformation Report," New Knowledge, December 17, 2018, https://www.newknowledge.com/articles/the-disinformation-report/.

15. Donie O'Sullivan and Dylan Byers, "Exclusive: Even Pokémon Go Used by Extensive Russian-Linked Meddling Effort," *CNN Money*, October 13, 2017, https://money.cnn .com/2017/10/12/media/dont-shoot-us-russia-pokemon-go/index.html.

16. Clinton Watts in conversation with the author.

17. Barack Obama (@BarackObama), "Until all of us stand up and insist on holding public officials accountable for changing our gun laws, these tragedies will keep happening," August 5, 2019, Twitter status update and photo, https://twitter.com/BarackObama/ status/1158453079035002881/photo/1.

18. Jeremy Roebuck and Andrew Seidman, "'Being Patriotic'—How Russia Worked to Influence Pennsylvania Voters over Social Media in 2016," *Philadelphia Inquirer*, February 20, 2018, available online at https://www.post-gazette.com/news/politics-state/2018/02/20/ Russia-trolls-Pennsylvania-election-meddling-oters-trump-2016-social-media-influence-false -information/stories/201802200095.

19. "The Disinformation Report," New Knowledge, December 17, 2018, https://www.newknowledge.com/articles/the-disinformation-report/; Scott Shane and Sheera Frenkel, "Russian 2016 Influence Operation Targeted African-Americans on Social Media," *New York Times*, December 17, 2018, https://www.nytimes.com/2018/12/17/us/politics/russia-2016-influence-campaign.html.

20. Craig Timberg and Tony Romm, "New Report on Russian Disinformation, Prepared for the Senate, Shows the Operation's Scale and Sweep," The Switch, *Washington Post*, December 17, 2018, https://www.washingtonpost.com/technology/2018/12/16/new-report-russian-disinformation-prepared-senate-shows-operations-scale-sweep/.

21. Ben Popken, Richard Engel, Kate Benyon-Tinker, and Monika Ghosh, "Russia-Linked Twitter Accounts Promoted 'Doxxing' over Racial Tension Videos," NBC News, August 8, 2019, https://www.nbcnews.com/tech/tech-news/russia-linked-twitter-accounts-promoted-doxxing-over-racial-tension-videos-n1040596.

22. Scott Shane, "These Are the Ads Russia Bought on Facebook in 2016," *New York Times*, November 1, 2017, https://www.nytimes.com/2017/11/01/us/politics/russia-2016-election-facebook.html.

23. Samantha Bradshaw and Philip N. Howard, "Challenging Truth and Trust: A Global Inventory of Organized Social Media Manipulation," working paper 2018.1, Oxford Internet Institute, Oxford, UK, July 20, 2018, http://comprop.oii.ox.ac.uk/wp-content/uploads/sites/93/2018/07/ct2018.pdf.

24. Donald G. McNeil Jr., "Russian Trolls Used Vaccine Debate to Sow Discord, Study Finds," *New York Times*, August 23, 2018, https://www.nytimes.com/2018/08/23/health/russian-trolls-vaccines.html. And read the full report at David A. Broniatowski et al., "Weaponized Health Communication: Twitter Bots and Russian Trolls Amplify the Vaccine Debate," *American Journal of Public Health* 108, no. 10 (2018): 1378–84, https://ajph.aphapublications.org/doi/pdf/10.2105/AJPH.2018.304567.

25. "About VAERS," Vaccine Adverse Event Reporting System (website), accessed October 3, 2019, https://vaers.hhs.gov/about.html.

26. "Russian Trolls, Twitter Bots Stoked Vaccine Debate by Spreading Misinformation, Study Finds," *Hub*, Johns Hopkins University, August 24, 2018, hub.jhu.edu/2018/08/24/russian-trolls-bots-spread-vaccine-misinformation/.

27. Craig Timberg and Tony Romm, "These Provocative Images Show Russian Trolls Sought to Inflame Debate over Climate Change, Fracking and Dakota Pipeline," The Switch, *Washington Post*, March 1, 2018, https://www.washingtonpost.com/news/the-switch/wp/2018/03/01/congress-russians-trolls-sought-to-inflame-u-s-debate-on-climate-change-fracking-and-dakota-pipeline/.

28. Alexander Panetta, "Russian Troll Farm that Meddled in US Election Also Targeted Trudeau and Canadian Oil," *National Post*, March 18, 2018, https://nationalpost.com/news/world/notorious-russian-troll-farm-also-took-swipes-at-canadian-targets-oil-pm.

29. US House of Representatives Committee on Science, Space, and Technology, *Russian Attempts to Influence U.S. Domestic Energy Markets by Exploiting Social Media*, committee report (Washington, DC: US House of Representatives, 2018), https://republicans-science.house.gov/sites/republicans.science.house.gov/files/documents/SST%20Staff%20Report%20-%20Russian%20Attempts%20to%20Influence%20U.S.%20Domestic%20Energy%20Markets%20by%20Exploiting%20Social%20Media%2003.01.18.pdf; Bloomberg, "Russia Accused of Inciting U.S. Pipeline Project Protests," *Fortune*, March 1, 2018, https://fortune.com/2018/03/01/russia-social-media-energy-policy/.

30. Claudia Cattaneo, "Russian Meddling in Canadian Oil Pipelines Uses Old Soviet 'Useful Idiots' Ploy," *Financial Post*, March 5, 2018, https://business.financialpost.com/commodities/energy/russian-meddling-another-worry-for-canadian-energy-exports.

31. Paresh Dave and Christopher Bing, "Facebook, Twitter Dismantle Disinformation Campaigns Tied to Iran and Russia," Reuters, August 21, 2018, www.reuters.com/article/us-facebook- https://www.reuters.com/article/us-facebook-russia-usa/facebook-twitter-dismantle-disinformation-campaigns-tied-to-iran-and-russia-idUSKCN1L62FD.

32. April Glaser and Aaron Mak, "Iran's Social Media Propaganda Campaign Was Bad at Both Propaganda and Social Media," Future Tense, *Slate*, August 22, 2018, https://slate.com/technology/2018/08/the-iranian-false-news-posts-on-facebook-and-twitter-were-not-very-convincing-or-good.html.

CHAPTER 4: THE MANIPULATORS AND THEIR METHODS

1. Global Threat Intelligence Center, "2018 Cyber Threat Intelligence Estimate," Optiv Security, Inc. (website), May 15, 2018, available for download at https://www.optiv.com/explore-optiv-insights/downloads/2018-cyber-threat-intelligence-estimate.

2. Dean Jackson, "Issue Brief: Distinguishing Disinformation from Propaganda, Misinformation, and 'Fake News,'" National Endowment for Democracy (website), October 17, 2017, https://www.ned.org/wp-content/uploads/2018/06/Distinguishing-Disinformation-from-Propaganda.pdf.

3. ZeroFOX Research, "Russia Just Used Trump's Favorite Social Network to Hack the US Government," *ZeroFOX Blog*, May 18, 2017, https://www.zerofox.com/blog/russia-just-used-trumps-favorite-social-network-hack-us-government/.

4. "Internet Growth Statistics: History and Growth of the Internet from 1995 till Today," table, *Internet World Stats*, https://www.internetworldstats.com/emarketing.htm.

5. Daniel Rutledge, "Vladimir Putin Hunts Topless, Cuddles Kitten in 2018 Calendar," *Newshub*, November 23, 2017, https://www.newshub.co.nz/home/entertainment/2017/11/vladimir-putin-hunts-topless-cuddles-kitten-in-2018-calendar.html; Anton Troianovski, "Branding Putin: How the Kremlin Turned the Russian President into a Global Icon," *Washington Post*, July 12, 2018, https://www.washingtonpost.com/graphics/2018/world/putin-brand/.

6. Anton Troianovski, "Branding Putin: How the Kremlin Turned the Russian President into a Global Icon," *Washington Post*, July 12, 2018, https://www.washingtonpost.com/graphics/2018/world/putin-brand/.

7. Issie Lapowsky, "Iran's New Facebook Trolls Are Using Russia's Playbook," *Wired*, October 26, 2018, https://www.wired.com/story/iran-facebook-trolls-using-russia-playbook/.

8. Lori Grisham, "Timeline: North Korea and the Sony Pictures Hack," *USA Today*, updated January 5, 2015, https://www.usatoday.com/story/news/nation-now/2014/12/18/sony-hack-timeline-interview-north-korea/20601645/.

9. "Security Council Calls on Member States to Address Threats against Critical Infrastructure, Unanimously Adopting Resolution 2341 (2017)," United Nations, February 13, 2017, https://www.un.org/press/en/2017/sc12714.doc.htm.

10. Shawn Henry in interview with the author, conducted via telephone, June 3, 2019.

11. Sanja Kelly, Mai Truong, Adrian Shahbaz, Madeline Earp, and Jessica White, *Freedom on the Net 2017: Manipulating Social Media to Undermine Democracy* (Washington, DC: Freedom House, 2018), https://freedomhouse.org/report/freedom-net/freedom-net-2017.

12. *Wikipedia*, "WannaCry ransomeware attack," last edited October 9, 2019, https://en.wikipedia.org/wiki/WannaCry_ransomware_attack.

13. Kacy Zurkus, "Nation-State Threats from Unexpected Countries," *Infosecurity Magazine*, May 15, 2018, https://www.infosecurity-magazine.com/news/nation-state-threats-from/. And download the full report at Global Threat Intelligence Center, "2018 Cyber Threat Intelligence Estimate," Optiv Security, Inc. (website), May 15, 2018, https://www.optiv.com/explore-optiv-insights/downloads/2018-cyber-threat-intelligence-estimate.

14. Zach Beauchamp, "It Happened There: How Democracy Died in Hungary," *Vox*, September 13, 2018, https://www.vox.com/policy-and-politics/2018/9/13/17823488/hungary-democracy-authoritarianism-trump.

15. Ibid.

16. Emily Dreyfuss, "The Internet Became Less Free in 2018. Can We Fight Back?" *Wired*, December 26, 2018, https://www.wired.com/story/internet-freedom-china-2018/. And find the full report at Mai Truong, Jessica White, and Allie Funk, *Freedom on the Net 2018*, ed. Tyler Roylance, research assistance by Cheryl Yu and Andrew Greco (Washington, DC: Freedom House, 2018), https://freedomhouse.org/sites/default/files/FOTN_2018_Final%20Booklet_11_1_2018.pdf.

17. Natalie Edmundson, "To Catch a Criminal: Hacking into the Dark Web and International Law Implications," *GlobalJusticeBlog.com*, December 4, 2017, https://law.utah.edu/to-catch-a-criminal-hacking-into-the-dark-web-and-international-law-implications/.

18. Louise Matsakis and Issie Lapowsky, "Don't Praise the Sri Lankan Government for Blocking Facebook," *Wired*, April 23, 2019, https://www.wired.com/story/sri-lanka-bombings-social-media-shutdown/.

19. Ilya Khrennikov and Stepan Kravchenko, "Putin Wants His Own Internet," Bloomberg, March 4, 2019, https://www.bloomberg.com/news/articles/2019-03-05/vladimir-putin-wants-his-own-internet.

20. Yanan Wang, "Chinese Cyberattack Hits Messaging App during HK Protest," Associated Press, June 13, 2019, https://apnews.com/5f14d84762a049e990f808d1718feb93.

21. Josh Summers, "What Websites and Apps Are Blocked in China in 2019?" *Travel China Cheaper*, updated October 2019, https://www.travelchinacheaper.com/index-blocked-websites-in-china.

22. Emily Dreyfuss, "The Internet Became Less Free in 2018. Can We Fight Back?" *Wired*, December 26, 2018, https://www.wired.com/story/internet-freedom-china-2018/.

23. Josh Chin, "New Target for China's Censors: Content Driven by Artificial Intelligence," *Wall Street Journal*, April 11, 2018, https://www.wsj.com/articles/new-target-for-chinas-censors-content-driven-by-artificial-intelligence-1523446234.

24. "Indonesia," *Freedom on the Net 2018* (online version), Freedom House (website), 2018, https://freedomhouse.org/report/freedom-net/2018/indonesia.

25. Andrea Kavanough, Steven D. Sheetz, Riham Hasan, Seungwon Yang, Hicham G. Elmongui, Edward A. Fox, Mohamed Magdy, and Donald J. Shoemaker, "Between a Rock and a Cell Phone: Social Media Use during Mass Protests in Tunisia and Egypt," *International Journal of Information Systems for Crisis Response and Management* 5, no. 1 (July 2013), text available online with subscription at https://www.microsoft.com/en-us/research/publication/

between-a-rock-and-a-cell-phone-communication-and-information-technology-use-during -the-2011-uprisings-in-tunisia-and-egypt/.

26. *Graham Pough,* "Ahmed Mansoor Targeted by UAE Government Hacking," *Americans for Democracy & Human Rights in Bahrain,* September 6, 2016, https://www.adhrb .org/2016/09/ahmed-mansoor-targeted-hacking-uae/.

27. Berhan Taye, "Benin Heads to Elections without Social Media and Opposition Parties," *Accessnow,* updated May 1, 2019, https://www.accessnow.org/benin-heads-to-elections -without-social-media-and-opposition-parties/.

28. Sanja Kelly, Mai Truong, Adrian Shahbaz, Madeline Earp, and Jessica White, *Freedom on the Net 2017: Manipulating Social Media to Undermine Democracy* (Washington, DC: Freedom House, 2018), https://freedomhouse.org/report/freedom-net/freedom-net-2017.

29. Emily Dreyfuss, "The Internet Became Less Free in 2018. Can We Fight Back?" *Wired,* December 26, 2018, https://www.wired.com/story/internet-freedom-china-2018/.

30. Netizen Report Team, "Netizen Report: Saudi Arabian Authorities Arrest Three Bloggers and Execute 37 Prisoners, Several of Them Protesters," *Global Voices Advox,* April 26, 2019, https://advox.globalvoices.org/2019/04/27/netizen-report-saudi-arabian-authorities -arrest-three-bloggers-and-execute-37-prisoners-several-of-them-protesters/.

31. "Uganda: Detention of Feminist Academic for Criticizing President a Travesty," Amnesty International (website), April 10, 2017, https://www.amnesty.org/en/latest/news/ 2017/04/uganda-detention-of-feminist-academic-for-criticizing-president-a-travesty/.

32. "South Korea's Spy Agency Admits Trying to Influence 2012 Poll," BBC, August 4, 2017, https://www.bbc.com/news/world-asia-40824793.

33. Siobhán O'Grady, "An Indian Journalist Has Been Trolled for Years. Now UN Experts Say Her Life Could Be at Risk," *Washington Post,* May 26, 2018, https://www.washingtonpost .com/news/worldviews/wp/2018/05/26/an-indian-journalist-has-been-trolled-for-years-now-u -n-experts-say-her-life-could-be-at-risk/.

34. Rana Ayyub, as told to Lucy Pasha-Robinson, "I Was the Victim of a Deepfake Porn Plot Intended to Silence Me," *Huffington Post,* updated November 21, 2018, https://www .huffingtonpost.co.uk/entry/deepfake-porn_uk_5bf2c126e4b0f32bd58ba316?; "UN Experts Ask Govt to Protect Journalist Rana Ayyub from Online Threats," *Hindustan Times,* May 27, 2018, https://www.hindustantimes.com/india-news/un-experts-ask-govt-to-protect-journalist -rana-ayyub-from-online-threats/story-GM1AkwJKLGN9S897HbO0kJ.html.

35. *Graham Pough,* "Ahmed Mansoor Targeted by UAE Government Hacking," Americans for Democracy & Human Rights in Bahrain (website), September 6, 2016, https://www .adhrb.org/2016/09/ahmed-mansoor-targeted-hacking-uae/; Nicole Perlroth, "iPhone Users Urged to Update Software after Security Flaws Are Found," *New York Times,* corrected August 25, 2016, https://www.nytimes.com/2016/08/26/technology/apple-software-vulnerability -ios-patch.html.

36. *Graham Pough,* "Ahmed Mansoor Targeted by UAE Government Hacking," *Americans for Democracy & Human Rights in Bahrain,* September 6, 2016, https://www.adhrb .org/2016/09/ahmed-mansoor-targeted-hacking-uae/.

37. Gabrielle Lim, Etienne Maynier, John Scott-Railton, Alberto Fittarelli, Ned Moran, and Ron Deibert, "Burned after Reading: Endless Mayfly's Ephemeral Disinformation Campaign," The Citizen Lab, May 14, 2019, https://citizenlab.ca/2019/05/burned-after-reading -endless-mayflys-ephemeral-disinformation-campaign/.

38. Jeff Yates, Kaleigh Rogers, and Roberto Rocha, "How a Suspected Iran-Based Campaign Tried to Get Canadian Media to Spread Fake News," CBC News, May 24, 2019,

https://www.cbc.ca/news/technology/how-a-suspected-iran-based-campaign-tried-to-get
-canadian-media-to-spread-fake-news-1.5143913.

39. Gabrielle Lim, Etienne Maynier, John Scott-Railton, Alberto Fittarelli, Ned Moran, and Ron Deibert, "Burned after Reading: Endless Mayfly's Ephemeral Disinformation Campaign," The Citizen Lab, May 14, 2019, https://citizenlab.ca/2019/05/burned-after-reading
-endless-mayflys-ephemeral-disinformation-campaign/.

40. Dan Tynan, "Facebook Removes Hundreds of US Political Pages for 'Inauthentic Activity,'" *Guardian*, October 11, 2018, https://www.theguardian.com/technology/2018/oct/11/facebook-purge-page-removal-spam.

41. Peter Salisbury, "The Fake-News Hack That Nearly Started a War This Summer Was Designed for One Man: Donald Trump," *Quartz*, October 20, 2017, https://qz.com/1107023/the-inside-story-of-the-hack-that-nearly-started-another-middle-east-war/.

42. Nicholas Confessore, Gabriel J. X. Dance, Richard Harris, and Mark Hansen, "The Follower Factory," *New York Times*, January 27, 2018, https://www.nytimes.com/interactive/2018/01/27/technology/social-media-bots.html.

43. Lion Gu, Vladimir Kropotov, and Fyodor Yarochkin, *The Fake News Machine: How Propagandists Abuse the Internet and Manipulate the Public*, TrendLabs research paper ([Tokyo]: Trend Micro, 2017), https://documents.trendmicro.com/assets/white_papers/wp-fake-news
-machine-how-propagandists-abuse-the-internet.pdf, p. 7. And see Zeljka Zorz, "Fake News Services and Tools Proliferate on Online Markets," Help Net Security, June 15, 2017, https://www.helpnetsecurity.com/2017/06/15/fake-news-services-tools/.

44. Barbie Latza Nadeau, "Anti-vaxxers Targeting Pro-vaccine Doctors with Fake Bad Reviews," *The Daily Beast*, May 12 2019, https://www.thedailybeast.com/anti-vaxxers-targeting
-pro-vaccine-doctors-with-fake-bad-reviews.

45. Zeljka Zorz, "Fake News Services and Tools Proliferate on Online Markets," Help Net Security, June 15, 2017, https://www.helpnetsecurity.com/2017/06/15/fake-news
-services-tools/.

46. Leo Benedictus, "Invasion of the Troll Armies: From Russian Trump Supporters to Turkish Stage Stooges," *Guardian*, November 6, 2016, https://www.theguardian.com/media/2016/nov/06/troll-armies-social-media-trump-russian.

47. Joel Harding, "Ukrainian Minister of Information Rallies Internet Army," *To Inform Is to Influence*, February 24, 2015, https://toinformistoinfluence.com/2015/02/24/ukrainian
-minister-of-information-rallies-internet-army/.

48. Shan Li, "Facebook Sues Chinese Companies for Creating Fake Accounts," *Wall Street Journal*, updated March 4, 2019, https://www.wsj.com/articles/facebook-sues-china
-companies-for-creating-fake-online-accounts-11551702165.

49. Sean Sullivan, "LinkedIn Sockpuppets Are Targeting Security Researchers," *News from the Lab*, September 3, 2015, https://labsblog.f-secure.com/2015/09/03/linkedin-sockpuppets
-targeting-security-researchers/.

50. Alfred Ng, "Oscars Scams Ran Wild Thanks to Twitter Bots," *CNET*, March 5, 2018, https://www.cnet.com/news/oscars-scams-running-wild-thanks-to-twitter-bots-impersonating
-celebrities/.

51. Nicholas Thompson and Issie Lapowsky, "How Russian Trolls Used Meme Warfare to Divide America," *Wired*, December 17, 2018, https://www.wired.com/story/russia-ira
-propaganda-senate-report/.

CHAPTER 5: HACKERS IN THE TRENCHES

1. Ed Pilkington, "LulzSec Hacker 'Sabu' Released after 'Extraordinary' FBI Cooperation," *Guardian*, May 27, 2014, https://www.theguardian.com/technology/2014/may/27/hacker-sabu-walks-free-sentenced-time-served.

2. Eden Estopace, "Massive Data Breach Exposes All Philippines Voters," *Telecom Asia*, April 12, 2016, http://www.telecomasia.net/content/massive-data-breach-exposes-all-philippines-voters; Phil Muncaster, "Every Voter in Philippines Exposed in Mega Hack," *Infosecurity Magazine*, April 8, 2016, https://www.infosecurity-magazine.com/news/every-voter-in-philippines-exposed/.

3. Michael Bueza and Wayne Manuel, "Experts Fear Identity Theft, Scams Due to Comelec Leak," *Rappler*, updated April 2, 2016, http://www.rappler.com/newsbreak/in-depth/127870-comelec-leak-identity-theft-scams-experts.

4. Andy Greenberg, "He Perfected a Password-Hacking Tool—Then the Russians Came Calling," *Wired*, November 9, 2017, https://www.wired.com/story/how-mimikatz-became-go-to-hacker-tool/.

5. Jane Lytvynenko, "The El Paso and Dayton Shootings Show How Disinformation Spreads on Messaging Apps," BuzzFeed, August 7, 2019, https://www.buzzfeednews.com/article/janelytvynenko/telegram-disinformation-fake-news.

6. US Senate Committee on Foreign Relations, "Putin's Asymmetric Assault on Democracy in Russia and Europe: Implications for U.S. National Security," Minority Staff Report (Washington, DC: US Government Publishing Office, 2018), https://www.foreign.senate.gov/imo/media/doc/FinalRR.pdf.

7. Lytvynenko, Jane, "The El Paso And Dayton Shootings Show How Disinformation Spreads On Messaging Apps." *BuzzFeed News*, BuzzFeed News, 8 August 2019, www.buzzfeednews.com/article/janelytvynenko/telegram-disinformation-fake-news.

8. Burgess, Matt, "Here's the First Evidence Russia Used Twitter to Influence Brexit." WIRED, WIRED UK, 14 November 2017, www.wired.co.uk/article/brexit-russia-influence-twitter-bots-internet-research-agency.

9. Karoun Demirjian and Colby Itkowitz, "Russians Probably Targeted Election Systems in All 50 States, Senate Panel's Report Says," *Washington Post*, July 25, 2019, https://www.washingtonpost.com/national-security/senate-intelligence-panel-releases-first-chapter-of-bipartisan-report-into-russian-meddling/2019/07/25/63bce4f4-af0c-11e9-bc5c-e73b603e7f38_story.html.

10. US Senate Select Committee on Intelligence, *Report of the Select Committee on Intelligence, United States Senate, on Russian Active Measures Campaigns and Interference in the 2016 U.S. Election*, vol. 1: Russian Efforts against Election Infrastructure with Additional Views (Washington, DC: US Government Publishing Office, 2019), redacted text available at https://www.intelligence.senate.gov/sites/default/files/documents/Report_Volume1.pdf.

11. Washington Post staff, "The Mueller Report, Annotated," *Washington Post*, updated July 23, 2019, https://www.washingtonpost.com/graphics/2019/politics/read-the-mueller-report/.

12. Woolf, Nicky. "DDoS Attack That Disrupted Internet Was Largest of Its Kind in History, Experts Say." *The Guardian*, October 26, 2016, www.theguardian.com/technology/2016/oct/26/ddos-attack-dyn-mirai-botnet.

13. Benjamin Wofford, "The Hacking Threat to the Midterms Is Huge. And Technology Won't Protect Us," *Vox*, October 25, 2018, https://www.vox.com/2018/10/25/18001684/2018-midterms-hacked-russia-election-security-voting.

14. Robert S. Mueller, *Report on the Investigation into Russian Interference in the 2016 Presidential Election* (Washington, DC: US Department of Justice, 2019), https://www.justice.gov/storage/report.pdf.

15. "The Dark Web: Where Cyber-Criminals Buy Guns, Drugs And Hacking Tools to Subvert Elections," CBS Denver, September 27, 2018, https://denver.cbslocal.com/2018/09/27/the-dark-web-where-cyber-criminals-buy-guns-drugs-and-hacking-tools-to-subvert-elections/.

CHAPTER 6: EXCLUSIVE INTERVIEW

1. *The Wire*, "More with Less," HBO, January 6, 2008, written by David Simon and Ed Burns, directed by Joe Chappelle.

2. *The Big Short*, screenplay by Charles Randolph and Adam McKay, directed by Adam McKay, produced by Regency Enterprises and Plan B Entertainment, 2015, based upon the book by Michael Lewis.

CHAPTER 7: THE US ELECTIONS, 2016 TO 2018

1. Abby Vesoulis, "States Are Trying to Stop Election Meddling. But the Real Risk Is Public Confidence," *Time*, March 5, 2019, https://time.com/5543649/2020-elections-voter-security-states/.

2. "Full Transcript and Video: James Comey's Testimony on Capitol Hill," *New York Times*, June 8, 2017, https://www.nytimes.com/2017/06/08/us/politics/senate-hearing-transcript.html.

3. Benjamin Wofford, "The Hacking Threat to the Midterms Is Huge. And Technology Won't Protect Us," *Vox*, October 25, 2018, https://www.vox.com/2018/10/25/18001684/2018-midterms-hacked-russia-election-security-voting.

4. *Wikipedia*, s.v. "List of controversial elections," last edited September 22, 2019, https://en.wikipedia.org/wiki/List_of_controversial_elections.

5. Author in conversation with Shawn Henry, via telephone, June 3, 2019.

6. Louis Nelson "Obama Says He Told Putin to 'Cut It Out' on Russia Hacking," Politico, December 16, 2016, https://www.politico.com/story/2016/12/obama-putin-232754; William M. Arkin, Ken Dilanian, and Cynthia McFadden, "What Obama Said to Putin on the Red Phone about the Election Hack," NBCNews.com, December 20, 2016, https://www.nbcnews.com/news/us-news/what-obama-said-putin-red-phone-about-election-hack-n697116.

7. "DHS assessed that the [Russian] searches [of US state voter systems], done alphabetically, probably included all 50 states, and consisted of research on 'general election-related web pages, voter ID information, election system software, and election service companies.'" US Senate Select Committee on Intelligence, *Report of the Select Committee on Intelligence, United States Senate, on Russian Active Measures Campaigns and Interference in the 2016 U.S. Election. Volume I: Russian Efforts against Election Infrastructure with Additional Views* (Washington, DC: US Senate, 2017), https://www.intelligence.senate.gov/sites/default/files/documents/Report_Volume1.pdf, page 8.

8. Robert S. Mueller, *Report on the Investigation into Russian Interference in the 2016 Presidential Election* (Washington, DC: US Department of Justice, 2019), https://www.justice.gov/storage/report.pdf, p. 19.

9. United States of America v. Viktor Borisovich Netyksho et al., 18 U.S.C. §§ 2, 371, 1030, 1028A, 1956, and 3551 et seq. (2018), https://www.justice.gov/file/1080281/download, pp. 2–3.

10. Julia Ioffe, "What Putin Really Wants," *The Atlantic* (January/February 2018), updated, https://www.theatlantic.com/magazine/archive/2018/01/putins-game/546548/.

11. Office of the Director of (US) National Intelligence, "Background to 'Assessing Russian Activities and Intentions in Recent US Elections': The Analytic Process and Cyber Incident Attribution," January 6, 2017, https://www.dni.gov/files/documents/ICA_2017_01.pdf.

12. Matt Apuzzo, Michael S. Schmidt, Adam Goldman, and Eric Licthbau, "Comey Tried to Shield the F.B.I. from Politics. Then He Shaped an Election," *New York Times*, April 22, 2017, https://www.nytimes.com/2017/04/22/us/politics/james-comey-election.html.

13. Natasha Bertrand, "'None of It Makes Much Sense': Experts Are Baffled by Comey's Use of a Fake Russian Document to Skirt the DOJ," *Business Insider*, May 31, 2017, https://www.businessinsider.com/james-comey-fake-document-russia-fbi-clinton-email-2017-5.

14. Robert S. Mueller, *Report on the Investigation into Russian Interference in the 2016 Presidential Election* (Washington, DC: US Department of Justice, 2019), https://www.justice.gov/storage/report.pdf, p. 50.

15. Miles Parks, "Florida Governor Says Russian Hackers Breached 2 Counties in 2016," NPR, May 14, 2019, https://www.npr.org/2019/05/14/723215498/florida-governor-says-russian-hackers-breached-two-florida-counties-in-2016.

16. Cynthia McFadden, William M. Arkin, Kevin Monahan, and Ken Dilanian, "US Intel: Russia Compromised Seven States Prior to 2016 Election," NBC News, updated February 28, 2018, https://www.nbcnews.com/politics/elections/u-s-intel-russia-compromised-seven-states-prior-2016-election-n850296; Tara Law and Abby Vesoulis, "Robert Mueller Showed Us How U.S. Elections Broke in 2016. Here's How to Fix Them," *Time*, updated April 18, 2019, https://time.com/5572927/mueller-report-elections-fixes/.

17. US Senate Select Committee on Intelligence, *Report of the Select Committee on Intelligence, United States Senate, on Russian Active Measures Campaigns and Interference in the 2016 US Election. Volume I: Russian Efforts against Election Infrastructure with Additional Views* (Washington, DC: US Government Publishing Office, 2019), redacted text available at https://www.intelligence.senate.gov/sites/default/files/documents/Report_Volume1.pdf, pp. 10–11.

18. Ibid., 21.

19. *United States of America v. Viktor Borisovich Netyksho et al.*, 18 U.S.C. §§ 2, 371, 1030, 1028A, 1956, and 3551 et seq. (2018), https://www.justice.gov/file/1080281/download, p. 26.

20. Nicas, Jack. "Does Facebook Really Know How Many Fake Accounts It Has?" *The New York Times*, January 30, 2019, www.nytimes.com/2019/01/30/technology/facebook-fake-accounts.html.

21. Zach Whittaker, "Four Things We Learned When Facebook, Google, Twitter Testified in Russia Inquiry," *ZDNet*, October 31, 2017, https://www.zdnet.com/article/what-we-learned-facebook-twitter-google-testified-senate-in-russia-probe/.

22. "Full Transcript and Video: James Comey's Testimony on Capitol Hill," *New York Times*, June 8, 2017, https://www.nytimes.com/2017/06/08/us/politics/senate-hearing-transcript.html.

23. *Wikipedia*, s.v. "Voter turnout," last edited September 19, 2019, https://en.wikipedia.org/wiki/Voter_turnout.

24. Foo Yun Chee and Gabriela Baczynska, "EU Election Turnout Rises for the First Time, Hits 50%," Reuters, May 26, 2019, www.reuters.com/article/us-eu-election-turnout-estimate/eu-election-turnout-rises-for-the-first-time-hits-50-idUSKCN1SW0QV.

25. *Wikipedia*, "Foreign electoral intervention," last edited September 20, 2019, https://en.wikipedia.org/wiki/Foreign_electoral_intervention.

26. Gregory Wallace, "Voter Turnout at 20-Year Low in 2016," CNN, updated November 30, 2016, https://www.cnn.com/2016/11/11/politics/popular-vote-turnout-2016/index.html.

27. Staff, *Washington Post*. "Mueller Report Findings: Mueller Rejects Argument That Trump Is Shielded from Obstruction Laws." *The Washington Post*, April 18, 2019, www.washingtonpost.com/politics/mueller-report-russia-investigation-findings/2019/04/18/b07f4310-56f9-11e9-814f-e2f46684196e_story.html.

28. Gustavo López and Antonio Flores, "Dislike of Candidates or Campaign Issues Was Most Common Reason for Not Voting in 2016," Pew Research Center, June 1, 2017, https://www.pewresearch.org/fact-tank/2017/06/01/dislike-of-candidates-or-campaign-issues-was-most-common-reason-for-not-voting-in-2016/.

29. Michael Wines and Julian E. Barnes, "How the US Is Fighting Election Interference," *New York Times*, August 2, 2018, https://www.nytimes.com/2018/08/02/us/politics/russia-election-interference.html.

30. Donald J. Trump, "Executive Order on Imposing Certain Sanctions in the Event of Foreign Interference in a United States Election," *Whitehouse.gov*, executive order, September 12, 2018, https://www.whitehouse.gov/presidential-actions/executive-order-imposing-certain-sanctions-event-foreign-interference-united-states-election/.

31. Julian E. Barnes, "Russians Tried, But Were Unable to Compromise Midterm Elections, US Says," *New York Times*, December 21, 2018, https://www.nytimes.com/2018/12/21/us/politics/russia-midterm-election-influence-coates.html.

32. Ellen Nakashima, "US Cyber Command Operation Disrupted Internet Access of Russian Troll Factory on Day of 2018 Midterms," *Washington Post*, February 27, 2019, https://www.washingtonpost.com/world/national-security/us-cyber-command-operation-disrupted-internet-access-of-russian-troll-factory-on-day-of-2018-midterms/2019/02/26/1827fc9e-36d6-11e9-af5b-b51b7ff322e9_story.html.

33. Ilya Khrennikov and Stepan Kravchenko, "Putin Wants His Own Internet," Bloomberg, March 4, 2019, https://www.bloomberg.com/news/articles/2019-03-05/vladimir-putin-wants-his-own-internet.

34. John Myers, "Hackers Attacked California DMV Voter Registration System Marred by Bugs, Glitches," *Los Angeles Times*, April 9, 2019, https://www.latimes.com/politics/la-pol-ca-california-motor-voter-problems-investigation-20190409-story.html.

35. Susan Shelley, "More Reasons to Be Concerned with Election Integrity in California," *Los Angeles Daily News*, updated April 30, 2019, https://www.dailynews.com/2019/04/30/more-reasons-to-be-concerned-with-election-integrity-in-california/.

36. Danielle Root, Liz Kennedy, Michael Sozan, and Jerry Parshall, "Election Security in All 50 States," Center for American Progress, February 12, 2018, https://www.americanprogress.org/issues/democracy/reports/2018/02/12/446336/election-security-50-states/.

37. Jen Schwartz, "The Vulnerabilities of Our Voting Machines," *Scientific American*, November 1, 2018, https://www.scientificamerican.com/article/the-vulnerabilities-of-our-voting-machines/.

38. Rob Leathern, "Shining a Light on Ads with Political Content," Facebook Newsroom, May 24, 2018, https://newsroom.fb.com/news/2018/05/ads-with-political-content/;

39. "Facebook Ad Library Report: United States; Ad Library Totals," Facebook, visited October 39, 2019, https://www.facebook.com/ads/library/report/?source=archive-landing-page&country=US.

40. Erin Corbett, "As Midterm Elections Get Underway, Facebook's Election Meddling Problem Is Worse than Ever," *Fortune*, November 5, 2018, https://fortune.com/2018/11/05/before-midterms-facebook-election-meddling-worse-than-ever/.

41. Natasha Bertrand, "DOJ Says Russian Trolls Are Interfering Online with the Midterms," *The Atlantic*, October 19, 2018, https://www.theatlantic.com/politics/archive/2018/10/doj-says-russian-trolls-interfering-midterm-elections/573526/.

42. Tim Starks, "Iran-Linked Campaign Impersonated GOP Midterm Candidates Online," Politico, updated May 29, 2019, https://www.politico.com/story/2019/05/28/iran-fake-accounts-facebook-twitter-1479189.

43. "Elections in America: Concerns over Security, Divisions over Expanding Access to Voting," Pew Research Center, October 29, 2018, https://www.people-press.org/2018/10/29/elections-in-america-concerns-over-security-divisions-over-expanding-access-to-voting/.

44. *Wikipedia*, s.v. "Electronic voting: By Country: Brazil," last edited October 28 22, 2019, https://en.wikipedia.org/wiki/Electronic_voting#Brazil.

45. *Wikipedia*, s.v. "Electronic voting in Belgium," last edited September 19, 2019 https://en.wikipedia.org/wiki/Electronic_voting_in_Belgium.

46. Laurens Cerulus, "Europe's Most Hackable Election," Politico, updated April 19, 2019, https://www.politico.eu/article/europe-most-hackable-election-voter-security-catalonia-european-parliament-disinformation/.

47. Ibid.

48. Lawrence Norden, "America's Voting Machines at Risk," Brennan Center for Justice, September 15, 2014, https://www.brennancenter.org/our-work/research-reports/americas-voting-machines-risk.

49. J. M. Porup, "Want to Hack a Voting Machine? Hack the Voting Machine Vendor First," CSO, March 30, 2018, https://www.csoonline.com/article/3267625/want-to-hack-a-voting-machine-hack-the-voting-machine-vendor-first.html.

50. Danielle Root, Liz Kennedy, Michael Sozan, and Jerry Parshall, "Election Security in All 50 States," Center for American Progress, February 12, 2018, https://www.americanprogress.org/issues/democracy/reports/2018/02/12/446336/election-security-50-states/.

51. Ibid.

52. Kevin Kelleher, "Microsoft Says Russia Has Already Tried to Hack 3 Campaigns in the 2018 Election," *Fortune*, July 19, 2018, https://fortune.com/2018/07/19/microsoft-russia-hack-2018-election-campaigns/.

CHAPTER 8: AMERICA ISN'T THE ONLY TARGET

1. Jean-Baptiste Jeangène Vilmer, Alexandre Escorcia, Marine Guillaume, and Janaina Herrera, *Information Manipulation: A Challenge for Our Democracies*, English translation of original French report (Paris: CAPS [Policy Planning Staff, Ministry for Europe and Foreign Affairs] and IRSEM [Institute for Strategic Research, Ministry for the Armed Forces], 2018), https://www.diplomatie.gouv.fr/IMG/pdf/information_manipulation_rvb_cle838736.pdf.

2. Samantha Bradshaw and Philip N. Howard, "Challenging Truth and Trust: A Global Inventory of Organized Social Media Manipulation," working paper 2018.1, Oxford Internet Institute, Oxford, UK, July 20, 2018, http://comprop.oii.ox.ac.uk/wp-content/uploads/sites/93/2018/07/ct2018.pdf.

3. Bakamo, "Patterns of Disinformation in the 2017 French Presidential Election," 2017, https://static1.squarespace.com/static/58495e3329687f8bfbb3f25c/t/590904cb15cf7da7d c3b15d8/1493763322834/Patterns+of+Disinformation+in+the+2017+French+Presidential +Election+-+Report+2+-+Bakamo.pdf; "Methods of Spreading Misinformation and Russian Influences on the French Presidential Elections," Bakamo, May 3, 2017, https://www .bakamosocial.com/whatsnew/2017/5/methods-of-spreading-misinformation-and-russian -influence-on-the-french-presidential-elections.

4. Christine Schmidt, "How France Beat Back Information Manipulation (and How Other Democracies Might Do the Same)," Nieman Lab, September 19, 2018, https://www .niemanlab.org/2018/09/how-france-beat-back-information-manipulation-and-how-other -democracies-might-do-the-same/.

5. Associated Press, "Hackers Have Targeted Election Campaign of Macros, Says Cyber Firm," *Guardian*, April 25, 2017, https://www.theguardian.com/world/2017/apr/25/hackers -have-targeted-election-campaign-of-macron-says-cyber-firm.

6. Nicolas Vincour, "Macron Confirms 'Massive' Hack Just Ahead of Election," Politico, updated May 7, 2017, https://www.politico.eu/article/macron-confirms-massive-hack-just -ahead-of-election/.

7. Laurens Cerulus, "Europe's Most Hackable Election," Politico, updated April 19, 2019, https://www.politico.eu/article/europe-most-hackable-election-voter-security-catalonia -european-parliament-disinformation/. The WikiLeaks page with the manipulated Macron information, https://wikileaks.org/macron-e-mails/, is no longer active.

8. Christine Schmidt, "How France Beat Back Information Manipulation (and How Other Democracies Might Do the Same)," Nieman Lab, September 19, 2018, https://www .niemanlab.org/2018/09/how-france-beat-back-information-manipulation-and-how-other -democracies-might-do-the-same/.

9. Zachary Young, "French Parliament Passes Law against 'Fake News,'" Politico, updated July 4, 2018, https://www.politico.eu/article/french-parliament-passes-law-against-fake-news/.

10. "Against Information Manipulation," Gouvernement.fr, visited October 31, 2019, https://www.gouvernement.fr/en/against-information-manipulation; Nicholas Boring, "France," in *Initiative to Counter Fake News in Selected Countries: Argentina, Brazil, Canada, China, Egypt, France, Germany, Israel, Japan, Kenya, Malaysia, Nicaragua, Russia, Sweden United Kingdom*, 29–32 (Washington, DC: The Law Library of Congress, 2019), https://www.loc .gov/law/help/fake-news/counter-fake-news.pdf.

11. *Wikipedia*, s.v. "Yellow vest movement," last edited October 31, 2019, https://en .wikipedia.org/wiki/Yellow_vests_movement.

12. Paul Carrel and Andrea Shalal, "Germany Says Its Government Computers Secure after 'Isolated Attack,'" Reuters, February 28, 2018, https://in.reuters.com/article/ germany-cyber-russia/russian-hacker-group-breached-german-ministries-took-data-media -idINKCN1GC2HB.

13. *Wikipedia*, "Criminal Case of Lisa. F.," last edited June 21, 2018, https://en.wikipedia .org/wiki/Criminal_case_of_Lisa_F.

14. Ibid.; Stefan Meister, "The 'Lisa Case': Germany as a Target of Russian Disinformation," *NATO Review Magazine*, July 25, 2016, https://www.nato.int/docu/review/2016/Also -in-2016/lisa-case-germany-target-russian-disinformation/EN/index.htm.

15. Andrea Shalal, "Russian-Germans in Focus amid Fears of Moscow Propaganda," Reuters, August 16, 2017, https://www.reuters.com/article/us-germany-election-russian -germans/russian-germans-in-focus-amid-fears-of-moscow-propaganda-idUSKCN1AW1NA;

Kadri Liik, "Europe, Russia, and the Laws of Nature: Importance of the EP Election," European Council on Foreign Relations, March 11, 2019, https://www.ecfr.eu/article/commentary _europe_russia_importance_of_european_parliament_election.

16. Stefan Meister, "The 'Lisa Case': Germany as a Target of Russian Disinformation," *NATO Review Magazine*, July 25, 2016, https://www.nato.int/docu/review/2016/Also-in -2016/lisa-case-germany-target-russian-disinformation/EN/index.htm.

17. Ibid.

18. Rowena Mason, "Theresa May Accuses Russia of Interfering in Elections and Fake News," *Guardian*, November 14, 2017, https://www.theguardian.com/politics/2017/nov/13/ theresa-may-accuses-russia-of-interfering-in-elections-and-fake-news.

19. Patrick Wintour, "Russian Bid to Influence Brexit Vote Detailed in New US Senate Report," *Guardian*, January 10, 2018, https://www.theguardian.com/world/2018/jan/10/russian -influence-brexit-vote-detailed-us-senate-report; US Senate Committee on Foreign Relations, *Putin's Asymmetric Assault on Democracy in Russia and Europe: Implications for U.S. National Security*, Minority Staff Report (Washington, DC: US Government Publishing Office, 2018), https://www.foreign.senate.gov/imo/media/doc/FinalRR.pdf; UK Digital Culture, Media, and Sport Committee, "Russian Influence in Political Campaigns," chap. 5 in *Disinformation and 'Fake News'* (London: Parliament of the United Kingdom, 2018), https://publications .parliament.uk/pa/cm201719/cmselect/cmcumeds/363/36308.htm#_idTextAnchor033.

20. "89up Releases Report on Russian Influence in the EU Referendum," 89up, February 10, 2018, https://89up.org/russia-report.

21. Julie Posetti and Alice Matthews, *A Short Guide to the History of 'Fake News' and Disinformation: A Learning Module for Journalists and Journalism Educators* (Washington, DC: International Center for Journalists, 2018), https://www.icfj.org/sites/default/files/2018 -07/A%20Short%20Guide%20to%20History%20of%20Fake%20News%20and%20 Disinformation_ICFJ%20Final.pdf.

22. Matthew Field and Mike Wright, "Russian Trolls Sent Thousands of Pro-Leave Messages on Day of Brexit Referendum, Twitter Data Reveals," *Telegraph*, October 17, 2018, https://www.telegraph.co.uk/technology/2018/10/17/russian-iranian-twitter-trolls-sent-10 -million-tweets-fake-news/.

23. Harriet Alexander and James Badcock, "Why Does Catalonia Want Independence from Spain?" *Telegraph*, October 10, 2017, https://www.telegraph.co.uk/news/0/does-catalonia -want-independence-spain/.

24. *Wikipedia*, "2017 Catalan Independence Referendum," last edited October 27, 2019, https://en.wikipedia.org/wiki/2017_Catalan_independence_referendum; Spanish Constitution, §155, English translation, pp. 47–48, https://www.boe.es/legislacion/documentos/ ConstitucionINGLES.pdf.

25. "Spain Warns EU of Russian Meddling in Catalan Separatist Movement," Deutsche Welle, November 13, 2017, https://p.dw.com/p/2nYRl.

26. Susana Urra, providing English version of original Spanish article by Raffa de Miguel, "Key Catalan Ideologue Met with Julian Assange in London," *El País* (Madrid), November 13, 2017, https://elpais.com/elpais/2017/11/13/inenglish/1510565565_636373.html; Susana Urra, providing English version of original Spanish article by David Alandete, "NATO Intelligence Reports Show Spike in Disinformation about Catalonia," *El País* (Madrid), November 20, 2017, https://elpais.com/elpais/2017/11/20/inenglish/1511166287_468181.html.

27. Susana Urra, providing English version of original Spanish article by David Alandete, "NATO Intelligence Reports Show Spike in Disinformation about Catalonia,"

El País (Madrid), November 20, 2017, https://elpais.com/elpais/2017/11/20/inenglish/1511166287_468181.html.

28. Ibid.

29. David Alandete and Daniel Verdú, "How Russian Networks Worked to Boost the Far Right in Italy," *El País*, March 1, 2018, https://elpais.com/elpais/2018/03/01/inenglish/1519922107_909331.html.

30. Joanna Plucinska and Mark Scott, "How Italy Does Putin's Work," Politico, March 4, 2018, https://www.politico.eu/article/italy-election-fake-news-sunday-bufale-misinformation-vladimir-putin-russia/.

31. Stephanie Kirchgaessner, "Russia Suspected over Hacking Attack on Italian Foreign Ministry," *Guardian*, February 10, 2017, https://www.theguardian.com/world/2017/feb/10/russia-suspected-over-hacking-attack-on-italian-foreign-ministry.

32. Paul Harrison, "Italy's Vote: Fake Claims Attempt to Influence Election," BBC News, March 3, 2018, https://www.bbc.com/news/world-europe-43214136.

33. Ibid.

34. J. Michael Cole, "Will China's Disinformation War Destabilize Taiwan?" *The National Interest*, July 30, 2017, https://nationalinterest.org/feature/will-chinas-disinformation-war-destabilize-taiwan-21708.

35. Chris Horton, "China Uses Taiwan as R&D Lab to Disrupt Democracies," *Nikkei Asian Review*, December 27, 2018, https://asia.nikkei.com/Politics/International-relations/China-uses-Taiwan-as-R-D-lab-to-disrupt-democracies.

36. Ibid.

37. J. Michael Cole, "Will China's Disinformation War Destabilize Taiwan?" *The National Interest*, July 30, 2017, https://nationalinterest.org/feature/will-chinas-disinformation-war-destabilize-taiwan-21708.

38. Chris Horton, "China Uses Taiwan as R&D Lab to Disrupt Democracies," *Nikkei Asian Review*, December 27, 2018, https://asia.nikkei.com/Politics/International-relations/China-uses-Taiwan-as-R-D-lab-to-disrupt-democracies.

39. "Fake News at Work: President Tsai 'Persecutes Religion' in Taiwan,'" *Taiwan Sentinel*, July 28, 2017, https://sentinel.tw/fake-news-tsai-persecutes-religion/.

40. "Against the Manipulation of Information," Gouvernement.fr, November 20, 2018, https://www.gouvernement.fr/en/against-information-manipulation.

41. Robin Emmott and Gabriela Baczynska, Reuters, "EU Leaders to Seek Cyber Sanctions, Press Asia for Action: Draft Statements," October 7, 2018, https://www.reuters.com/article/us-eu-asia-cyber-sanctions/eu-leaders-to-seek-cyber-sanctions-press-asia-for-action-draft-statements-idUSKCN1MR1Z2; National Coordinator for Security and Counterterrorism, "Cyber Security Assessment Netherlands 2018," English translation, Ministry of Justice and Security, Netherlands, August 7, 2018, available for download at https://english.nctv.nl/documents/publications/2018/08/07/cyber-security-assessment-netherlands-2018; UK House of Commons Digital, Culture, Media and Sport Committee, *Disinformation and "Fake News": Final Report*, 8th report of session 2017–19 (London: UK House of Commons, 2019), https://publications.parliament.uk/pa/cm201719/cmselect/cmcumeds/1791/1791.pdf; Ministry of Defence of Finland, *Security Strategy for Society: Government Resolution 16.12.10* (Helsinki: The Ministry of Defence of Finland, 2010), English translation, https://www.defmin.fi/files/1883/PDF.SecurityStrategy.pdf; German Federal Ministry of the Interior and Federal Ministry of Justice, "German Government Takes Action against Right-Wing Extremism and Hate Crimes," Federal Government of Germany, October 30, 2019, https://www.bundes

regierung.de/breg-en/search/gegen-extremismus-und-hass-1687190; Yasmeen Serhan, "Italy Scrambles to Fight Misinformation Ahead of Its Elections," *The Atlantic*, February 24, 2018, https://www.theatlantic.com/international/archive/2018/02/europe-fake-news/551972/.

42. "Call for Applications for the Selection of Members of the High Level Group on Fake News," European Commission, November 12, 2017, https://ec.europa.eu/digital-single -market/en/news/call-applications-selection-members-high-level-group-fake-news.

43. The group's final report is available for download at https://ec.europa.eu/digital-single -market/en/news/final-report-high-level-expert-group-fake-news-and-online-disinformation.

44. Ibid.

45. Ibid.

46. Article 19, *Germany: The Act to Improve Enforcement of the Law in Social Networks* (London: Article 19, 2017), https://www.article19.org/wp-content/uploads/2017/09/170901-Legal -Analysis-German-NetzDG-Act.pdf.

47. "Rapid Alert System," fact sheet, European Union, March 15, 2019, https://eeas .europa.eu/sites/eeas/files/ras_factsheet_march_2019_0.pdf ; "Member Countries," North Atlantic Treaty Organization (website), last updated: May 14, 2019, https://www.nato.int/ cps/en/natohq/topics_52044.htm.

48. Daniel Funke, "Misinformation Transcends Platforms, Languages and Countries. How Can Fact-Checkers Stop It?" *Poynter*, May 15, 2019, https://www.poynter.org/fact -checking/2019/misinformation-transcends-platforms-languages-and-countries-how-can -fact-checkers-stop-it/.

CHAPTER 9: THE NEXT TARGET

1. "FBI Fiscal Year 2020 Budget Request," C-Span video, 1:29:34, May 7, 2019, https://www.c-span.org/video/?460435-1/fbi-director-wray-word-spying-describe -surveillance&live=.

2. "Robert Mueller Testifies before Two House Committees" C-SPAN video, 2:41:42, July 24, 2019, https://www.c-span.org/video/?462629-1/robert-mueller-testifies-house -intelligence-committee.

3. Dan Patterson, "Election Hacking Has Never Been Cheaper, Easier or More Profitable," *CNET*, June 15, 2019, https://www.cnet.com/news/election-hacking-has-never-been -cheaper-easier-or-more-profitable/.

4. Natasha Korecki, "'Sustained and Ongoing' Disinformation Assault Targets Dem Presidential Candidates," Politico, February 20, 2019, https://www.politico.com/story/ 2019/02/20/2020-candidates-social-media-attack-1176018.

5. Clint Watts, in phone interview with the author, July 15, 2019.

6. Richard A. Clarke, in phone interview with the author, July 31, 2019.

7. Macy Bayern, "How Credential Stuffing Contributed to 8.3B Malicious Botnet Logins in Early 2018," *TechRepublic*, September 19, 2018, https://www.techrepublic.com/article/ how-credential-stuffing-contributed-to-8-3b-malicious-botnet-logins-in-early-2018/.

8. Olivia Solon, "Richard Dawkins on the Internet's Hijacking of the Word 'Meme.'" *Wired UK*, October 4, 2017, https://www.wired.co.uk/article/richard-dawkins-memes; Merriam Webster, s.v. "Meme," accessed October 7, 2019, https://www.merriam-webster.com/ dictionary/meme.

9. Benjamin T. Decker, "What a Kamala Harris Meme Can Teach Us about Fighting Fake News in 2020," Politico, March 3, 2019, https://www.politico.com/magazine/story/2019/03/03/what-a-kamala-harris-meme-can-teach-us-about-fighting-fake-news-in-2020-225515.

10. "What Is a Deepfake?" *The Economist*, August 7, 2019, https://www.economist.com/the-economist-explains/2019/08/07/what-is-a-deepfake.

11. Benjamin T. Decker, "What a Kamala Harris Meme Can Teach Us about Fighting Fake News in 2020," Politico, March 3, 2019, https://www.politico.com/magazine/story/2019/03/03/what-a-kamala-harris-meme-can-teach-us-about-fighting-fake-news-in-2020-225515.

12. Natalia Drozdiak, "Facebook Didn't Uphold Political Ads Policy, Rights Group Says," Bloomberg, June 6, 2019, https://www.bloomberg.com/news/articles/2019-06-06/facebook-didn-t-uphold-political-ads-policy-rights-group-says.

13. Craig Timberg, Tony Romm, and Elizabeth Dwoskin, "Russian Disinformation Teams Targeted Robert S. Mueller III, Says Report Prepared for Senate," *Washington Post*, December 18, 2018, http://www.msn.com/en-xl/northamerica/northamerica-top-stories/russian-disinformation-teams-targeted-robert-s-mueller-iii-says-report-prepared-for-senate/ar-BBR7qYi.

14. Ibid.

15. Donie O'Sullivan, "Exclusive: Russian-Linked Group Sold Merchandise Online," *CNN Money*, October 6, 2017, https://money.cnn.com/2017/10/06/media/blacktivist-merchandise-facebook-russia/index.html.

16. Shawn Musgrave, "White House 'Antifa' Petition Written by Pro-Trump Troll," Politico, August 24, 2017, https://www.politico.com/story/2017/08/24/antifa-white-house-petition-trump-troll-241990.

17. Caitlin O'Kane, "Russian Trolls Fueled Anti-Vaccination Debate in US by Spreading Misinformation on Twitter, Study Finds," CBS News, May 31, 2019, www.cbsnews.com/news/russian-trolls-fueled-anti-vaccination-debate-in-us-spreading-misinformation-online-study/.

18. Abigail Summerville, "'Deepfakes' Trigger a Race to Fight Manipulated Photos and Videos," *Wall Street Journal*, July 27, 2019, https://www.wsj.com/articles/deepfakes-trigger-a-race-to-fight-manipulated-photos-and-videos-11564225200.

19. James Vincent, "New AI Deepfake App Creates Nude Images of Women in Seconds," The Verge, June 27, 2019, https://www.theverge.com/2019/6/27/18760896/deepfake-nude-ai-app-women-deepnude-non-consensual-pornography .

20. Michael Zollhöfer, "Deep Video Portraits: Siggraph 2018," website of Michael Zollhöfer, http://web.stanford.edu/~zollhoef/papers/SG2018_DeepVideo/page.html.

21. Corinne Reichert, "Congress Investigating Deepfakes after Doctored Pelosi Video, Report Says," *CNET*, June 4, 2019, https://www.cnet.com/news/congress-investigating-deepfakes-after-doctored-pelosi-video-report-says/.

22. Emily Tillett and Olivia Gazis," House Holds Hearing on 'Deepfakes' and Artificial Intelligence amid National Security Concerns," CBS News, updated June 13, 2019, https://www.cbsnews.com/news/house-holds-hearing-on-deepfakes-and-artificial-intelligence-amid-national-security-concerns-live-stream/.

23. Tom Costello, "How 'Deepfake' Videos Are Manipulating People Online," video, 3:09, *Today*, May 3, 2019, https://www.today.com/video/how-deepfake-videos-are-manipulating-people-online-58785349692.

24. Donie O'Sullivan, "Russian Accounts Pushed Fake Rubio Tweet Warning of British Spy Threat to US Elections," CNN, updated June 23, 2019, https://www.cnn.com/2019/06/22/politics/russia-fake-rubio-tweet/index.html.

25. Steve Contorno, "Marco Rubio Says Russians Made Fake @marcorubio Tweets," *Tampa Bay Times*, June 19, 2019, https://www.tampabay.com/florida-politics/buzz/2019/06/19/marco -rubio-says-russians-made-fake-marcorubio-tweets/.

26. Sabrina Siddiqui, "Half of Americans See Fake News as Bigger Threat Than Terrorism, Study Finds," *Guardian*, June 7, 2019, https://www.theguardian.com/us-news/2019/jun/06/ fake-news-how-misinformation-became-the-new-front-in-us-political-warfare.

27. Tom Simonite, "Is This Photo Real? AI Gets Better at Faking Images," *Wired*, December 28, 2018, https://www.wired.com/story/is-this-photo-real-ai-getting-better-faking -images/.

28. Michael C. Bender, "Paul Winfree Under Consideration for Federal Reserve," *Wall Street Journal*, updated May 3, 2019, https://www.wsj.com/articles/paul-winfree-under -consideration-for-federal-reserve-11556912790.

29. Raphael Satter, "Experts: Spy Used AI-Generated Face to Connect with Targets," Associated Press, June 13, 2019, https://apnews.com/bc2f19097a4c4fffaa00de6770b8a60d.

30. Mashadi Kekana, "New App Developed to Detect Twitter Bots—in Any Language," *Mail & Guardian* (Johannesburg), June 13, 2019, https://mg.co.za/article/2019-06-13-new -app-developed-to-detect-twitter-bots-in-any-language.

31. Daniel R. Coats, "Statement for the Record: Worldwide Threat Assessment of the US Intelligence Community," Senate Select Committee on Intelligence, January 29, 2019, https://www.dni.gov/files/ODNI/documents/2019-ATA-SFR—-SSCI.pdf.

32. Lawrence Norden, "How to Secure Elections for 2020 and Beyond," Brennan Center for Justice, November 12, 2019, https://www.brennancenter.org/our-work/research-reports/ how-secure-elections-2020-and-beyond.

33. Julian E. Barnes, "US Begins First Cyberoperation against Russia Aimed at Protecting Elections," *New York Times*, October 23, 2018, https://www.nytimes.com/2018/10/23/us/ politics/russian-hacking-usa-cyber-command.html.

34. Visit the EI-ISAC online at https://www.cisecurity.org/ei-isac/ei-isac-charter/.

35. Dave Lewis, "The DDoS Attack against Dyn One Year Later," *Forbes*, October 23, 2017, https://www.forbes.com/sites/davelewis/2017/10/23/the-ddos-attack-against-dyn-one -year-later/#580bd27b1ae9.

36. Robert Hackett, "Data Breeches Now Cost $4 Million on Average," *Fortune*, June 15, 2016, https://fortune.com/2016/06/15/data-breach-cost-study-ibm/; "How Much Would a Data Breach Cost Your Business? Cost of a Data Breach Report Highlights," report compiled by the Ponemon Institute on behalf of IBM Security, visited November 19, 1019, https:// www.ibm.com/security/data-breach.

37. Letter from George Washington to John Trumbull, dated June 25, 1799, and found online at *Founders Online*, US National Archives, accessed November 19, 2019, https:// founders.archives.gov/documents/Washington/06-04-02-0120.

CHAPTER 10: YOUR WORST NIGHTMARE

1. Dan Pfeiffer on *Pod Save America*.

2. Benjamin Wofford, "The Hacking Threat to the Midterms Is Huge. And Technology Won't Protect Us," *Vox*, October 25, 2018, https://www.vox.com/2018/10/25/18001684/2018 -midterms-hacked-russia-election-security-voting.

3. Flash Eurobarometer 464 (Fake news and disinformation online) and Special Euro-barometer 477 (Democracy and elections), "Activation Plan against Disinformation: Understanding the Threat and Stepping Up European Response," March 2019, https://eeas.europa.eu/sites/eeas/files/disinformation_factsheet_march_2019_0.pdf.

4. Sabrina Siddiqui, "Half of Americans See Fake News as Bigger Threat Than Terrorism, Study Finds," *Guardian*, June 7, 2019, https://www.theguardian.com/us-news/2019/jun/06/fake-news-how-misinformation-became-the-new-front-in-us-political-warfare.

5. Peter Steiner, "On the Internet, Nobody Knows You're a Dog," cartoon, *The New Yorker*, July 45, 1993, section G, p. 8; "Cartoons," *Peter L Steiner* (website), accessed November 19, 2019, https://www.plsteiner.com/cartoons#/newyorker; and see *Wikipedia*, s.v. "On the Internet, Nobody Knows You're a Dog," last edited October 28, 2019, en.wikipedia.org/wiki/On_the_Internet,_nobody_knows_you%27re_a_dog.

6. Michael H. Keller, "The Flourishing Business of Fake YouTube Views," *New York Times*, August 11, 2018, https://www.nytimes.com/interactive/2018/08/11/technology/youtube-fake-view-sellers.html.

7. Tauhid Zaman, "Even a Few Bots Can Shift Public Opinion in Big Way," *Salon*, November 6, 2018, https://www.salon.com/2018/11/06/even-a-few-bots-can-shift-public-opinion-in-big-way_partner/.

8. Kathleen Jamieson Hall, *Cyberwar: How Russian Hackers and Trolls Helped Elect a President: What We Don't, Can't, and Do Know*. Oxford, UK: Oxford University Press, 2018.

9. "The Partisan Divide on Political Values Grows Even Wider," Pew Research Center, October 5, 2017, http://www.people-press.org/2017/10/05/the-partisan-divide-on-political-values-grows-even-wider/.

10. Susan Page and Bill Theobald, "Poll: Americans Can Agree That the Nation Is Divided. Beyond That, They Don't Agree on Much," *USA Today*, updated December 20, 2018, https://www.usatoday.com/story/news/politics/2018/12/20/poll-democrats-republicans-agree-us-divided-worry-trump-health-border-issues/2349589002/.

11. Tim Cook, "Commencement Address by Apple CEO Tim Cook," prepared text of address delivered at Stanford's 128th commencement, June 16, 2019, https://news.stanford.edu/2019/06/16/remarks-tim-cook-2019-stanford-commencement/.

12. Max Read, "How Much of the Internet Is Fake? Turns Out, a Lot of It, Actually," Intelligencer, *New York Magazine*, December 26, 2018, http://nymag.com/intelligencer/2018/12/how-much-of-the-internet-is-fake.html.

13. Rob Copeland and Katherine Bindley, "Millions of Business Listings on Google Maps Are Fake—and Google Profits," *Wall Street Journal*, updated June 20, 2019, https://www.wsj.com/articles/google-maps-littered-with-fake-business-listings-harming-consumers-and-competitors-11561042283.

14. Ibid.

15. Copeland, Rob, and Katherine Bindley. "Millions of Business Listings on Google Maps Are Fake-and Google Profits." *The Wall Street Journal*, Dow Jones & Company, June 20, 2019, www.wsj.com/articles/google-maps-littered-with-fake-business-listings-harming-consumers-and-competitors-11561042283.

16. Phillip N. Howard, Bharath Ganesh, and Dimitra Liotsiou, "The IRA, Social Media and Political Polarization in the United States, 2012–2018." The Computational Propaganda Project., 2018. https://comprop.oii.ox.ac.uk/research/ira-political-polarization/.

17. Olivia Beavers, "Hackers Increasingly Target Reputations through Reviews Sites, Experts Say," The Hill, September 1, 2018, https://thehill.com/policy/cybersecurity/404477-hackers-increasingly-target-reputations-through-reviews-sites-experts.

18. Sabrina Siddiqui, "Half of Americans See Fake News as Bigger Threat Than Terrorism, Study Finds," *Guardian*, June 7, 2019, https://www.theguardian.com/us-news/2019/jun/06/fake-news-how-misinformation-became-the-new-front-in-us-political-warfare.

19. Adi Robertson, "Virginia's 'Revenge Porn' Laws Now Officially Cover Deepfakes," The Verge, July 1, 2019, https://www.theverge.com/2019/7/1/20677800/virginia-revenge-porn -deepfakes-nonconsensual-photos-videos-ban-goes-into-effect.

20. Chris Hoffman, "Touch ID and Face ID Don't Make You More Secure," *How-To Geek*, October 2, 2018, https://www.howtogeek.com/368114/touch-id-and-face-id-dont-make-you -more-secure/.

21. LastPass, *The Password Exposé: 8 Truths about the Threats—and Opportunities—of Employee Passwords* (Budapest: LogMeIn, 2017), https://lp-cdn.lastpass.com/lporcamedia/document-library/lastpass/pdf/en/LastPass-Enterprise-The-Password-Expose-Ebook-v2.pdf.

22. Shawn Henry in an interview with the author, conducted via telephone, June 3, 2019.

CHAPTER 11: WHAT CAN YOU DO?

1. "How Do I Mark a Facebook Post as False?" Facebook, accessed October 7, 2019, https://www.facebook.com/help/572838089565953.

2. "Election Integrity Policy," Twitter, April 2019, https://help.twitter.com/en/rules-and -policies/election-integrity-policy.

3. The Electoral Integrity Project's website can be accessed at https://sites.google.com/site/electoralintegrityproject4/home.

4. Clint Watts, senior fellow at the Center for Cyber and Homeland Security at George Washington University and Foreign Policy Research Institute fellow, in phone conversation with the author, July 15, 2019.

5. Katy Steinmetz, "How Your Brain Tricks You Into Believing Fake News," *Time*, August 9, 2018, https://time.com/5362183/the-real-fake-news-crisis/.

6. Visit the Fact Checker's Guide to Manipulated Video online at https://www .washingtonpost.com/graphics/2019/politics/fact-checker/manipulated-video-guide/?utm _term=.6d7ecc9c45bb.

7. "About the Observatory on Social Media," The Observatory on Social Media, accessed October 7, 2019, http://osome.iuni.iu.edu/about/.

8. Play Fakey online at https://fakey.iuni.iu.edu/.

9. Play Hoaxy online at https://hoaxy.iuni.iu.edu/. See also "Hoaxy, Fakey and Botometer Are Three Powerful Tools for Studying and Countering Online Misinformation and Manipulation," *Innovation Toronto*, June 24, 2018, https://www.innovationtoronto.com/2018/06/hoaxy-fakey-and-botometer-are-three-powerful-tools-for-studying-and-countering-online -misinformation-and-manipulation/.

10. To play Which Face Is Real, visit http://www.whichfaceisreal.com/.

11. Find a computer-generated face here: https://thispersondoesnotexist.com.

12. Visit, respectively, https://www.newsguardtech.com, https://trusted-news.com, and. And for more about how these plug-ins work, see Patrick Nohke, "Fighting Deep Fakes with Digital Signatures," *Hashed Out*, August 24, 2018, https://www.thesslstore.com/blog/fighting-deep-fakes-with-digital-signatures/.

13. To read more about how ProPublica's plug-ins work, see Julia Angwin and Jeff Larson, "Help Us Monitor Political Ads Online," ProPublica, September 7, 2017, https://www .propublica.org/article/help-us-monitor-political-ads-online.

14. Jeremy B. Merrill, Ally J. Levine, Ariana Tobin, Jeff Larson, and Julia Angwin, "Facebook Political Ad Collector: How Political Advertisers Target You," ProPublica, first posted July 17, 2018, updated hourly, https://projects.propublica.org/facebook-ads/.

15. Read the latest edition, *Democracy at Risk: Threats and Attacks against Media Freedom in Europe; Annual Report 2019* ([Strasbourg, France]: Council of Europe, 2019), at https://cpj.org/blog/COE_JournalistsReport_2019.pdf.

Index

About the Author

Theresa Payton served as the first female chief information officer for the White House during the George W. Bush administration and is currently CEO and founder of Fortalice Solutions, a boutique cybersecurity and intelligence services company that's listed in the Global Cybersecurity Top 500. She starred as the deputy commander of Intelligence on the CBS TV series, "Hunted", is a frequent guest on national and international news outlets, and is featured in the book *100 Fascinating Females Fighting Cybercrime*. Among her many accolades are the FBI director's award for community service. She has coauthored two other books with Ted Claypoole.